Einige Artikel wurden auf einer Konferenz usw.
Sexualität etc. in SF präsentiert. s.b.
~~www~~ http://iasscs.sfsu.edu
weitere Konferences
x Masculinities in Southern Africa (1997, Durban
x   -   & Manhood (2004, Wits)

Men Behaving Differently

Men Behaving Differently

edited by Graeme Reid and Liz Walker

DOUBLE STOREY
a juta company

Published in 2005 by Double Storey Books,
a division of Juta & Co. Ltd, Mercury Crescent, Wetton, Cape Town

© 2005 the authors and editors

ISBN 1 919930 98 1

All rights reserved. No part of this book may be reproduced or utilised in any form and by any means, electronic or mechanical, including photocopying and recording, or by any information storage or retrieval system, without permission in writing from the publisher.

Editing by Andrew van der Spuy
Typesetting by Christabel Hardacre
Printing by Paarl Print, Paarl

Contents

List of contributors   vii

Foreword   *Robert Morrell*   ix

Acknowledgements   xv

1   Masculinities in question   *Graeme Reid & Liz Walker*   1

2   'Baby rape': Unmaking secrets of sexual violence in post-apartheid South Africa   *Deborah Posel*   21

3   Masculine domination in sexual violence: Interpreting accounts of three cases of rape in the South African lowveld   *Isak Niehaus*   65

4   Rules of engagement: Structuring sex and damage in men's prisons and beyond   *Sasha Gear*   89

5   'You have to change and you don't know how!': Contesting what it means to be a man in a rural area of South Africa   *Tina Sideris*   111

6   Cultural politics and masculinities: Multiple-partners in historical perspective in KwaZulu-Natal   *Mark Hunter*   139

7   Negotiating the boundaries of masculinity in post-apartheid South Africa   *Liz Walker*   161

8   Male-male sexuality in Lesotho: Two conversations   *Marc Epprecht*   183

9   'A man is a man completely and a wife is a wife completely': Gender classification and performance amongst 'ladies' and 'gents' in Ermelo, Mpumalanga   *Graeme Reid*   205

Index   231

List of contributors

Marc Epprecht is an Associate Professor in the Department of History and the Development Studies Program, Queen's University, Kingston, Canada.

Sasha Gear is a researcher in the Criminal Justice Programme at the Centre for the Study of Violence and Reconciliation (CSVR), Johannesburg, South Africa.

Mark Hunter is a doctoral candidate in the Department of Geography, University of California at Berkeley and a research associate in the School of Development Studies, University of KwaZulu-Natal.

Isak Niehaus is Professor in Anthropology at the University of Pretoria, South Africa.

Deborah Posel is Director of the Wits Institute for Social and Economic Research (WISER) and Professor in Sociology at the University of the Witwatersrand, South Africa.

Graeme Reid (Co-editor) is a researcher at the Wits Institute for Social and Economic Research (WISER), University of the Witwatersrand, Johannesburg and a doctoral candidate in the Amsterdam School for Social Science Research, University of Amsterdam.

Tina Sideris is a post-doctoral research fellow at the Wits Institute for Social and Economic Research (WISER), University of the Witwatersrand.

Liz Walker (Co-editor) is a lecturer in the Faculty of Health and Social Care, University of Hull and research associate at the Wits Institute for Social and Economic Research (WISER), University of the Witwatersrand, Johannesburg, South Africa.

Foreword

by Robert Morrell

In the last ten years, viewers of South African television will have become acquainted with the British TV comedy series 'Men Behaving Badly'. It is a show that follows the doings of two white, working-class Englishmen as they engage with alcohol, women and work. The main characters, Gary, Dermot and later Tony, have come to represent a form of laddish masculinity, uncouth, insensitive, fun-loving, incompetent and politically incorrect. We are asked to laugh with them, love them and forgive them but not really to understand them. Liz Walker and Graeme Reid have put together a collection of essays which pick up on media concerns about and representations of men and masculinity. Instead of taking a position that, with furrowed brow, notes the concern for women's interests but asks 'what about the boys?' the contributors take a serious look at sex, sexuality and the construction of masculinity among men in contemporary South Africa.

A lot has changed in South Africa over the last ten years. We get a sense of this by looking at two political snapshots involving white men. In 1994, three white members of the AWB (Afrikaner Weerstandsbeweging) were shot dead by a black member of the security forces in Bophuthatswana as they tried to prevent the shift in the political balance of power by supporting the bantustan government. Ten years later, the leader of the AWB was released from prison having served a sentence for attempted murder. In a racist rage, he had attacked a petrol pump attendant. It is tempting to read these developments – the decline in the fortunes of Afrikaner right-wing movements, coinciding with the formal end of apartheid, and of those white men who were politically formidable prior to 1990 – as symptomatic of the political shifts and of a particular gendered transition. And, in a way, these events indeed tell this story. But this is only one of the narratives about the country's recent past.

Another narrative has been generated by the spread of AIDS. In the last ten years, South Africa has joined the countries of central Africa as having levels of HIV infection amongst the highest in the world. In the period from 1997 to 2002, the number of deaths per year increased from 318 000 to 499 000 (in a population of 44 million people) (Wines 2005). The gender bias of the pandemic is well known – women tend to get infected earlier and to die earlier than men do, though men are heavily affected as well.

In Botswana, South Africa and Zimbabwe, an estimated 60 per cent of boys now 15 years old will eventually become infected (GENDER-AIDS 2003).

The AIDS pandemic has contributed to a process by which sex has become very visible (Posel in this volume). Since HIV infection occurs primarily via unprotected sexual intercourse, the South African public has become accustomed to hearing about condoms and has lost some of its squeamishness in discussing sexual acts and orientations. This has been assisted by the constitutional protection of gay rights and the proliferation of shops which in some or other way deal in sex.

The collection of essays in *Men Behaving Differently* engages with themes that have been around for a while. Papers on masculinity and sexuality were presented at the 1997 Colloquium on 'Masculinities in Southern Africa' in Durban and, since then, there have been many notable publications on the subject. What marks the collection as highly significant in the development of studies on men and masculinity is the way in which new theories are brought to bear and the way in which the lens of research has been widened to cover those areas hitherto under-researched. The book presents some of the best research in the last few years on masculinity and sexuality.

The editors and the authors draw on a literature that has dramatically advanced understandings of sexuality in the last two decades. Contributors highlight the way in which sex has become an arena of contestation and accommodation in relationships. Men (and women) have always brought their strengths and weaknesses to intimate relationships but now the stakes are higher. Men no longer have the law on their side. Marital rape is a crime and domestic violence has become a priority area in policing and the criminal justice system. The situation is compounded for some men by unemployment or underemployment. They feel vulnerable and some express themselves by assaulting their partners while others search for a more harmonious way to relate to their partners and a more peaceful way of expressing their masculinity (Sideris in this volume).

South African men are confronting new material, political and social circumstances. Family structures are changing under the influence of AIDS deaths and illnesses, and poverty, and as a result of the gradual rise in the economic fortunes of women (Hunter in this volume).

In a society so rapidly changing and with established power relations being challenged (in gender and race terms, if not exactly in social class terms) it is to be expected that constructions of masculinity will change as well. This book offers new insights into the way in which sexuality is understood and performed. It suggests that intimate relations are undergoing important reconstitution though it notes that unequal gender relations still limit the extent to which change is possible. In showing that men are behaving differently, it echoes the important point made in Bob Connell's seminal *Masculinities* (1995), that there are many masculinities, that masculinities are fluid and can and do change. In posing the question 'Crisis, what crisis?' the editors in their introduction address two important questions: is there a crisis of masculinity, and what are the motors of gender change?

The editors are careful not to hook into a literature which threatens to privilege the affairs of men over those of women. The idea of a 'crisis of masculinity' is rightly treated with suspicion by feminists. It is regarded as a Trojan Horse intended to roll back the advances of women under the pretence of concern for the (declining) fortunes of men. The editors acknowledge that the fortunes of some men have changed for the worse but note that their responses to challenge are not uniform. Some have seemed able to respond positively to the opportunity to live more harmoniously with women, children and themselves, while others have experienced crises of identity.

Men have not only responded in individualistic ways. In the last decade, South Africa has been drawn into a global world of gender work with men. In the last few years, this work has begun to stretch to address global issues (Breines, Connell & Eide 2000). In a highly significant development, the UN's Commission on the status of women in March 2004 adopted a position on 'The role of men and boys in achieving gender equality', to guide gender equity work with men (UN 2004). As a result masculinity has become a global issue and it has been taken forward in a variety of ways by organs of the UN as well as by state and donor-sponsored initiatives, which include promoting father–child work and ending violence (Barker et al. 2004; Ferguson et al. 2004).

Organisations established to work with men are relatively new. Among the first was the White Ribbon campaign, an organisation founded in Canada in 1989. It now has a presence in Southern Africa (Kaufman nd). Many local organizations have been established too and a variety of NGOs now work with men. Many of these have followed the pioneering work of ADAPT (Nkosi 1998; Madonsela nd) to address issues of domestic violence. Others have worked with youth in the context of HIV infections (Makhaye 1998; Peacock 2003). Yet others have worked to encourage men to be good fathers and husbands and responsible citizens – for example, the work of the South African Men's Forum and Getnet (Khumalo 1998; Getnet 2002; Richter and Morrell forthcoming). In other government and non-government arenas, working with men and masculinity is now well recognised. For example, the government's Commission for Gender Equality has created a focus on men while trade unions continue to explore issues affecting men, including paternity leave (Appolis 1998).

South Africa's men are behaving differently. In the realm of sexuality (gay and hetero), new expressions sit alongside the old, and all can be compared with styles and conventions from an earlier era. New theories make it possible both to analyse sexuality and to encourage greater tolerance within a framework of gender equity. But in South Africa, there are always other, deeply historically rooted, forces at work. And racial and class realities remain powerful. In this important collection, Reid and Walker have brought sophisticated theory, nuanced research and a political sensitivity to the study of men, masculinity and sexuality. They have avoided identifying men who behave badly, and have taken the much more helpful position of analysing the many different ways that South African men are expressing, negotiating and living their sexuality.

References

Appolis, P. (1998) Workers as Fathers. *Agenda*, 37, 78–81.

Barker, G., D. Bartlett, T. Beardshaw, J. Brown, A. Burgess, M.E. Lamb, C. Lewis, G. Russell & N. Vann. (2004) *Supporting Fathers: Contributions from the International Fatherhood Summit 2003* (The Hague: Bernard van Leer Foundation).

Breines, Ingeborg, Robert Connell & Ingrid Eide (eds.) (2000) *Male Roles, Masculinities and Violence: A Culture of Peace Perspective* (Paris: Unesco).

Connell, R.W. (1995) *Masculinities* (Cambridge: Polity).

Ferguson, Harry, Jeff Hearn, Oystein Gullvag Holter, Michael Kimmel, James Lang & Robert Morrell, (2004) *Ending Gender-based Violence: A Call for Global Action to Involve Men* (Stockholm: SIDA).

GENDER-AIDS eForum (2003) State of the World Population 2003: Making 1 billion Count: Investing in Adolescents' Health and Rights. (GENDER-AIDS eForum 2003: gender-aids@healthdev.net posted 15 October 2003).

Getnet. (2002) *Masculinities in the Making of Gendered Identities: A Getnet Guidebook for Trainers* (Bellville: Getnet).

Kaufman, Michael. (nd) The White Ribbon Campaign. *Namibian Men against Violence against Women* (Windhoek: Legal Assistance Centre).

Khumalo, B. (1998) Restoring the Soul of the Nation. *Agenda*, 37, 46–48.

Madonsela, Samokelo. (nd) South Africa's Experience: The Work of Adapt. *Namibian Men against Violence against Women* (Windhoek: Legal Assistance Centre)

Makhaye, Gethwana. (1998) Shosholoza's Goal: Educate Men in Soccer. *Agenda*, 39, 93–96.

Nkosi, T. (1998) Young Men Taking a Stand! *Agenda*, 37, 30–31.

Peacock, Dean. (2003) Building on a Legacy of Social Justice Activism: Enlisting Men as Gender Justice Activists in South Africa. *Men and Masculinities*, 5, 3, 325–28.

Richter, L. and R. Morrell (eds.) (forthcoming) *Baba? Fathers and Fatherhood in South Africa* (Pretoria: HSRC)

United Nations Commission on the Status of Women. (2004) The Role of Men and Boys in Achieving Gender Equality. (Forty-eighth session, 1–12 March 2004 at http://www.peacewomen.org/un/ecosoc/CSW/FinalACMenBoysCSW2004.pdf).

Wines, Michael. (2005) South Africa Reports Deaths Increased 57% over 5 Years. *New York Times*, 19 February 2005 reported af-aids@eforums.healthdev.org, 25 February 2005).

Acknowledgements

Many of the chapters in this book were first presented at *Sex and Secrecy*, the 4th International Conference of the International Association for the Study of Sexuality, Culture and Society (IASSCS), which took place at the University of the Witwatersrand in June 2003. The conference was co-hosted by the Wits Institute for Social and Economic Research (WISER), the Graduate School for Humanities and Social Sciences, and the Gay and Lesbian Archives (GALA).

The impetus behind the creation of the IASSCS was the perceived need to address the fragmentation of studies in sexuality and to provide a forum for expanding and developing sexuality as a legitimate area of scholarship. The IASSCS encourages interdisciplinary and cross-cultural studies of sexuality, and its international bi-annual conference provides an opportunity for the presentation of research findings (http://iasscs.sfsu.edu).

Peter Aggleton and his team at *Culture, Health and Sexuality* compiled a special issue of the journal (vol. 7, no. 3, 2005) in which several of the chapters first appeared. We are grateful to Peter Aggleton for his extensive and meticulous editorial work, to Janet Remmington for her ongoing support, and to Taylor and Francis (http://www.tandf.co.uk/journals) for permission to republish.

The editors and publishers would like to thank the following journals for permission to reproduce chapters in this book or earlier versions of them:

African Studies, vol. 63, no. 1 (2004), published by Taylor and Francis, for chapter 5 by Tina Sideris

Culture, Health and Sexuality, vol. 7, no. 3 (2005), published by Taylor and Francis, for the introduction by Graeme Reid and Liz Walker (pp 185–94), and chapters 6 by Liz Walker (pp 225–38), 2 by Deborah Posel (pp 239–52), 4 by Sasha Gear (pp 195–208) and 6 by Mark Hunter (pp 209–23)

Journal of Men's Studies, vol. 10, no. 3 (2002) © 2002 by the Men's Studies Press, LLC, for chapter 8 by Marc Epprecht

1
Masculinities in question
Graeme Reid and Liz Walker

Introduction

The transition to democracy in South Africa has been accompanied by changes in the gendered ordering of society. An unquestionably patriarchal system has given way to new ideals of equality between men and women, which are enshrined in the Constitution. The first decade of democracy in South Africa has thus exposed previously hidden sexual practices and abuses, confronted and unseated traditional gender hierarchies, created the space for the construction and expression of new masculinities and catapulted matters of sexuality into the spotlight. This collection, *Men Behaving Differently: South African Men Since 1994*, explores some of these concerns. South African men have for some time now been the subject of academic enquiry, although often in relation to issues other than gender, such as the economy, work and broader process of social change. In his groundbreaking collection, *Changing Men in Southern Africa*, Morrell (2001) brought together many of these studies. One key thrust of Morrell's collection was to suggest that 'there is no one, typical South African man' (2001:33), but rather many different masculinities. Some men challenge gender hierarchies, others oppose any attempt to democratise gender relations, and some are happy to support the status quo. *Changing Men* served to invigorate and stimulate an important area of enquiry; in Morrell's words:

> This book, then, is prompted by two, interrelated concerns: the first intellectual, and the second, political. The first concern is to identify and explore the different forms in which masculinity as a collective social form is expressed in South Africa. Related to this is an investigation of the way in which masculinity is implicated in gender inequalities and of how masculinities are changing. The second concern is to widen the debates about gender and to promote

a rethinking of masculinity which offers new ways of imagining masculinity and, for men, suggests new ways of being a man. (2001:xiv)

This collection, appearing as it does in the immediate aftermath of that symbolic threshold, ten years of democracy, focuses on changing concepts of masculinity in a period marked by rapid social transition. In *Men Behaving Differently* we take up the challenge of examining the relationship between sexuality and social transition, in different institutional and geographical locations, and look at new masculinities which have been forged in post-apartheid South Africa. Authors in this collection reflect on masculinities of the past, and how they are refracted into the present and mediated through new possibilities opened up by democratisation.

One opportunity to engage systematically with some of these issues was at the *Sex and Secrecy* Conference, where many of the chapters included in this collection were first presented as papers. The conference was an international forum which addressed issues pertaining to sexuality in a South African and international context. *Sex and Secrecy*, the fourth conference of the International Association for the Study of Sexuality, Culture and Society, was held at the University of the Witwatersrand, Johannesburg in June 2003. One of the strong themes to emerge from the conference was that of masculinity and sexuality. This theme was contained in a provocative set of papers, clustered together under the title *Unsettling Sexual and Gender Identities*. In this collection we have sought to bring together some of the highlights from the conference as well as additional work that explores the troubled, unsettled world of masculinity and sexuality in a country in transition. *Men Behaving Differently* is about masculinity in a state of flux, reconfiguration and change. This includes immediate and tangible changes in South Africa's political landscape, transitions in academic enquiry into gender and sexuality, and also emerging possibilities for alternative sexual and gender identities. As Connell (1995) pointed out as a truism (which Morrell adapted to the South African context), men can be expected to react to change in a variety of ways, from embracing and supporting new ideas about manhood and masculinity, to violently defending the status quo. In this collection men are seen to be behaving differently across this spectrum of anticipated possibilities. Social transformation has brought about ambiguous circumstances in which brutal violence may coexist with previously unimaginable levels of integration and acceptance of sexual minorities, for example. One of the intellectual transitions that is still taking place is change in the ways in which sexuality and masculinities are studied in an African context.

The study of sexuality in Africa

In his provocatively entitled critique of the colonial encounter, *Black Skin, White Masks* (first published in 1952), Fanon remarks that 'The sexual potency of the negro is hallucinating' (1986:157). Indeed the sexuality of the African – including as it does the fears, desires and fantasies projected onto men and women on the continent – provides a powerful metaphor for the colonial encounter. The image of polymorphous perversity embodied in the virile and promiscuous African man and the primary object of his desires, the subordinate, child-bearing African woman, are familiar tropes that announce the African sexual subject as quintessentially 'other'. Stereotypes about the 'other' serve to construct ideas about the 'self'. Thus images of 'African sexuality' as pathological, perverse and primitive construct the sexuality of the European, in opposition, as healthy, normal and civilised (Mohanty 1991, Vaughan 1991, Arnfred 2004). The study of sexuality in Africa has been shaped by this false dichotomy between 'us' and 'them'. European discourse on African sexuality has thus tended to reveal more about the observer than the observed, more about the author than the subject (Vaughan 1991, Bleys 1995, Heald 1999, Arnfred 2004).

The legacy of these stereotypes lingers to this day and is evident in the nature and focus of research on sexuality that has been undertaken in Africa, for example, in the tendency to view tradition as static and ahistorical rather than dynamic and subject to change; and in the ways in which European perceptions and preoccupations with the nature of sexuality, morality and sin are often imposed on 'the African'. The tendency to generalise for the whole of Africa in the form of a model of 'African sexuality' is also evident in an approach to research in Africa that lacks cultural nuance and historical specificity. These shortcomings are at the heart of the 'African sexuality' thesis developed by the Caldwells (1987, 1989), which seeks to construct an overarching interpretation from patterns of sexuality 'diverse enough for us to doubt whether there is any point at all in talking of an "African sexuality"' (Heald 1999:130).

Sexuality, where it has featured as part of social science enquiry, has tended to do so in a context of development discourse that has focused almost exclusively on the experience of women. The 'universal female subordination' hypothesis has formed the theoretical basis for important scholarly work and feminist activism (Ortner 1974, Rosaldo 1974). This theoretical framework has informed approaches to the empowerment of women in oppressive patriarchal and gerontocratic social systems. However, this model, which has been highly influential in 'gender and development' discourse, has often been transposed and applied to diverse situations in Africa as if it has universal applicability, and without recognising the cultural biases that inform this particular understanding of the nature and circumstances of women's subordinate social position. Some have argued that, by eliding the cultural specificities of women's experiences, Western feminists have had a tendency to undervalue African women's agency in creatively responding to social and cultural circumstances. These reactions can lead to an uncomfortable 'cultural relativist position' which tends to downplay criticism of practices such as virginity testing or female genital mutilation. Yet, as Signe Arnfred (2004) points out, female genital mutilation has become the overarching framework for understanding all forms of female initiation involving the manipulation or modification of the genitalia, even when these are designed to greatly enhance women's capacity for sexual pleasure and enjoyment.

Megan Vaughan (1991) has shown how medical discourses in a colonial context were crucial in constructing 'the African' as an object of knowledge. Not only was medical discourse highly sexualised, reflecting 'male sexual imagery of conquest, penetration and subjugation' (1991:19), but it also played an important role in articulating and specifying ideas about African sexuality. The influence of medical discourse on the study of sexuality in Africa is evident to this day. In a continent where health issues remain a pressing priority, public health priorities and models have tended to shape the research agenda in the social sciences. For example, reproductive health, including issues of fertility, contraception and maternal mortality, has been at the top of the research agenda, displaced only recently by a growing awareness of women's particularly vulnerable position within the largest health crisis on the continent – the HIV/AIDS pandemic. The recognition that women are more vulnerable than men to HIV infection has led to a focus in social science research on the role of gender in HIV transmission. This research is much needed and has proved indispensable to shaping public health interventions. However, it has also meant that the study of sexuality in Africa has been dominated by biomedical discourse relating to women and reproduction, often infused with normative assumptions about women's needs, again derived from a European context. A consequence of this perspective has been a dearth of research on sexuality and pleasure, especially for women. The HIV/AIDS pandemic in the sub-Saharan region has redefined understandings of sexuality and given a renewed impetus and urgency to the study of sexuality in all its complexity. More recently, research into gender and AIDS has highlighted the importance of including men, male sexuality and masculinity in HIV/AIDS prevention and education programmes (Mane & Aggleton 2002).

The public health crisis precipitated by HIV/AIDS has also brought social science, biomedical and development research into closer collaboration and renewed dialogue. The indelible stamp of public-health-related sexuality research in Africa can be seen in the emphasis on demography, population and fertility studies, on quantitative research strategies and on 'knowledge, attitudes and practices'.

Political change in South Africa has coincided with an upsurge in work on same-sex identities, focusing on social aspects of law, history, cultural geography and social anthropology (Epprecht 1998, Dirsuweit 1999, De Vos 2000, Reid 2004). This builds on earlier work in labour studies and historical accounts of migrant labour in the southern African region that have focused on the role of homoeroticism in the construction of masculinity (Moodie 1989, Harries 1990). This work, examining the complex interplay between gender, sexuality and identity, is relatively recent. Historically, same-sex relations in Africa have either been largely ignored or concealed in inaccessible texts such as travel writings, missionary reports and obscure anthropological journals. 'Among the many myths Europeans have created about Africa, the myth that homosexuality is absent or incidental in African societies is one of the oldest and most enduring' (Murray & Roscoe 1998:xi). Perceptions of homosexuality in Africa usually reveal more about the preoccupations of Europeans than the experiences of Africans. Early writings tended to cast Africans as closer to nature, their sexuality devoted to the 'natural' functions of reproduction, and therefore free of 'degenerate and perverse' European practices such as homosexuality. However, evidence of widespread same-sex experience has been used by homophiles to demonstrate that homosexuality must be a natural variant of human sexuality. In this argument, Africans are still seen as closer to nature and free of the corrupting influences of European civilisation. Alternatively, the same evidence is used by homophobes to suggest that homosexuality is indeed perverse. From this vantage point, Africans are seen as morally lax and sexually indiscriminate (Murray & Roscoe 1998). All of these interpretations are based on the idea of African sexual exceptionalism, characteristic of European perceptions of African sexualities.

The role of contemporary research on sexualities in Africa is to challenge the dualities and dichotomies of the colonial gaze that has been so influential in shaping an understanding of 'African sexuality', and to deepen and broaden the narrow public health perspective that sees sexuality primarily as a medical issue. Recent work reflects this move towards a more nuanced and holistic understanding of African sexualities. *Men Behaving Differently* contributes to this understanding by focusing explicitly on African sexualities, with a primary emphasis on men and masculinities in South Africa.

Masculinity studies

International scholarship on men and masculinities has grown exponentially within the past few decades. 'Today there are no areas of men's activities that have not been subject to some research and debate by both women and men' (Whitehead & Barrett 2001:1). At one level, this is born of a recognition that early feminist and gender theory focused almost exclusively (and for obvious political reasons) on the position and experience of women. Men, except where they were situated as part of the problem (the abuser, the oppressor, the patriarch), were neither the object nor the subject of study; and scholarship on gay men was accommodated under the rubrics of queer studies and gay and lesbian studies. Sociological enquiry into the changing nature of work and family, at least in a Western context, resulted in a focus on the changing position of men (Segal 1990). 'Men and masculinity' has become the subject of intense theorisation, and the work of Bob Connell (1995) is seminal here. His typologies of hegemonic and non-hegemonic masculinities inaugurated an intense and ongoing debate (Hearn & Morgan 1990, Seidler 1994, Hood-Williams 2001). Critically, this debate has dismantled monolithic notions of men's power by demonstrating that men wield and access power differently, depending on their racial, class and sexual locations (Connell 1995, Morrell 2001, Whitehead 2002, McDowell 2003).

In a South African context, scholars have pointed to the influence of colonialism and apartheid on men and the study of masculinity. Morrell argues that 'masculinity and violence have been yoked together in South African history' (2001:12). He suggests that masculinity (especially for African men) has been shaped by two key experiences in the twentieth century, namely, the workplace, in particular mining, and rural life. The latter legitimated a gender (and generational) system in which men dominated at all levels, from the system of chieftaincy, which controlled all access to the land, to the sexual division of labour within the household. The social and gendered organisation of rural life was reflected in urban areas, particularly in the early years of proletarianisation, where African urban life was dominated by men. Morrell (2002) suggests that African men in urban centres survived lives of extreme hardship by combining prior knowledge with new strategies. Work, and patterns of residential formation structured along existing friendship and ethnic lines, gave rise to forms of masculinity characterised by violence.

Others also point to the interconnectedness of masculinity and violence, partly imprinted in social and economic conditions. Breckenridge (1998:668–94), for example, argues that the ubiquity of violence in South Africa can be traced back to gold mining, which he aptly terms a 'world without women'. Diamond mining and gold mining, the backbone of the South African economy, were developed on the back of the migrant labour system, and, as Campbell observed in her study of Basotho migrants on the gold mines of Carltonville in the 1990s (1997:227–8), 'masculinity emerged as a master narrative'.

The system of compounds or single-sex hostels formed an environment in which pleasure was hard to find. Conditions were humiliating, violent and brutal. Within the confines of the compound it was a world of men, and high levels of risk at work were often matched by high-risk behaviour socially (Campbell 2002, Walker et al. 2004). The masculine figure of the mineworker is an enduring symbol of bravery and fearlessness, yet it also represents the hard edge of poverty and exploitation.

Masculinities in South Africa have been profoundly shaped by closed institutions such as compounds and hostels. The prison is another such institution which creates and reinforces violent masculinities, particularly through prison gangs (Niehaus 2002, Gear 2003). As Morrell (2001) argues, masculine identities have been forged through work and entrenched gender systems in rural areas. Yet masculine identities were also constructed through opposition to apartheid. Soldiers fighting against the apartheid government in the ANC's and PAC's armed wings Umkhonto we Sizwe and APLA were regarded as figures of heroic masculinity, as were young men (comrades) who were involved in anti-apartheid struggles in the townships. The latter kind of masculinity, often referred to as 'struggle masculinity', developed in the late 1970s and 1980s and was marked by high levels of militancy and violence, legitimated as a necessary response to the apartheid government (Xaba 2001). Unterhalter (2000) has also identified a form of heroic masculinity associated with the work setting of political struggle, the characteristics of which are personal heroism, bravery, adventure, hardship and male camaraderie.

If colonialism and apartheid shaped the masculinities of the past, the transition to democracy in South Africa in the 1990s has had the effect of unsettling and unseating entrenched masculinities: masculinities, which were, in the main, patriarchal, authoritarian and steeped in violence.

Recent South African scholarship points to the visibility of sex and sexuality after 1994 (Posel 2003a, 2003b). Contemporary South African society is saturated with matters sexual. The high levels of gender-based violence, and the growing prevalence of child sexual abuse and rape have occupied centre stage in the media and have become the preoccupation of key government ministers and departments. HIV/AIDS, which has exploded over the past ten years, has resulted in widespread and very explicit advertising around negotiating sex and safer-sex practices. Reid & Dirsuweit (2002) argue that in the period of democratic transformation, gay people had never been so visible in South Africa. They claim that:

> increased visibility, the political climate of the time and the promise of equality enshrined in the Constitution, created an environment conducive to 'coming out' and many people did so, sometimes in the full glare of the public eye. (2002:4)

Access to previously unavailable books, films, and magazines (including pornographic material) and the rapid growth in 'adult sex shops' accompanied the period of democratic transition and were legally sanctioned.

The transition to democracy simultaneously ushered in changes to the existing gender order. These are reflected in the South African Constitution, in key changes in legislation and in the widely held perception that 'women are better off in the new South Africa', succinctly summed up in a dialogue from a film made recently about two men who want to get married:

> Is it okay if two men want to marry?
> If men want to marry, it's fine. A wife can change into a man in your house. You may have to cook, although you are a man. Now that this rotten government gives women rights, you can't solve your problems at home, because your wife will run to the government. I'd rather be with a man.[1]

Not surprisingly, the publicness of sex and sexuality and the shifting gender order have had significant consequences for men and masculinities. Men are centrally implicated in the shifting sexual landscape. The HIV/AIDS epidemic is driven by men, and men are blamed for the prevalence of domestic violence and child sexual abuse, and more recently baby-rape (Walker et al. 2004).

Crisis? What crisis?

The idea of 'crisis', or more specifically 'crisis tendencies', has emerged as a central trope for understanding the pressures, reactions and responses to the changing nature of power relations between men and women, embedded in the vagaries of economic power and precipitated by changes in the social structure of sexuality and emotions (Connell 1995). In other words, the conditions for 'crisis tendencies' have been identified in public and private spheres: in the public sphere, through shifts in economic and political power towards a more gender-equitable arrangement; and in the private or intimate sphere by changes in what was expected of men both sexually and emotionally. Connell thus distinguishes between 'crisis tendencies', which include broader shifts in the gender order, and 'masculinities in crisis', which involve crises in terms of men's roles, tasks and identity. In a convincing study of the interrelationship between socioeconomic change and male sexual behaviour in rural and urban East Africa, Margrethe Silberschmidt shows how these two spheres are inextricably interconnected (2004). The interplay between broader social and gender change and individual men's responses is complex. Such complexities and dichotomies are evident in the context of political/gender transitions in South Africa where shifts in the gender order are embedded in a liberal discourse of human rights which puts the onus of claiming rights and of meeting responsibilities onto the individual. Although gender transitions occur at the level of the social, the locus of change rests with the individual. Failure to fulfil masculine ideals (socially and economically constructed) can be played out at a personal level, resulting in crises of identity – an idea developed by both Niehaus and Sideris in this volume.

The idea of a 'crisis of masculinity' originated as an analytic device and soon permeated popular consciousness, thus feeding moral panics about men and boys. Clearly 'crisis' was a fertile term for public panic. Boys were seen to be underperforming at school, men's health was seen to be at dire risk and the traditional model of fatherhood was under increasing strain through the 'absent father' syndrome (Dowsett 2003). In public panics, hegemonic masculinity was seen to reassert itself by implication – women's advances and achievements, which remained statistically insignificant, became the scapegoat for popular understandings of 'masculinity in crisis'. This perception has led some academics working in the field to caution against the 'crisis of masculinity' theory (Dowsett 2003, Sideris 2004). Dowsett (2003) suggests that 'men are in trouble collectively' but stops short of arguing that masculinity is in crisis.

'Masculinities and its crises' was a theme that allowed for the idea of 'crisis' to be tackled head-on at the symposium *Masculinity and Manhood: Struggles with Change*,² which took place at the Wits Institute for Social and Economic Research (WISER) in September 2004. As Bob Connell reiterated at the symposium, it is undoubtedly true that the serious academic engagement with masculinity as an object of study arose as a result of 'cultural turbulence' associated with the rise of the women's movement, the reorganisation of gender relations and changing systems of relating between men and women. These factors have placed in question the presumed nature of masculinity. In her symposium paper, Tina Sideris, while cautious of the 'crisis' model, nevertheless asserted that expressions of insecurity amongst men should be taken quite seriously, while Deborah Posel, in her presentation, suggested that a reading of popular moral panics alerts us to important underlying tensions in gender relations.

Throughout the present volume the authors show that men in South Africa have responded differently to social and gender change. Indeed, some masculinities have responded well to the demands of political transformation, yet others reveal deep crises of identity. This reiterates the now well-established notion that there are many different masculinities and certainly many different forms and experiences of crisis.

Crisis or no crisis, there have been seismic shifts in the worlds of men and masculinities, changes which are keenly felt in a country that has undergone a period of rapid political change and economic transformation. It is men's prominent yet uncertain and changing position in South Africa that constitutes the focus of this collection.

Men behaving differently

Many of these papers focus on change arising out of a challenge to the status quo – a challenge to existing patriarchal norms and values. In this respect, the chapters by Liz Walker, Tina Sideris and Mark Hunter give nuanced insight into the ways in which men grapple with change, over time, in the social context and in the intimate sphere. The chapters by Isak Niehaus and Sasha Gear are linked through an analysis of violence as an attempt to bridge the gap between fantasies of masculine domination and the harsh demeaning conditions of everyday life. Deborah Posel explores the implications of violent masculinist rhetoric in the political domain. New possibilities for the public expression of sexual and gender identities are presented in the chapter by Graeme Reid. Marc Epprecht highlights the historical bias of sexuality research and suggests new ways of exploring male sexuality. The book is intended to provide sharp glimpses into 'men behaving differently', in various parts of the country, in rural and urban environments, in familial and institutional settings, in public and private spheres, amongst gay men and straight men.

Deborah Posel puts the phenomenon of baby rape and the more general phenomenon of sexual violence into historical perspective, highlighting the manner in which sexuality, particularly male sexuality, has become politicised in contemporary South Africa. She argues that in apartheid South Africa, sexual violence was concealed: by the very narrow legal definitions of rape, by the racist state's lack of interest in the growing problem of gender-based violence in black communities, and by family members who were often economically dependent on 'the rapist' or abuser within the family. In this context, the perpetrator of sexual violence was a 'deviant stranger', and rape and sexual abuse were aberrant or deviant acts. Posel demonstrates how sexual violence becomes a matter of public concern and condemnation in post-apartheid South Africa, where sexuality is much more visible. Rape cases, particularly those involving babies and young children, are highly publicised and become the yardstick by which the 'moral fibre' of the nation is measured. In this discourse of moral shame, Posel shows how it is men – fathers, brothers, sons – who are blamed. The most profound threat to babies and children is now coming from within – the sexual predator is no longer the stranger. The country's moral crisis can thus be seen as a crisis of manhood. These issues are engaged through an analytical exploration of the nature and structure of secrecy. Posel argues that the 'internal structure of the secrecy of sexual violence has been dislodged' and has broken down. She invokes the 'politics of confession and truth-telling' to understand and explain the ways in which sexual violence, masculinity and sexuality have entered into public conversation.

Isak Niehaus provides fresh insight into the shockingly high levels of rape in contemporary South Africa through an ethnographic study based in Impalahoek, a village of 20 000 people located in the Bushbuckridge area of the South African Lowveld. Drawing on Henrietta Moore's distinction between 'gender as it is constructed' and 'gender as it is lived', Niehaus delves into the lives and circumstances of the men and women involved in three different accounts of rape. He considers the nature of masculine domination in sexual violence and questions the common understanding of rape as 'an expression of patriarchy' and as an attempt by dominant men to control assertive women through the violent expression of sexual entitlement. Instead he focuses on rape as a brutal and symbolic assertion of masculine domination in a context where there is a dramatic rift between men's ideals and the diminished realities of their everyday lives. Niehaus shows that it is often socially marginal and weak men who engage in rape in a futile attempt to assert painfully unrealisable ideals of masculine prowess and heterosexual virility. His cases are shocking, not only in the cruel detail but also in the informants' recounting of events that convey the everyday nature of sexual violence in the area. As Niehaus reflects:

> The information provided in this chapter is extremely sensitive, potentially harmful and even incriminating. Yet I believe that in a country afflicted by horrendous sexual violence, silence is a far more serious abuse of academic freedom than the exposure of secrets.

Sex, gender and masculine identity in a men's prison is the focus of Sasha Gear's paper. Gear argues that sex (with whom and how) in prison shapes many dimensions of an inmate's experience, in particular the sex/gender identity of the prisoner. Sex in prison is highly regulated and controlled by the gangs. In the main, male prisoners are divided into 'men' and 'women' (or *wyfies*). The *wyfies* are forced (and tricked) into becoming 'women', where they perform many of the submissive roles expected of women, including always being the receptive or penetrated sexual partner. In this way, Gear argues, their outside masculine identity is subverted and ruptured, yet their inside sexual identity is constructed within the confines of patriarchal heterosexuality and it is here that the continuity lies. Prison, in these terms, is an institution that facilitates the creating of new identities, while never completely breaking with those of the past. Gear also details the presence of sexual encounters between male inmates which are neither coercive nor transactional, but rather pursued for pleasure and intimacy. This chapter demonstrates that men's sex/gender identity in closed institutions reflects aspects of the old (or the outside), which combine with contingencies for managing the new. For Gear, negotiating sex in prison thus represents continuity, adaptation and rupture.

Tina Sideris documents changes in gender relations in the Nkomazi region, a rural area situated in south-eastern Mpumulanga province. Drawing on fieldwork and clinical work conducted over the past eight years, Sideris examines how a small group of men have reflected upon their practices and redefined themselves as 'different'. In this area, as in many in South Africa, violence against women is ubiquitous: expected by women and meted out as the norm by men. Economic deprivation, poverty and uncertainty characterise the lives of these men, shaping their sense of themselves as men, and their relations with their families. Gender relations in this setting are structured along patriarchal lines where the status of manhood is conferred by having a wife and children, and the establishment of an independent household where the man is unambiguously the head. Here, authority over women is maintained through violence. Yet Sideris shows that patriarchal gender relations in the Nkomazi region are being redefined in the wake of the transition to democracy and subsequent legislation which seeks to promote the rights of women. In this chapter she outlines the lives and practices of men who have rejected violence as a means of resolving conflict. These men seek to promote equality in their households in relation to the domestic division of labour and the distribution of financial resources in the home, thus fundamentally recasting family and gender relations. They embrace a discourse of human rights which is regarded as deviant by family, friends and the community, thus making their 'difference' all the more remarkable.

Drawing on ethnographic and documentary research in KwaZulu-Natal, Mark Hunter points to the necessity to locate contemporary understandings of sexuality within the context of historical and cultural processes. He situates the notion of the isoka in an historical frame and examines how the meanings of Zulu manhood and patterns of sexual networking more generally have changed over time and in response to changing social and economic conditions. Although having multiple sexual partners has always been sanctioned for men (and legitimated for them though polygamy), until quite recently, manhood was achieved through the ability to establish an independent household, to marry and have children. Marital rates began to drop from the 1960s, and Hunter argues that, since the 1980s, owing to increasing levels of unemployment, men have been increasingly unable to afford to pay *lobola* (bridewealth). Men have found it very difficult to assert their manhood through traditional avenues. In this context, alternative means of achieving manhood, such as violence and having multiple sexual partners, take on exaggerated significance. Hunter also points to the contradictions of isoka masculinity in a time of AIDS where men who are 'successful with women' are also dying. Valorising alternative attributes of successful masculinity such as sporting prowess and independence are, Hunter suggests, important strategies. Yet he also cautions that they may be at odds with the lived experience of the majority of poor South Africans.

In a similar vein, Liz Walker argues that in contemporary South Africa traditional notions of masculinity have been destabilised. She suggests that the transition to democracy has precipitated a crisis of masculinity in which some men are defending established masculinities and others are seeking to explore new possibilities – in short, constructing new and different masculinities. She discusses the findings of research conducted amongst urban, working-class African men who have previously been perpetrators of violence, particularly against women. The men interviewed speak of role confusion, shifting expectations and demands placed on them as men and the pressures and possibilities they have encountered in the new social order. Walker argues that the new democratic order has created a legitimate space for men to embark on reflective and introspective journeys, giving rise to new notions of manhood.

Certainly democracy and a precedent set by the Constitution in relation to gay equality have had a profound influence on the public expression of gay identities in post-apartheid South Africa, so much so, in fact, that it is not uncommon for gay lifestyles to be associated in the public imaginary with 'fashion', and for gay visibility to be regarded as almost inextricably linked to South Africa's transition to democracy. Graeme Reid explores the tension between creativity and constraint in the making of gendered identities amongst 'ladies' and 'gents' in an ethnographic study based in the town of Ermelo, Mpumalanga. In a context where there is a high level of innovation and creativity in the making of gay identities, why is it that there is such a rigid adherence to masculine and feminine ideals? Or, to paraphrase the words of an informant used in the title of the chapter, why is it that 'a man is a man completely and a wife is a wife completely' even in male same-sex relationships? Reid looks at the performance of masculinity and femininity amongst men, highlighting the fact that masculinity is understood and defined by what it is not – in this case, 'not female' and 'not gay'. He shows how ideas about gender are developed in everyday practices as well as through ritual performances such as engagement and marriage ceremonies. What it means to be a 'gent', a 'lady' or a 'Greek salad' in small-town South Africa is explored through the experiences of young men in Ermelo for whom these questions are of immediate and compelling interest and the main focus of workshops designed to teach people 'how to be real gays'.

Marc Epprecht highlights the gaps and silences that exist in ethnographic research on male–male sexual relationships as a result of bias and myopia amongst researchers. He situates his argument in the 'assertively masculinist culture' of Basotho men and in contrast to their 'enduring reputation for heterosexual virility'. He argues that this reputation is in part due to the 'blindness, myth-making and self-censorship of heterosexist or homophobic Western and Western-trained scholars'. Epprecht's chapter draws on the author's encounter with a small community of self-identified gay men in the outskirts of Maseru whom he engages on questions of masculinity and same-sex sexuality. His use of transcripts from these discussions gives voice to a small and largely ignored group of men in Lesotho, and simultaneously serves a larger purpose both by questioning the academic bias which gives rise to a particular construction of masculinity and by exposing some of the reasons behind the invisibility of non-normative sexuality in African studies as a whole.

Our intention in bringing these diverse chapters together in *Men Behaving Differently: South African Men Since 1994* is to broaden existing horizons in masculinity and sexuality studies in Africa by focusing on men's varied, contradictory and unpredictable responses, in intimate and social spheres, to transition and change in the public realm.

Acknowledgements

Thanks to Tina Sideris and Rachel Spronk for their useful input, comments and suggestions.

Notes

1 Interview at Springs Station, Johannesburg. (Njinge 2002).
2 *Masculinity and Manhood: Struggles with Change Symposium.* Wits Institute for Social and Economic Research (WISER), 5–7 September 2004.

References

Arnfred, S. (ed.) (2004) *Rethinking Sexuality in Africa*. (Uppsala: Nordic Africa Institute).

Bleys, Rudi C. (1995) *The Geography of Perversion: Male-to-Male Sexual Behaviour outside the West and the Ethnographic Imagination, 1750–1918* (New York: New York University Press).

Breckenridge, K. (1998) The allure of violence: men, race and masculinity on the South African goldmines, 1900–1950. *Journal of Southern African Studies*, 24, 4, 669–94.

Caldwell, J.C. and Caldwell, P. (1987) The cultural context of high fertility in sub-Saharan Africa. *Population and Development Review*, 13, 409–37.

Caldwell, J.C., Caldwell, P. and Quiggin, P. (1989) The social context of AIDS in sub-Saharan Africa. *Population and Development Review*, 15, 185–234.

Campbell, C. (1997) Migrancy, masculine identities and AIDS: the psychosocial context of HIV transmission on the South African gold mines. *Social Science and Medicine*, 45, 2, 273–81.

Campbell, C. (2002) *Letting Them Die*. (Cape Town: Double Storey Books).

Connell, R. (1995) *Masculinities*. (Cambridge: Polity).

De Vos, P. (2000) The Constitution made us queer: the sexual orientation clause in the South African Constitution and the emergence of gay and lesbian identity. (Herman & Stychin 2000: 194–202).

Dirsuweit, T. (1999) Carceral spaces in South Africa: a case study of institutional power, sexuality and transgression in a women's prison. *Geoforum*, 30, 71–83.

Dowsett, G. (2002) 'Uncovering the Men' in men's health: working with desire, diversions and demons. Paper presented at the Wits Institute for Social and Economic Research (WISER).

Duberman, M.B., Vicinus, M. and Chauncey, G. Jr. (eds.) (1989) *Hidden from History: Reclaiming the Gay and Lesbian Past*. (New York: New American Library).

Epprecht, M. (1998) 'Good God Almighty, what's this!': homosexual 'crime' in early colonial Zimbabwe. (Murray & Roscoe 1998: 197–221).

Fanon, F. (1986) (1952) *Black Skin, White Masks*. (London: Pluto).

Gear, S. (2003) An exploration of sex, violence and gender in South African men's prisons. Paper presented at the *Sex and Secrecy* Conference, University of the Witwatersrand, Johannesburg, 22–25 June.

Harries, P. (1990) Symbols and sexuality: culture and identity in the early Witwatersrand mines. *Gender and History*, 11, 3, 318–36.

Heald, S. (1999) *Manhood and Morality. Sex, Violence and Ritual in Gisu Society*. (London and New York: Routledge).

Hearn, J. and Morgan, D. (eds.) (1990) *Men, Masculinity and Social Theory*. (London: Unwin Hyman).

Herman, D. and Stychin, C. (eds.) (2001) *Sexuality in the Legal Arena*. (London: Athlone Press).

Hood-Williams, J. (2001) Gender, masculinities and crime: from structures to psyches. *Theoretical Criminology*, 5, 1, 37–60.

Mane, P. and Aggleton, P. (2001) Gender and HIV/AIDS: What do men have to do with it? *Current Sociology* 49, 23–37

McDowell, L. (2003) *Redundant Masculinities. Employment, Change and White Working Class Youth*. (Oxford: Blackwell).

Mohanty, C. (1991) Under western eyes: feminist scholarship and colonial discourses. (Mohanty et al. 1991:51–80).

Mohanty, C., Russo, A. and Torres, L. (eds.) *Third World Women and the Politics of Feminism*. (Bloomington: Indiana University Press).

Moodie, T.D. (1989) Migrancy and male sexuality in the South African gold mines. (Duberman et al. 1989: 411–425).

Moore, H. (1994) *A Passion for Difference: Essays in Anthropology and Gender*. (Cambridge: Polity Press).

Morrell, R. (2001) *Changing Men in Southern Africa*. (London: Zed Press).

Morrell, R. (2002) Men, movement and gender transformation in South Africa. *Journal of Men's Studies*, 10, 3, 309–321.

Murray, S.O. and Roscoe, W. (eds.) (1998) *Boy-Wives and Female Husbands. Studies of African Homosexualities*. (London: Macmillan).

Niehaus, I. (2002) Renegotiating masculinity in the South African Lowveld: narratives of male-male sex in labour compounds and in prisons. *African Studies* 61, 1, 77–98.

Njinge, M. (director) (2002). *My Son the Bride*. Video Documentary. (Johannesburg: South African Broadcasting Corporation).

Ortner, S. (1974) Is female to male as nature is to culture? (Rosaldo & Lamphere 1974:67–87).

Posel, D. (2003a) Getting the nation talking about sex: reflections on the politics of sexuality and 'nation-building' in post-apartheid South Africa. Paper presented at the WISER seminar series, *On the Subject of Sex*, 25 February.

Posel, D. (2003b) The scandal of manhood: unmaking secrets of sexual violence in post-apartheid South Africa. Paper presented at the *Sex and Secrecy* Conference, University of the Witwatersrand, Johannesburg, 22–25 June.

Reid, G. (2004) 'It's just a fashion!' Linking homosexuality and 'modernity' in South Africa. *Etnofoor*, 16, 2, 7–25.

Reid, G. and Dirsuweit, T. (2002) Understanding systemic violence: homophobic attacks in Johannesburg and its surrounds. *Urban Forum*, 13, 3, 99–126.

Rosaldo, M. (1974) Woman, culture and society: a theoretical overview. (Rosaldo and Lamphere 1974:17–14).

Rosaldo, M. and Lamphere, L. (1974) *Woman, Culture and Society*. (Stanford: Stanford University Press).

Segal, L. (1990) *Slow Motion. Changing Masculinities, Changing Men*. (London: Virago).

Seidler, V. (1994) *Unreasonable Men. Masculinity and Social Theory.* (London: Routledge).

Sideris, T. (2004). 'You have to change and you don't know how!': Contesting what it means to be a man in rural areas of South Africa. *African Studies,* 63, 1, 29–50

Silberschmidt, M. (2004) Masculinities, sexuality and socio-economic change in rural and urban East Africa. (Arnfred 2004:233–48).

Unterhalter, E. (2000) The work of the nation: heroic masculinity in South African autobiographical writing of the anti-apartheid struggle. *The European Journal of Development Research,* 12, 2, 157–177.

Vaughan, M. (1991) *Curing their Ills. Colonial Power and African Illness.* (Cambridge: Polity).

Walker, L., Reid, G. and Cornell, M. (2004) *Waiting to Happen. HIV/AIDS in South Africa.* (Cape Town: Double Storey Books).

Whitehead, S. and Barrett, F. (2001) *The Masculinities Reader.* (Cambridge: Polity).

Whitehead, S. (2002) *Men and Masculinities.* (Cambridge: Polity).

Xaba, T. (2001) Masculinity and its malcontents: the confrontation between 'struggle masculinity' and 'post-struggle masculinity' (1990–1997). (Morrell 2001:105–24).

2
'Baby rape':
Unmaking secrets of sexual violence in post-apartheid South Africa

Deborah Posel

> 'Actually it's not a new phenomenon; it's been something that you hide, you regard it as an embarrassment within the family. But now people have started to talk, they've decided that they've had enough.'
>
> (South African women protesting against child rape, speaking on BBC News, UK, 11 December 2001)

Introduction

Before the mid-1990s, the issue of sexual violence[1] in South Africa had languished on the margins of public debate and political engagement. Intermittent media foci on rape excited some brief episodes of public concern and interest, but these receded quickly. Nor was any of this the subject of much political discussion or engagement. From the early 1980s, some women's groups and NGOs strove to publicise and politicise what they saw as a serious and worsening social problem of sexual violence in many spheres and settings;[2] but they largely failed to arouse sustained attention or intervention. Throughout the apartheid era, some sexual crimes were more visible than others, particularly if the victim was white and the perpetrator was black, but in the main, sexual violence was shrouded in varying orders of secrecy and silence, and the politics of sexual violence was largely inert.

By the end of 2001, however, public talk about sexual violence – and rape in particular – was incessant and prominent: a preoccupation of media talk shows; writ large in the investigative press; and regularly the subject of magazine feature articles, letters to editors, documentaries and other forms of social commentary. As one magazine article put it, 'day after day, television, radio and newspapers are full of horrifying accounts of lives being destroyed by brutish rapists'.[3]

This media blitz both echoed and orchestrated resounding calls from members of the public to 'break the silence' and bring the 'dark unspoken secrets'[4] of sexual violence into the open. Waves of popular anger brought protest marches to the streets. 'Respect our mothers and sisters', read the placards of protesting men.[5] Much of the popular outrage focused on the sexual behaviour of men. 'Men of South Africa, why do we allow lust and greed to turn us into beasts without emotions?' implored the author of a letter in the press on the subject of punishing 'rape monsters'.[6] And within the polity, the issue of rape had been thrust to the forefront of debates about the meaning of democracy and justice, and the manner of the national subject. 'Why is there such moral degeneration in our new-found democracy?' asked a lead article in the *Saturday Star*. As various NGOs and community organisations 'challenged the politicians' to take the lead in combating 'the scourge of rape', government spokespeople scrambled to express their 'disgust' and 'despair' at the unfolding saga of sexual assault. Parliament called for public hearings on child rape and abuse; the Deputy President initiated a 'national convention to plan a mass regeneration campaign';[7] debates about punishment for sexual crimes raged fiercely in parliament and in the media, with many calling vehemently for the reinstatement of the death penalty for rapists; and several vigilante groups took matters into their own hands and dispensed 'peoples' justice' to suspected perpetrators of rape.

Of course, resistances to the visibility and politicisation of sexual violence have persisted, not least within the state and among leading politicians. The increased volume and intensity of debate about rape and sexual abuse is not in itself a measure of the scale of concern or the change of views within the population at large, and for all the talking, the practice of sexual violence has remained brutal and endemic. Still, we have witnessed important shifts in the public discourse[8] and politics of sexual violence, linked to some powerful and urgent impulses to bare, and grapple with, the enormity of its perpetration in the country.[9]

In many respects, these recent efforts to confront sexual violence have taken on the character of a public confessional, of admitting a problem which was, at least in some sense and to some extent, known all along. The revelations of widespread and terrible sexual violence have not been wholly new and surprising, therefore. Indeed, part of the contemporary anxiety and flurry of debate is exactly an urge to revisit the past: how much of it is new, how much of it has always been there but hidden from public view?

This chapter, as an attempt to decipher how and why the politics of sexual violence has changed in South Africa, is therefore an exploration of the process of unmaking secrets (uneven and incomplete though this unmaking undeniably is).

The chapter has four parts. The first gives a brief account of the politico-legal, social and cultural production of secrecy with respect to sexual violence prior to 1994. The second considers the form which the new public confrontation with sexual violence has taken, by tracking the genealogy of the process of exposing practices previously shrouded from public view. The third looks more analytically at the nature of secrecy, with a view to identifying the key points of rupture with the past. And the fourth seeks to explain why these changes occurred, and why they occurred in the particular form identified in part 3.

In so doing, the chapter has several aims. In the absence of a substantial history of the politics of sexual violence in this country, it provides an inevitably brief historical account, tracing the making of a political issue in the shift from the marginalisation and minimisation of the problem of sexual violence, to the point where it came to occupy the centre stage of public debate. As a study in the unmaking of secrets, the chapter has an interest in the epistemological conditions of secrecy and its unmaking, showing how – in the case of sexual violence – reconceptualisations of violation and victimhood were fundamental to the new politics of exposé. The chapter is also an analysis of the politicisation of secrecy, in relation to wider questions about the politics of confession more generally, locally and internationally. I have argued elsewhere that sexuality has unexpectedly become one of South Africa's principal sites of political contestation (Posel forthcoming). The exposé of sexual violence has been part of this process, in ways which demonstrate the interconnectedness of these modalities of politicisation with other facets of the recent local and global investment in the redemptive powers of 'speaking out'.

Making secrets of sexual violence

Long-standing habits of secrecy and silence with respect to sexual violence have had profound effects on the production of historical research. In South Africa, as has been the case in many other parts of the world,[10] historians have shown relatively little interest in exploring the subject. Until recently, there was similarly little by way of a local anthropology or sociology of sexual violence, with a small archive of research having been assembled largely in the fields of law and psychology.[11]

There is little, then, by way of an established historical account to draw on; even less by way of analysis. The statistical corpus is patchy, and even then, inherently unreliable, given many blockages and imponderables in the data-gathering process (See for example Statistics South Africa (2000:3). The apartheid state displayed relatively scant interest in the surveillance of sexual violence, and the efforts at quantifying the problem by organisations dealing with sexual violence are estimates, more than reliable measures (although they undoubtedly provide some evidence, often more local than national).

The discussion which follows, therefore, is scant and tentative. Yet it is uncontroversial to anchor it in the claim that there has been a long-standing and serious problem of sexual violence across different races and classes in this society, which has been intertwined with powerful impulses to conceal it socially and marginalise it politically.

In the first instance, the history of sexual violence in South Africa has been shaped by habits of patriarchal thought, which have spanned the society and state at large. Prior to 1994, South African law made a series of familiarly patriarchal assumptions about gender and sexual violence, across all races, which were seldom publicly challenged.[12] Both law and custom buttressed the authority of men over women, in ways which severely constricted women's claims to legal and police protection from sexual violence. Rape was legally defined as the imposition of unwanted vaginal sex by an adult man upon an adult woman (Ross 1993:8). The omission of coercive oral or anal sex precluded homosexual rape from the scope of the law. The definition also excluded sexual violence within marriage.

A tacit hierarchy thus informed the legal conceptualisation and adjudication of sexual violence. The moral censure associated with rape, as the most extreme and reprehensible form of sexual violence, was limited to heterosexual encounters, and even here, the perceived extremity of the violence was *inversely proportional* to the degree of emotional and sexual intimacy involved. Rape could only occur outside the home; the figure of the rapist was that of the predatory stranger.

The law offered protection from sexual violence within the home in terms of provisions against 'indecent assault'. Not only was this a lesser order of offence, it was also difficult for women or children to invoke the support of police in laying charges (Wits Historical Papers 1990a).[13] Police were reluctant to venture into the supposedly 'private' spaces of 'the home', as the domain within which, as far as possible, men should be left to discipline 'their' women and children without legal interference. As the Ministry of Law and Order put it, in an extraordinarily revealing statement of the gendered logic of policing priorities:

> the apparent reluctance of the South African Police to act on charges of assault brought by women against their husbands is based on moral and humanitarian grounds and must generally not be regarded as insensitive behaviour.

The moral entitlements of citizenship were unashamedly unequal; police acted first and foremost to respect and uphold the dignity and authority of the husband.

The policing of rape – even in its attenuated legal definition – was saturated with other prejudicial versions of gender. As a memorandum on rape compiled by the South African Police put it, 'it must always be kept in mind that the complainant in a rape case or a case of immoral nature must be treated with great circumspection (caution) [sic]…'[14] Generally regarded as more unreliable complainants than men, women were considered particularly suspect in the case of sexual crimes, either because of a deep-rooted suspicion that the woman provoked the sexual encounter in the first place (tempting the man beyond reasonable restraint of his natural lust)[15] or because the accusation would probably be withdrawn 'owing to rationalisation' by the complainant (coming to her senses) (Wits Historical Papers 1990b).

These state practices fitted comfortably with the dominant predilections within South Africa's citizenry, where cultures of male authority are long established and deeply rooted. Particularly in respect of sexual violence in zones of domestic or familial intimacy, social impulses to secrecy colluded with politico-legal reluctances, so that such violations were seldom reported to the police, and even less frequently investigated to the point of prosecution. In the seemingly one and only year in which the Minister of Law and Order was challenged in parliament to produce 'the latest available statistics in respect of cases of incest brought to the police' – symptomatic in itself of the abiding political uninterest in issues of this sort – all he could muster for the period from January to December 1984 was a national total of 118.[16]

The prism of race also had a powerful effect on the state's limited sightings of sexual violence. With visions of 'black sexuality' steeped in familiar colonial myths and stereotypes about the rapacious lust of black men and essential lasciviousness of black women,[17] state institutions were particularly uninterested in the problem of worsening sexual violence within black communities, and police were all the more disinclined to act on reports of such violence when the complainants were black. Recognition that sexual violence was widespread became exactly the basis on which the issue was ignored. As the Ministry of Law and Order put it:

> experience has proved that assault within the family occurs mainly amongst the lower socio-economic groups,[18] very often due to the uncontrolled use of intoxicating liquor. The behaviour of these families is usually habitual and well known to the police. Policewomen usually deal with such female complainants in private, where possible, but circumstances often make this impossible ... Police members are often assaulted, in some instances even by the complainants when trying to arrest the assailants. (Wits Historical Papers 1990b)

So 'habitual' sexual violence in the home was better left a private matter, since apparently no amount of police intervention would make a difference – indeed, the victims themselves would resent it. And, as the police liked to point out, many perpetrators of sexual violence were also 'habitual' drinkers, and since 'it [was] not an offence under our laws for a person to be drunk in his own home'(Wits Historical Papers 1990b), there was little to be done to deter the predictable consequences.

Rendered invisible by various strategies of legal and judicial minimisation fashioned by the patriarchal politics of the apartheid state, sexual violence was also the site of other, more culturally specific, practices of secrecy. And in the same vein as the politico-legal, the more intimate the setting of the violence, the greater the urge to secrecy – but with different orders of interest insinuated into the logic of secret-making.

In African communities, if 'contemporary research suggests an awkward inter-generational silence on issues of sexuality' generally (Delius & Glaser 2002:30), the secrecy attached to sexual violence was that much more forceful, particularly within marriage and the family. The practice of lobola (giving bride wealth) created a marital contract between families, which structured reciprocal entitlements and obligations. Exposing sexual violence within the marriage – particularly if seriously physical harmful to the woman – jeopardised the contract. Familial interests in keeping the contract in place therefore created powerful incentives to suppress unpalatable exposures, putting intense pressure on women to hide their pain and retreat into silence. Here, the impulse to secrecy was also a sign of the moral shame and cultural stigma attached to the public revelation of sexual violence, particularly if severe. It was because the moral and cultural stakes for the family were high that the practice of secrecy kicked in; if sexual violence had been seen as trivial, there would have been no need to conceal it. And the more harmful the act of violence, the greater the familial imperative to keep it hidden.

Although little is known about the history of child sexual abuse in the country, similar cultural logics of secrecy have been suggested in such cases too: that in the knowledge that such practices were shameful and offensive, family members were complicit in efforts to conceal them from public exposure – and in the process, in order to minimise the moral and psychological discomfort within the family, to banish the issue from zones of more intimate acknowledgement and intervention as well (Lewis 1997).

As Sowetan resident and mother Mary Mabaso put it, African parents maintained an anxious silence about child rape because its exposure threatened further victimisation of the child and the humiliation of the family:

> We are afraid that ... the whole life of the poor child is damaged and there is no future for her. If people know a girl was raped, no-one will marry her. And others can come now and rape her because she has been raped before. She will never be safe. (Russell 1991:12)[19]

Mothers of child rape victims interviewed by researcher Sharon Lewis made similar points:

> I even told them [the child] not to tell anyone, because they will abuse her too ... I won't tell anyone. I'll keep it to myself as I have been keeping this to myself. (Lewis 1997:37)

In Lewis's language, 'there is a suggestion of a paranoid element in the mothers' concern about the "contamination" of their daughters. Their concern appears to go beyond realistic ones'. As a psychologist, Lewis (1997:39) identified here a 'cognitive distortion driven by anxiety'; but from a more sociological and anthropological perspective, it is also possible to recognise here the powerful effects of cultural myths of sexual purity and pollution, and the pressures they created to conceal the 'defilement' of girls for the sake of their marriageability, social integration, and the respectability of their families.

The informal economy of sex and sexual transactions further reinforced the cultural incentives to secrecy. If exposing rape within a relationship or within the home threatened to jeopardise the rapist's contribution to the woman's or family's livelihood, this created overwhelming material incentives to conceal the violence and accommodate it along with the other burdens of everyday life.

With law, politics, cultures of marriage and sexuality, and the strictures of poverty intersecting to banish sexual violence to the margins of public discourse and attention – and with particular force within the terrains of marriage and family – it's not surprising that the victims of such violence were often powerless to defy the threats of death or further harm by perpetrators if the crimes were publicly disclosed. The forces keeping the lid on sexual violence firmly held down were clearly substantial, and bore down especially heavily in the domains of the home.

The creation of a public issue: from secrecy to moral panic

It was feminist groups that were the first to grapple publicly with the issue of sexual violence. The Cape Town Rape Crisis Centre was established in 1977. Its Durban counterpart followed in 1979, with the first national rape crisis conference held in 1980. Outside feminist circles, it seems that the first stirrings of a wider public debate about rape were felt in 1982, as a consequence of stories in the English and Afrikaans media about the trauma of rape, and the secondary victimisation suffered by complainants at the hands of the South African Police. This sudden flurry of interest provoked the Minister of Justice to convene an inquiry by the South African Law Commission into 'the procedure for the laying of rape charges and the medico-forensic aspects of rape' (SA Law Commission 1985: para. 1.1). The Commission in turn felt it 'necessary to undertake a more wide-ranging investigation … to include related offences, such as indecent assault' (SA Law Commission 1985: para. 1.2). But the promise of a more ambitious project amounted to little. Significantly, the Commission's sensitivity to rape as a source of trauma to the victim marked the beginning of an overtly psychological conceptualisation of victimhood, which would ultimately bear directly on the ways in which the horrors of sexual violence were represented and exposed (see part 3). But at this stage, the implications of this shift were largely invisible. While recognising that 'there is growing public awareness of the frequency of rape' (SA Law Commission 1985: para. 1.3), the Commission was nevertheless intent on producing a suitably modest and contained formulation of the extent of the problem. Anxious to dispel 'the impression that something is radically wrong with the social order and with the law and with the process of law relating to rape' (SA Law Commission 1985: para. 1.7), the Commission dismissed claims that 'the figure for rape in South Africa was astronomically high by comparison with that in other countries' (SA Law Commission 1985: para 1.6). Such data, it alleged, was mere feminist propaganda, driven by 'the campaign for an improvement in the status of women, rather than from an honest appraisal of defects in existing law and practice' (SA Law Commission 1985: para. 1.10).

Most of the Commission's recommendations were worthy but limited: rape cases could be heard in camera; and the identity of the victim could be kept anonymous until judgement had been reached. More significant was its recommendation that some legal definition be given to the possibility of rape within marriage, but with the proviso that 'only the Auditor-General may institute such legal proceedings' (House of Assembly Debates 1985: vol. 4, col. 6759).

Overall, however, rape was not seen to be a fundamental social problem; the recommended responses were easily accommodated within the established framework of legal, moral and cultural thinking on the subject. So the Commission's report excited little debate in parliament,[20] and not much media interest. The changes which ensued were modest. In 1986, the first rape unit staffed entirely by female police was created. It was only in 1993, with the passage of the Prevention of Family Violence Act, that the conviction of a husband for the rape of his wife became possible.

Popular mobilisation beyond the women's movement – itself rather attenuated – was slow to develop. The conditions producing high levels of sexual violence within the country were deep-rooted and long established. And, as retrospective readings of the past now reveal, the realities of sexual violence have long been known,[21] particularly in poorer communities subject to harsh living conditions. By the late 1970s, rape had taken on particularly insidious forms among township youth, with the advent of 'jack-rolling' (seen as 'a game of the kidnap and rape' (Russell 1991:65) of girls by gangs of youths). Rape had become 'a new style' (Andersson 2000) for the assertion of a brutalising masculinity. Signs of a 'culture of sexual violence' (Russell 1991:65) were becoming prominent.

Yet it seems it was only in February 1990 that the first march against sexual assault in the history of South Africa occurred (Russell 1991:63). Spearheaded by community leader Mary Mabaso, under the auspices of the Interdenominational Prayer Women's League, and with the support of the South African Council of Churches as well as People Against Women Abuse, the march took to the streets of Soweto 'to show the rapists that we are not happy' (Russell 1991:63). Alarmed at the extent of rape and sexual abuse in Soweto, the organisers mobilised the support of other 'concerned mothers' who 'cannot stand this any more ... worried about the lives and futures of our children'. The rape of teenagers and children was uppermost in their minds. As Mary Mabaso explained:

> we asked everyone to make their own placards, and there were lots of different ones. 'Stop Rape because You are Damaging the Future of the Young Girls.' 'Sexual Abuse is a Curse.' 'Don't Think this is the Right Approach to the Young Ones.' 'Sexual Abuse Can Cause Abnormalities in Young Females.' And 'Hands off Our Children.' The last one referred particularly to the fathers because of the crisis we have of fathers abusing their own children (Russell 1991:70).

Culminating in a prayer service, the march made the evening television news. Some township-based women's organisations then organised 'take back the night' marches, in the aftermath of the protest (Gouws & Kadalie 1994:221). But their impact was short-lived and the issue slipped from public view once again.

Feminist lobbying against sexual violence (with more of a focus on adult than on child victims) intensified in the wake of the constitutional negotiations process during the early 1990s, bearing fruit in the provisions for gender equality and protection from physical harm (including sexual violence) which would become entrenched in the new Bill of Rights. In 1993, three draft bills on women's rights issues were tabled in parliament, including the Prevention of Domestic Violence Draft Bill, which criminalised sexual violence within married couples. But, according to feminist activists Gouws & Kadalie (1994:221):

> the debate in parliament was embarrassing in its irrelevance and by the patronising attitudes of its male members. Apart from a few women members who clearly knew what was at stake, and what the omissions, shortcomings and strength of these bills were, the debate did not enlighten the condition of women at all.

So, notwithstanding the few moments of recognition and concern, the problem of sexual violence, particularly in familial settings, was still largely a non-issue: the butt of sexist stereotyping and political disinterest – in parliament as much as within the wider society.

The issue began to come into public view more intensely and acutely after 1994, in the post-apartheid milieu. Typically, it was a focus on the violent sexual abuse of children that excited the highest orders of concern. But even then, until 2001, it remained a story of intermittent sightings of sexual violence, with faint to moderate signs of activism and vehemence attached to these fleeting moments of public acknowledgement and debate.

The removal of apartheid's media censorship regime[22] created new public spaces within which to represent and grapple with the realities of sexual violence. A series of television dramas – with huge audiences across races, genders and generations – were crafted as social exposés of violence in urban black townships, including sexual violence of various types. In 1994, Soul City, a large NGO, launched what it called a 'multimedia edutainment health project', in the form of a long-running local television soap opera series dramatising a host of difficult social problems. The first series of programmes, broadcast in 1994, dealt head-on with the problem of child sexual abuse – the first time a drama scheduled for family viewing on national television had broached this subject.

The same issue made a brief headline appearance again in 1997, when a media release by the Human Sciences Research Council on the International Day of the Child announced that 'in South Africa child abuse [including sexual abuse] had reached epidemic proportions' (HSRC 1997). But there seems to have been little sustained take-up of, or public interest in, the issue at that point.

It was in June 1998 that the beginnings of a more sustained shift in public mood became evident. This was in response to the sentencing of police sergeant Mandisi Mpengesi for the murder of a man who had raped one of his twin daughters in January 1997. A survivor of childhood sexual abuse, who then became a child-abuse investigator in the sprawling township of Khayelitsha, Mpengesi briefly captured the public imagination as a heroic vigilante warrior in a lax justice system which failed the child victims of sexual assault. Angry crowds protesting his nine-year prison sentence for the murder picketed the Western Cape High Court.

With the high profile afforded to this court case, the issue of child rape received more sustained media coverage than had typically been the case in the past. The South African National Council for Child Welfare claimed that reports of child rape had increased by 74 percent since 1994. But still, no one seemed to panic. An activist NGO, Resources Aimed at the Prevention of Child Abuse and Neglect (RAPCAN), announced with horror that it had discovered schoolboys playing a game called 'catch and rape'. Patience Tshabalala, founder of Project Child at Risk in Soweto, declared it 'time to challenge other men on child abuse'.[23] But the call did not yet strike much of a chord.

While the problem of adult rape hit the headlines early in 1999 with the much-publicised rape of journalist Charlene Smith, the issue of child rape also surfaced again in that year, in relation to the AIDS pandemic and allegations that HIV-positive men were raping young girls in the belief that this would 'cleanse' them of the disease. A feature article in the national newspaper *Sunday Times* cited Dr Nono Simelela, director of the National AIDS programme in the national government Department of Health, as agreeing with research findings produced by medical anthropologist Suzanne Leclerc-Madlala, that 'the myth that AIDS could be cured by having sex with a virgin is prevalent thinking in KwaZulu-Natal.' And a magistrate at Camperdown, in the KwaZulu-Natal midlands, was quoted as reporting that 'at least five child rape victim cases are being dealt with every day.' Yet, according to the article, the issue was largely suppressed by the 'overwhelming silence over AIDS'.[24]

The issue of the virgin myth then became the site of some heated controversy, one which has lasted to the present day, with political leaders, researchers and community activists joining the fray. It was the first public insight into the close connections which have developed between sexual violence and AIDS: sexual violence exacerbated the spread of the HI virus, and the secrecy which attaches to AIDS compounded the urge to hide the prevalence of sexual violence, particularly the rape of virgins whose 'purity' could allegedly cleanse the 'contamination' of AIDS.[25]

The first large public march by men protesting against sexual violence took place in Cape Town on Saturday 25 November 2000. Organised by an inter-religious forum to condemn violence against women and to call for stricter sentences for perpetrators, the march apparently drew 'thousands of men' onto the streets.[26]

So, by 2000, the problem of worsening sexual violence, and particularly the sexual victimisation of children, was clearly on the agenda of the press, and increasingly a subject of political engagement. The signs of critical public scrutiny of male sexuality, in particular, were becoming apparent, even among some groups of men themselves. But it was in October 2001 that an unprecedented storm broke, and the issue of sexual violence first achieved saturation coverage, provoking nothing less than a moral panic.[27]

In late October 2001, six men, aged between 24 and 66, were arrested on charges of gang-raping a nine-month old baby girl, in Louisvale, a small and impoverished community in the Northern Cape. Information about the details of the crime was scant: the baby's mother had gone to buy food, leaving the baby in the care of another (unnamed) person; later, the child's grandmother had seen the baby covered in blood, and called the police. But the moral horror was absolute. It rendered the six suspects immediately and thoroughly guilty in the eyes of the media and public opinion,[28] and triggered a media frenzy on the subject of 'baby rape'. The first newspaper reports of the Louisvale incident were carried on 30 October. By 1 November, the press had suddenly uncovered two more cases of the rape of the very young – all the more alarming because the perpetrators were members of the baby's family.[29] Equally rapidly, the press was also awash with a litany of 'shocking statistics' of child rape cases, going all the way back to 1994. With sudden concern and certitude, *The Star* informed its readers that

> in 1994 a total of 7559 cases [of child rapes and attempted child rapes] were reported. The figure increased dramatically over the next three years, and in 1997, stood at 15 336. It is believed that a large percentage of incidents go unreported ... Police said research conducted over the past five years indicated that in 83% of sexual abuse cases the perpetrators were known to their victims
>
> .... In 1998 the SA National Council for Child Welfare reported that five children were abused every hour in South Africa and that child rape had increased by 74% since 1994.[30]

By 5 November, *The Star* announced that 'child rape had rocketed to a national crisis', with 58 child rape cases a day. And by the end of that month, a further 13 cases of child or baby rape had been documented.[31] Indeed, for the next year and more,[32] most newspapers carried stories about rapes – in dramatic contrast to the generally desultory, if intermittently more animated, coverage of the issue which had marked the post-1994 period until then.

Within the space of a month, sexual violence – and particularly the rape of the very young – had suddenly become a *national scandal*, and the focus of overt public anguish and political alarm. Members of the public dialling in to radio talk shows could speak of little else; letters columns in newspapers and magazines were consumed with the issue. 'After the brutal rape of 9-month-old baby, should we not be at war?' read the headline of a 'letters to the editor' column, quoting from one of the letters on the subject. An editorial in the influential newspaper, *The Sowetan*, deemed it a 'state of emergency'.[33] The office of the Minister for Justice and Constitutional Development was 'inundated with e-mails from people who are concerned and outraged by recent incidents of violence against children'.[34] Protest marchers took to the streets of Cape Town;[35] public vigils were held.[36] Calls for vengeance were loud and insistent. Groups of protestors picketing outside court during the trials of alleged rapists; participants in radio programmes and people writing to the press joined some political parties in calling for the return of the death penalty as an appropriate punishment for rape, particularly child rape.[37] In other instances, mob justice took over, as alleged rapists were attacked and punished by groups of vigilantes.

The political stakes, moreover, had grown dramatically and rapidly larger. The spate of rapes, particularly child and baby rapes, was now interpreted as evidence of profound failures of political leadership, along with the gross inadequacies of an under-resourced and unresponsive justice system. President Mbeki in particular was singled out for his initially conspicuous silence on the matter, and failure to provide 'moral leadership' at a time of perceived crisis. With the state under pressure to respond, a special parliamentary debate was rapidly convened to discuss the 'horrific rape' of Baby Tshepang (the pseudonym given to the nine-month-old baby raped in Louisvale); 'almost every speaker said South Africa had been shamed', and a 'unanimous motion committed MPs to fight and expose the scourge, and campaign for the harshest punishment permissible under the Constitution'.[38]

As had been the case in other societies – such as France (Vigarello 2001) and Namibia (Green 1999) – it was the effective exposé of *child* sexual abuse which had the effect of morally and politically electrifying the phenomenon of sexual violence more generally. Press coverage of rape across the board increased. During the course of the next year, television viewers saw graphic footage of rape in prisons; and dramatic revelations were made about the extent of sexual violence in schools, where schoolgirls were the victims of sexual coercion from teachers as much as from fellow pupils. Increasingly the scope of public judgements widened to condemn the full spectrum of sexual violence, as an indictment of the very 'moral fibre' of the nation.

With President Mbeki remaining reticent on the subject, Deputy President Zuma was forthright in pronouncing South African society 'sick', and declaring the need for a wholesale programme of 'moral regeneration'. Addressing the Moral Regeneration Movement National Consultative Meeting, convened in the immediate aftermath of the rape of Baby Tsephang, Zuma was emphatic:

> There is a consensus that there is something seriously wrong in our society. We are still haunted by the news of six adult men having raped a nine-month-old baby, and there are many other cases, which display barbarism and moral decay of the worst kind.[39]

His diagnosis overlapped directly with the mode of questioning which had been triggered across various sites of public debate. Journalists Thembisile Makgalemele and Lumka Oliphant asked, 'why is our society collapsing to the point where not even our babies and elders are safe? why is there such moral degeneration in our new-found democracy?'[40] 'What has become of us? Why have we – and more especially men – become sexual cannibals?' pondered journalist Lucky Mazibuko. Letters to newspapers protested the moral betrayal of the country's struggle: 'baby rape mocks liberation', ran one of the headlines.

The idea of South Africa's moral degeneracy in turn struck a powerful chord in other loci of public vigilance, as the recognition of a fundamental malaise grew to encompass other sorts of crime and degradation. In Zuma's words,

> the lack of respect for the sanctity of human life, for the next person, private property, disregard for the law of the land, lack of parental control over children, and the general blurring of the lines between right and wrong are continuing to plague our communities.[41]

The call for 'moral regeneration' galvanised by the baby rape, now encompassed the 'blurring of ... right and wrong' across the board.

Sexual violence, then, had become a trope of social violation, moral frailty and the challenges of governance more widely. Rape now exemplified the most fundamental political and moral challenges confronting the newborn democratic nation: the terms and conditions of the new nation's moral community, the manner of the national subject ('who are we that we can do such things to out children?'), and the meaning of liberation and democracy.

Within this sense of moral and political crisis – indeed, as one of the critical elements of the sense of crisis – the scandal of manhood loomed large. With the rape of a baby, there could be no question of the culpability or collusion of the victim; none of the familiar exonerations or qualifications of a rapist's behaviour ('she asked for it', '"no" really means "yes"', 'women like a bit of rough handling', etc.) had any purchase. The moral horror of the violation was absolute and undiluted, and it emanated unconditionally and unambiguously from the actions of the male rapists. *Drum* magazine, in an article on 'Rape – Our National Shame', therefore focused the spotlight of shame squarely on men:

> Baby rape ...is the most barbaric thing a man can do. It puts all men in a very precarious position. With men raping their daughters and sodomising their own sons, who can trust us?[42]

A letter to *Drum*, published a week later, echoed this newfound sense of the root of the problem: 'oh God, what is wrong with the man of this planet?'[43]

The most brutal threats to women and children had come from the men closest to them: no longer protectors, fathers, husbands, relatives and friends had been exposed as predators. And within this exposé, the most intimate settings were now the most dangerous ones: no longer a sanctuary, the home had become the zone of moral menace of the worst kind.

Public expressions of anger, guilt and shame from various groupings of men animated calls for social activism. The National Association of People Living with HIV/Aids (NAPWA)

> called on men and boys to join them in their campaign against the rape of children. 'Men of Africa, do you care enough to stand up against the sexual violation of women and children?'[44]

The South African Men's Forum, founded by Bongani Khumalo, was even more forthright in its challenge to men:

> Men form a large proportion of the moral degeneration that we see in our society. There is not a single crime – whether rape, robbery or abuse – where a man is not the common denominator. Until you address the issue of men, and the violence they perpetrate in our society, you will not begin to steer society towards moral regeneration.[45]

The sense of moral crisis included an anxious impulse to revisit the past. The newly intense awareness of sexual violence, particularly in its most horrifying forms, prompted questions about its history: how long had such things being going on? Had the abolition of apartheid exacerbated the problem? Various expert informants were consulted. Some declared 'a marked increase in young victims of rape and sexual assault', often on the basis of the 'sleeping with a virgin' myth;[46] others insisted that the reverse was true. National newspaper *The Sunday Independent* ran a poll on the subject: '87% of online and 80% of offline readers said that they thought that cases of child rape had escalated in SA'.[47]

The idea of turning the past into the subject of a poll is revealing. In the absence of reliable data, this is not centrally an argument in pursuit of robust historical truth. These competing pronouncements about the past speak more to the processes of historical myth-making which inhere in the social imaginary of the nation. Establishing who 'we' are – the manner of our imagined moral and social community – is partly a matter of where we have come from. The past becomes a biography of the national subject which produces a diagnosis of the present, and a judgement about the possibilities for the future.

It is significant, then, that the feature of the past which emerged most conspicuously from these reflections is the intensity and depths of its secrets. The past emerges as a dark, shameful and oppressive secret. Linked to this is the insistence that to liberate the present from its burdens thus requires a process of *confession*, a preparedness and commitment to bringing hidden truths into the open. For, with confession comes the promise of redemption; confession – unmaking the secrets of the past – becomes the hallmark of nation building.

In this way then, the terms in which the issue of sexual violence has been publicised and politicised have constituted the idea of a public confessional, based on the assumption that the catharsis of truth will help to expose the 'rot', heal the damage (individual and collective), and open the way to a more wholesome present, producing morally rejuvenated conditions of citizenship. The appeal of this confessional is neither uncontested nor complete, but it has spanned a spectrum from rape victims who had kept their experiences of rape secret,[48] and rapists[49] who confessed the newfound realisation that sexual violence was wrong, through to political leaders admitting that long-standing and serious problems of sexual violence had been allowed to persist by authorities who minimised their importance and resisted their public acknowledgement.[50]

The scope of the claims made in this discussion should not be misunderstood. The new perspectives and verdicts on sexual violence, while prominent and dramatic, are neither wholesale nor unanimous. The fact that the rape issue had amplified into an indictment of the fledgling nation – with family and fatherhood, two of the pillars of nationhood, both scandalised – was bound to intensify the resistances to its visibility among those who favoured other tactics of nation building. So, although there have been few public declarations of dissent from 'ordinary' members of the public, there is probably a wider public sympathy for those political leaders who have expressed their scepticism, anger and/or discomfort at the growing public fuss about rape and abuse – as much in their refusal to partake in the clamour of acknowledgement as in their spoken responses. President Thabo Mbeki, in particular, was slow to respond to the rape of Baby Tsephang, prompting accusations of indifference ('keeping silent ... on the abomination destroying not only the country but eating away at our nation's soul') from the editor of the influential newspaper, *The Sowetan*. NGOs offering support to victims and families of child abuse complained that the President ignored their calls for support. When Mbeki did express his 'disgust' at the incident – through his spokesman, a month later[51] – he refused to acknowledge any undue problem or sense of emergency. And on the wider issue of rape, Mbeki had already expressed his mistrust of the 'hysterical' measurements of the problem ('the very false figures about the incidence of rape in our country, that are regularly peddled by those who seem so determined to project a negative image of our country')[52] and his distaste for the political prominence of the issue as a symptom of the tenacity of racist stereotyping.[53] In similar vein, when the BBC announced its intention of making a documentary of the Baby Tsephang case, some MPs protested that the publicity afforded to rape would portray South Africa as 'the leader in all aspects of bad things.'[54]

Still, notwithstanding these dissonances, by the end of 2002, the issue of sexual violence had been the site of some dramatic – if contested – reversals. How do we account for these changes? Why the calls to confess, where previously the reasons to conceal were so powerful? What is the relationship between the urges to unmake these secrets and the shifts in the ways in which sexual violence has been conceptualised, particularly in the home? The rest of this chapter grapples with these questions, first by theorising the key points of contrast and change in an analysis of the modalities of secrecy, and then by contextualising the South African saga of sexual violence within more global registers of the politics of confession.

The structure of a secret
There are at least four modalities of secrecy, which help to analyse both the making and unmaking of a secret, and which can be usefully applied in the South African case.

Secrecy as a mode of knowledge

There are different types of secrets. The least interesting, for the purposes of this chapter, are the simplest kinds of secrets, the objects of which are fully known, but unspoken. More interesting, and more pertinent here, are those cases in which secrecy is not simply an act of withholding knowledge from the public domain through not speaking, but in which secrecy also involve elements of denial – a combination of knowing and refusing to know. Secrecy, in such cases, is associated with a retreat from full knowledge, through processes of denial and self-deception on the part of those who make and keep the secret. As Stanley Cohen (2001:21) puts it in his acute characterisation of the mechanisms of denial, 'self-deception is a way to keep secret from ourselves the truth we cannot face'. Yet this entails, paradoxically, a recognition of that which cannot be confronted: a simultaneity of knowing and not knowing, 'being in the light and in the dark' (Cohen 2001:39). And these patterns of light and dark are indicative, in turn, of particular ways of conceptualising the substance of the secret, bringing some aspects to the fore and pushing others into the background, which are shaped by wider orders of social, cultural and political knowledge-production.

Secrecy as a mode of speech

A secret is a particular kind of speech act, a way of speaking as much as a way of knowing. Keeping secrets is a practice of saying some things and not saying others, in respect of particular audiences. These patterns of speech and silence are shaped in the first instance by the epistemology of the secret (what is known and not known, and in what terms), but they are also immersed in cultural and political repertoires of disclosure and non-disclosure.

Secrecy as a site of shame and stigma

The drives to denial and silence are closely associated with cultural, political and psychic logics of shame and stigma. It is seldom that good, happy things are kept secret. Perceptions of shame and stigma – intertwined with the ways in which the object of the secret are conceptualised – are powerful in animating the urge to keep things hidden, in the hope of avoiding public censure.

Secrecy as a site of power

Along with the cognitive, performative and normative dimensions of a secret, patterns of secrecy are also produced and sustained by regimes of surveillance. And these are rooted in relations of power, and the configurations of interests and norms shaping them.

In the case of the production of secrets of sexual violence in South Africa, these four elements locked together robustly during the apartheid era; even after 1994, the structure of the secret loosened only incrementally, until the major disruption of October 2001.

If the four elements of the idea of a secret all interlock, it is the epistemological dimension – the secret as a mode of knowing and not knowing – which constitutes its foundation. Applying this analysis to the South African case, and drawing on part 1 of this chapter, we can now recognise that the secrecy of sexual violence was constituted on the basis of the following key conceptual motiefs.

First, it invoked a *tacit distinction between 'public' and 'private'*[55] *realms*, defined in gendered terms, From a sexual point of view, 'the home' – the space and place of family – was understood as a place of male authority, sanctioned both by law and custom. The authority of the patriarch was as much a matter of his responsibilities as his entitlements: men were seen as protectors of women and children, in ways which would make the home a safe haven. From this vantage point, provided family members were 'safe', their concerns were legitimately 'private' matters, with little need for recourse to state institutions such as courts or police. So the internal logic of this position hinged on the safety of home. To admit to the home as unsafe would be to subvert the logic of privacy, and with it the idea of a private haven governed by protective men. The impulse to protect the sanctity of the home thus produced the practices of denial ('not knowing') – which inhered in the production of these secrets of sexual violence. If an admission of danger within the home was made, the logic of privacy was subverted.

Within this conceptualisation, therefore, sexual violence was *least likely – and yet simultaneously most threatening* – in the domain of 'the home'. Hence the strongest urges to secrecy, as a combination of knowing and not knowing, in the cases of domestic sexual violence.

Second, the *perpetrator* was cast *as an antisocial deviant*. If the patriarch – instantiating adult men who were known to women – was depicted as essentially a protector, then the likelihood of rape was highest among men who were unknown and antisocial: stray beasts, roaming on the margins of society. Indeed, within this way of thinking, rape was a quintessentially antisocial act, the symptom of brute force and untamed lust. The rapist was therefore represented as a faceless, predatory stranger, without personality or motives other than an inchoate sexual menace.

Third, the victimisation inflicted through sexual violence was understood as *bodily harm, rather than psychological trauma*. Sexual violence was represented primarily as a crime against a woman's body. Again, it followed internally within the conceptual schema outlined. If the rapist was the antisocial brute whose innate lust had got the better of him – and whose actions were therefore spontaneously violent rather than rationally calculated and manipulative – then the object of his violence was the sexualised body of the woman, rather than her psyche. Her individuality, her self, were irrelevant to the act of brutal passion: she was simply an instance of the female physical form. Within this paradigm of the secret, then, there was little sense of the inner psychic trauma of rape – 'damage' which would deepen and worsen the longer it was suppressed and denied. Mary Mabaso's anxieties about incestuous child rape, for example, focused on the damage to the child's physical health:

> it is not a healthy thing to be sexually abused because at the end of the day you might become abnormal. You might become a cripple because some of your organs have been worn out before their time (Russell 1991:69)

Fourth, *sexual violence was represented as a marginal, and relatively superficial, social problem*. It was a position which followed directly from the understandings adduced in 1, 2, and 3 above. With the really serious sexual violence (in the domain of the home) largely hidden, and its publicly more visible forms associated with random acts of violence perpetrated by antisocial deviants, the society could safely ignore – and deny – that the problem was anything other than an irritant on the margins of the social order.

This cognitive and conceptual structure of the secrets of sexual violence was closely intertwined with particular patterns of speaking and not speaking, as well as stigma and shame. The understanding that sexual violence was simultaneously least likely and most threatening within the home meant that this was also the site where the taboos and stigmas associated with the exposure of such violations would be most intense. Therefore, the habits of silence developed most insistently in respect of the spaces of familiarity and intimacy. Keeping silent about sexual violence was both an expression of the disinterest which came from knowing about its more marginal forms, and a symptom of the alarm which derived from the knowledge-cum-denial of its more insidious, dangerous manifestations in the crucible of the family.

The political regime of the secret in turn buttressed this logic of disclosure and non-disclosure, with the law allocating the state diminishing powers of intervention in proportion to the intimacy of the violation. Cultural norms of surveillance worked the same way: families were just as ready as the police to settle any domestic accusations quietly and discreetly, with as little public acknowledgement and exposure as possible.

By 2002, each of these elements of the secret had been disrupted, and its interlocking structure destabilised. Sexual violence had been prominently (although not comprehensively or unanimously) reconstituted as an object of knowledge in ways which destabilised the performative, normative and political logics of its secrecy.

As the first part of the chapter suggested, there is a now newly prominent version of sexual violence as a fundamental (rather than a marginal) social problem and moral malaise, an indicator of nothing less than the social, psychic and cultural health of the nation as a whole. Perhaps the central measure of this perceived malaise is the scandal of manhood: the recasting of the figure of the perpetrator as the father, the brother, the uncle, the friend – the enemy *within* – as opposed to the brutal yet anonymous, socially deviant, stranger. Seen in this way, the sanctity of the home, as a domain of patriarchal privacy, has been violated – by the patriarch himself.

Both the perpetrator and the violation have been recast as psychologically more interesting and complex. The perpetrator is no longer a faceless stranger, but an individual man, identifiable as the member of a particular family and community – a self, with a history. A different set of assumptions and interests now attaches to the conceptualisation of his sexual violence. Particularly if the target of his attack was his own child, his wife or relative, his actions are redefined and re-evaluated as the manifestation of a troubled self, rather than simply a random surge of lust. It becomes interesting and important to ask questions about why men commit such crimes and which men commit them. The more intimate the crime, the greater the inclination to question the motives, mindset and psychological orientation of the perpetrator.

The reconceptualisation of the rapist and the manner of his violation has similarly reoriented the representation of victimhood, in more psychological terms. Being violated by a man whom the victim knows and has perhaps trusted in the past, and with whom she has lived and interacted on a regular basis, casts the impact of rape in a very different light. It cannot be viewed any longer as a primarily bodily violation; rather, it is the psychic trauma, causing much deeper and persistent harm, which looms largest. 'Trauma' replaces 'damage' as the principle modality of victimhood.

These newly psychologised ways of thinking about sexual violence are in turn associated with a different logic of speech and silence. The crime of sexual violence becomes more interesting and substantial as a topic of public conversation; after all, there is that much more to say and ponder when the subject under discussion is a complex psyche rather than simply the site of surges of lust. Speaking also becomes an urge to confess, on the assumption that breaking the silence will be an act of *healing*. Confronting the scandal of sexual violence promises to heal the nation and replenish its 'moral fibre'. And for the victim, the catharsis of speaking out becomes a way of dealing with the psychic trauma of the violation.

The idea that *speaking is healing* – the new common sense in the contemporary politics of sexual violence – then puts a somewhat different gloss on the sense of stigma and shame associated with sexual violation. Once confession is recast as therapeutic (rather than sullying), then it becomes an antidote to the stigma of exposure. Truth telling can trump shame.

The regulation and surveillance of the secret has also been disrupted. Even if patriarchal cultural norms are largely in place,[56] the constitutional changes ushered in with South Africa's transition from apartheid have exploded the legal basis for the 'privacy' of domestic sexual violence, by conferring the basic human right to 'be free from all forms of violence from either public or private sources.'[57] There is now a constitutional onus on the state to provide various forms of protection to women and children against the sexual predations of the men closest to them.[58]

In short, then, the internal structure of the secrecy of sexual violence has been dislodged.

The epistemological, legal, cultural and political shifts registered by these changes are profound, and in some respects, enigmatic. They destabilise long-standing habits of thought about masculinity, male authority and domesticity, in a milieu in which constitutional provisions for gender equality are far ahead of their cultural take-up. These new practices of thought are therefore by no means wholesale, uncontested or even representative of a majority view, and their adoption is not necessarily a sign of any systematic embrace of a feminist stance on gender. The last remaining question to be answered in this chapter, then, is: Why has this alternative epistemology of sexual violence gained some degree of prominence and power, particularly outside feminist circles?

The politics of confession

Sexual violence is now spoken – even if incompletely – where it was once silenced; it is the site of a politics of exposé where once it was rendered politically invisible. At least in some quarters, there is an urge to confess where once there were powerful reasons to keep quiet. As the discussion above has shown, the ways in which sexual violence is represented, along with the ways in which it is spoken and heard, bear fundamentally on these shifts. The question, then, is where do these new repertoires of representation and speech come from? And whence their purchase in the South African case?

The first, and most obvious, part of an answer to these questions lies in the discourses and politics of sexual violence elsewhere in the world, where the challenges to secrecy had been lodged some time before. Child sexual abuse, in particular, hit the headlines in other parts of the world before the South African furore, creating a more global repertoire and memory of ways of thinking about, and judging, the phenomenon.[59] Linked to this, the psychologisation of both victim and perpetrator has been well established in many other parts of the world for some time.[60] But the question remains of how and why these modalities of thought and speech took hold in the South African case.

The answer has to start with the major constitutional and legal changes presaged by the election of South Africa's first democratic government, and the spaces which were thus opened up for a redefinition and re-engagement with the issue of sexual violence. The particular forms which these shifts took must then be accounted for with reference to wider genres of political discourse and performance, both locally and globally.

South Africa's transition from apartheid produced two sets of constitutional changes of fundamental importance for the politics of sexual violence. The first exploded the apartheid regime of sexual censorship (as discussed earlier in the chapter). With extraordinary rapidity, the domain of sex was liberalised and 'modernised' in line with political and legal norms in the West. Suddenly, South Africans could say, see and hear things about sex which would previously have been vehemently forbidden. The catch-up has been dramatic and swift: South Africa is now party to the global networks of economic and cultural exchange which are saturated with sex, and which have produced increasingly explicit sexual imagery and ever more garrulous sex talk across the world (See Altman 2001 and Hennessy 2000). So there are new material forces, as well as juridico-legal spaces, for the increased visibility of sex and the banishment of old inhibitions about talking, displaying and inspecting the full spectrum of sexual behaviour.

If sex has become rapidly and dramatically more available as a topic of public conversation and representation, the new constitution has also impacted powerfully on the terms in which the subject of sex have been unveiled. The old version of the public–private divide, enshrined in the corpus of apartheid legislation, has been displaced, with the recognition of sex as a site of right. This has included the right to protection from sexual violence – 'harm' – no matter where it is inflicted or by whom. The constitutional space of 'the home' has therefore changed profoundly: what was once 'private' is now reconstituted, regulated and protected by the allocation of specific entitlements to citizens, and correlative responsibilities to the state. The status of allegations about sexual violence has thereby also changed dramatically: they now carry a more substantial legal weight, associated with the possibility of more robust orders of protection from the state. If the embrace of a doctrine of universal human rights has been marked as the signifier par excellence of South Africa's re-entry to the global community of modern nations, then the reconceptualisation of sexual violence as a violation of rights immediately intensifies the seriousness of the issue, and legitimises the politics of exposé.

These legal and constitutional changes constitute a field of possibilities, but do not determine the particular substance or intensity of their realisation. Indeed, these changes are in many respects at odds with the cultural paradigms of male authority which have persisted – even buoyed in some quarters by popular discomfort with, or outrage at, the tenets of gender and sexual equality enacted by the new constitution. What, then, has shaped the production of new representations and conversations about sexual violence within the field of constitutional possibilities?

At least two factors, both with global lineages, bear directly and powerfully on the process. The first is the HIV/AIDS pandemic; the second is the wider politics of memory and confession, borne of the drive to 'negative commemoration' and distilled in South Africa through the funnel of the Truth and Reconciliation Commission.

First, HIV/AIDS. Although evidence of the disease in South Africa was undeniable during the 1980s, the issue of HIV/AIDS has largely been a post-apartheid problem. As late as 1990, the estimated prevalence of HIV infection in South Africa was less than 1 percent. These figures grew dramatically more serious by the mid-1990s, reaching 22.8 percent by 1998 (and as high as 32.5 percent, according to some measurements, in parts of KwaZulu-Natal) (Marks 2001:16). In other words, during the apartheid era, the spread of the disease within South Africa remained relatively slow; its acceleration occurred in the wake of the transition from apartheid.

With the advance of the epidemic, and in the midst of the South African government's resistance to providing anti-retroviral drug treatments on a mass scale to those infected with the virus, predicted rates of death from AIDS have taken on genocidal proportions. The vastness of the problem, along with the political controversies after 1998 which have diluted (and in some respects shut down) effective political interventions from within the state, and the availability of substantial donor funding for public health campaigns, prompted the development of a vigorous NGO sector committed to tackling the spread of AIDS. A range of AIDS awareness campaigns were launched, using diverse media and educational techniques, across the length and breadth of the country.

A recent national survey of this plethora of anti-AIDS work revealed that the dominant focus was on the subject of sex, rather than on other aspects of the AIDS epidemic (HSRC 2002). Messages about practising 'safe sex' were writ large, in media campaigns which rank among the most lavishly funded of their kind in the world. In a country historically unaccustomed to any public disclosures or conversations about sex, the initiative to promote safe sex was embedded in a multitude of strategies to bring the subject of sex out into the open and to 'get the nation talking about sex' (Posel forthcoming).

The anti-AIDS initiative, therefore, made full use of the newly liberalised spaces for sex talk enabled by the constitutional changes. Indeed, the dominant genre of AIDS education was that of the exposé. Undoing deep-seated habits of sexual secrecy was emphasised as an absolutely critical part of the effort to disseminate knowledge of the sexual transmission of the virus. Leading politicians, religious leaders, media personalities and community spokespeople were drawn into media campaigns aimed at parents, urging them to 'love them [children] enough to talk about sex'. Pamphlets and broadsheets aimed at young audiences were full of articles, letters and questions which dealt openly and directly with a host of questions about sex, 'unsafe sex' and HIV/AIDS. In this mix, the issue of sexual violence had a prominent place as one of the factors which heightens the risk of the transmission of HIV through genital lesions inflicted in coercive sex.

So, the impulse to lift the lid on sexual violence had another powerful groundswell, in the proliferation of public messages on the subject of HIV/AIDS. If the discourse on rights and the removal of sexual censorship gave the society the space and reason to expose sexual violence, the anti-AIDS discourse gave social and psychological urgency to it.

The pulse and pace of these public-health campaigns also articulated with the momentum of the shifting politics of sexual violence discussed earlier in the paper. While the publicity surrounding AIDS was initiated well before 1994, it is in the post-1998 period that the visibility of the issue and its associated messaging has peaked – a function of both the epidemiology of the disease and the politics of AIDS, which grew considerably more prominent and heated with Mbeki's so-called 'denialism'. While Nelson Mandela largely ignored the problem of AIDS (and has subsequently apologised for this), Mbeki unwittingly maximised the visibility of the AIDS problem by his challenges to the orthodox scientific explanations of the causes of HIV and the onset of AIDS. Mbeki's position on AIDS foregrounded issues of poverty, rather than sexuality, in coming to grips with the disease.[61] The more emphatic he was in stating his view, the more insistent were the NGO campaigns on stressing the sexual dimensions of the epidemic, and the need to confront the realities of sex, the dangers of 'unsafe sex', sexual promiscuity and sexual violence. In short, the messages to 'lift the lid' on sexual violence grew louder and more insistent in the post-1998 period, which coincided with the gathering momentum of popular concern and anger in the face of rape, and child rape in particular. (Indeed, perhaps it is not coincidental that the political heat generated by the AIDS controversy peaked in 2000 and 2001, just before the furore of baby rape).

The impact of AIDS discourses and debates upon the unmaking of secrets of sexual violence goes deeper, however, than simply the echoing of calls to bring sexual violence out into the open. As we saw in the third part of this chapter, the secrecy of sexual violence was buttressed by an interlocking structure of conceptual, performative, normative and political elements – the combination of which was the production of internally logical barriers to public acknowledgement. The unmaking of the secrets is rooted in the rupture of this logic, through the production of alternative conceptualisations of victimhood, violation, and the effects of confession. It is here that the discourses on AIDS and the heightened publicity attached to them have arguably had a fundamental impact.

Within the various texts on AIDS produced by the NGO movement, the bodily risks inflicted by coercive and violent sex were linked to a notion of empowerment: to prevent infection, women and children were urged to 'say no' to unwanted sexual advances; to insist on the use of a condom; to speak out against their sexual intimidation – in short, to challenge the conventional assertion of male authority in the transaction and practice of sex. For example, in the campaigns mounted by 'loveLife', the largest and most prominent of these NGOs, there has been a consistent link between sex and issues of self-esteem and 'positive lifestyles'. Sexuality has been presented as a site of rational, individual choice and an opportunity for 'healthy positive living':

> Living a positive lifestyle is about taking care of yourself; having the information you need to make responsible decisions about your life; understanding the consequences of your actions; being assertive; talking about what bothers you; and having fun in a cool, responsible way.[62]

The idea of 'safe sex', then, is part of a more general discourse of agency, one which has been harnessed to what, in Foucaultian terms, are recognisably modern techniques of the self (Foucault 1979): ways of 'taking control of one's self', acting rationally, assertively and decisively, in the face of fears, appetites and urges which threaten to overwhelm and engulf the reasonable self. Indeed, in the NGO AIDS discourses, the key to 'safe sex' is the production of a modern subject: knowledgeable, rational, responsible and in control.

But there is more to this notion of the subject than its familiarly modern rationality. It also encompasses a rendition of psychic health, which bears directly on the reconceptualisation of victimhood and confession identified in part 3. The empowered sexual subject valorised by the anti-AIDS campaigns is also one with strong propensities to reflexivity in matters of sex (as much as in other areas of life): thinking through the consequences of sexual choices, monitoring the surges of sexual passion, 'speaking out' about any anxieties or problems. A tacit psychology, therefore, informs the production of selfhood: along with self-control and assertiveness, the key to psychic well-being is the capacity to 'speak out', to perform the healing catharsis of disclosure. In the case of AIDS, the emphasis has been placed on the need to acknowledge being HIV positive, or having AIDS, as the basis on which an infected person can accept and come to terms with his or her status, and which can likewise enable acceptance and support from the family and community. Keeping AIDS secret has been presented as psychologically harmful, as much as morally injurious.

Ultimately, it is this notion of the subject – as one who embraces the logic of speaking-as-healing – on which the politics of confession depends, and which underpins the alternative conceptualisation of sexual violence which explodes its secrecy.

The impulse to confess, buttressed by a psychology of the self which recognises the catharsis of speech, was even more strongly imprinted in the Truth and Reconciliation Commission, South Africa's version of the 'memoro-politics' (Hacking 1995) which has gained ascendancy globally.

As Hacking (1995:214) puts it:

> memoro-politics is above all, a politics of the secret, of the forgotten event that can be turned, if only by strange flashbacks, into something monumental. It is a forgotten event that, when it is brought to light, can be memorialised in a narrative of pain.

The global memoro-politics of the late twentieth century has dual intellectual and political trajectories. The first, and earliest, was powerfully articulated by Hannah Arendt, shortly after World War Two:

> We can no longer simply afford to take that which is good in the past and simply call it our heritage, to discard the bad and simply think of it as a dead load which by itself time will bury in oblivion. (Arendt 1967)

More recently, Taylor called it the imperative of 'negative commemoration': the need to acknowledge past moral wrongdoings, setting the historical record straight, as the basis on which to redeem a sense of moral community and the political legitimacy of democracies built in the name of a doctrine of rights.[63] Negative commemoration, argued Taylor, has become an integral part of the moral politics of democratic nations; and its audiences are increasingly global, as the currency of the notion of human rights has grown internationally.

Taylor, like Arendt before him, was speaking principally of the politics of memory in the stable democracies of the West in the aftermath of the second World War. The second trajectory of 'memoro-politics' emerged during the 1980s, fashioned in the crucible of 'transitional justice' – the search for justice and stability in the aftermath of the overthrow of violent, sometimes genocidal, authoritarian regimes. Overseen by what Klug (2000) calls the 'international human rights movement', the idea of transitional justice is informed by the idea that a commitment to human rights provides the glue by means of which to stick these unstable, newly democratising, societies together. The way to activate this commitment is through systematic processes of confession to past abuses of human rights. For within the catharsis of this confession lies the possibility of healing the rifts within the fledgling democracy, as well as overcoming the trauma of violence suffered by its victims. The psychologisation of trauma here finds its most powerful political mouthpiece. 'Lifting the lid' on a violent and abusive past becomes the key to redeeming the humanity of the victims and the perpetrators, enabling their 'reconciliation' on the strength of their shared commitment to a more open, truthful and just society.

The essential vehicle for this politics of confession, then, has been the truth commission. Since 1983 (with the inauguration of the Argentinian National Commission on the Disappeared), there have been 26 truth commissions, with others in the pipe-line. This recent proliferation of truth commissions is evidence in itself of the power and appeal of the discourse of confession and its perceived moral and political effects.

There is no single, uniform model for a truth commission, but they all share certain defining assumptions about the power of truth, which in turn rest on the notion of the rational, psychologically reflexive, subject identified earlier in relation to the production of anti-AIDS discourses. Truth commissions emanate from the confidence that truth-telling – in the form of the confession to past secrets of abuse and violation (and on the strength of exactly the notion of secrecy under discussion in this paper, of simultaneous knowledge and denial) – is redemptive. This makes sense only if the subject and audience of the confession are deemed able thereby to 'heal'. In other words, the political logic of truth telling depends on a psychology of victimhood, along with a tacit theory of the psychic mechanisms of denial and its transcendence.

South Africa's Truth and Reconciliation Commission (TRC) drew upon exactly this notion of the subject, as its agent and audience.[64] The

Commission began its deliberations after the promulgation of the Promotion of National Unity and Reconciliation Act of 1995. Its five-volume interim report was submitted in 1998, with a final report concluded in 2003. But arguably the most memorable – and memory-forming – facet of the TRC was its public hearings, overseen by a panel of Commissioners chaired by the charismatic Archbishop Desmond Tutu, who heard testimonies from selected victims of human rights abuses (or their spokespeople) and perpetrators of such abuses. Many of these hearings, widely televised nationally and internationally, were intense emotional dramas of the catharsis of confession. Testifiers wept, as did the Archbishop. They were held and hugged by people designated by the Commission to offer psychological support through the pain of speaking, prompted by the confidence that with the speaking would come a process of psychological healing. The script of this 'narrative of pain' (to use Arendt's phrase) also had another protagonist and subject of the healing process: the nation itself. The publicity of the hearings was based on the assumption that the more personal dramas of confession and healing would prompt the urge to 'reconcile' at a more national level. Reconciliation, in this sense, was based on the 'recognition of the humanity of the other', enabling the imagining of a new form of national community animated by a 'collective memory' of a 'shared', and newly bared, past (Posel 2002:149).

The extent to which the TRC was able to achieve its declared objectives was extremely uneven, and its public reception was mixed (Wilson 2002). For the purposes of this chapter, the more immediate terms of reference of the Commission, and its success or lack of success in accomplishing these goals, are less pertinent than the wider impact of the Commission's discourse. Arguably, the process of the Commission, and particularly its public hearings, produced a new political common sense which has been reproduced in various quarters of public conversation and commentary since then – namely, that talking about painful and hidden facets of the past is the key to national unity. This in turn rests on the more psychologically focused assumption about the psychically healing powers of confession. This is not to suggest a consensus on the matter; indeed, 'nation-building' is a contentious and divisive issue. Nevertheless, the degree to which the conviction that speaking is healing has become part of the public lingua franca has been striking. As one radio talk show host put it during a programme on racism, 'let's talk about it. Hear our pain. Then we'll all heal. How else can we expect reconciliation?'[65]

In short, therefore, the unmaking of secrets of sexual violence has been fuelled by a wider politics of confession, informed and animated by a common underlying notion of the subject, victimhood and violation. This epistemology of agency and violence has produced a logic of speech which challenges some long-standing habits of silence and denial. There is now a global political culture, along with a national juridico-legal system, which sets out to reward as well as support the act of disclosure – as a trope for nation-building itself.

The recognition of the scandal of manhood, and the expression of moral outrage at the 'scourge of rape' in South Africa, therefore, does not depend upon, or presuppose, any feminist predispositions. It derives more from a way of thinking about selfhood, victimhood and violation which already had a powerful global currency, and which became prominent in, and internal to, other sites of national public argument and political engagement after 1994.

Conclusion

On the strength of an historical account of the production of secrets of sexual violence, and the processes of their incomplete but dramatic and prominent unmaking in this country, this chapter has posited the structure of the secrecy of sexual violence – as a four-fold matrix of interlocking elements (cognitive, performative, normative and political). It has identified the substance of these elements as they developed during the apartheid era, and demonstrated their internal logic. This then enabled an analysis of the rupture represented by the recent public and political furore around rape, as well as an account of the ways in which the secret of rampant sexual violence has been destabilised. Within spaces opened up by the country's new democratic constitution, the secrecy of sexual violence has been disrupted by the growing appeal and purchase of new global discourses of confession and truth telling, which have entered the arena of public conversation and political engagement in South Africa as much through the politicisation of AIDS and the enactment of the TRC, as in the revelations of the horrors of baby rape.

Notes

1. I am using 'sexual violence' to encompass rape of men and women, vaginal as well as anal (whether or not these are recognised in terms of the law as 'rape'; child sexual abuse; and other orders of sexual assault. Under apartheid law, rape was defined as unlawful sexual (vaginal) intercourse with an adult women without her consent, but excluded the case of coersive sex within marriage. See Ross (1993:8–9). '

2. See for example, Gouws & Kadalie (1994:216–232).

3. *Drum* magazine, 15 November 2001, 'Child Rape: Social Workers Quit'.

4. *Sowetan*, 29 January 2002, 'Just Call me Lucky'.

5. *Daily Trust*, 26 November 2001, 'SA Men Protest Rape of Baby Girls'.

6. *Sowetan*, 15 November 2001, 'How do we punish rape monsters?' Letter to the editor.

7. *The Citizen*, 15 November 2001, 'Parliament united in outrage at baby rape'.

8. While there are always multiple publics, my focus in this chapter is limited to the production of a public debate in the most obvious and prominent of places. My access to the 'public' (in the sense in which I am using the term here) is largely through national and local media of various sorts (press, radio, television, magazines), all with substantial circulations and impact. It has not been possible within the scope of a single chapter to disaggregate different constituencies within this public.

9. The argument in the chapter is prompted by the public drama and impact of these shifts; it does not depend on, nor speak to, the proportion of their popular support.

10. Vigarello (2001) is an important exception. As the opening sentence of this study states, 'the history of rape has never been written' (2001:1) – at least in respect of societies not at war or in other states of emergency. The historical study of rape as a weapon of war seems to have sparked more scholarly interest than the 'normality' of rape in everyday settings.

11. According to Diana Russell, psychologist Lloyd Vogelman produced the first book on rape in South Africa, (Vogelman 1990), in which he cited only two published and two unpublished works on the psychology of rape or sexual abuse written in or of this country.

12. The issue of sexual violence was not publicly at the forefront of the politically dominant form of the women's movement (in the ANC-aligned anti-apartheid struggle).

13 The allegations concerned police reluctance to intervene in allegations of family violence, and were based on the extensive dealings with victims of domestic violence and police on the part of the South African National Institute for Crime Prevention and Rehabilitation of Offenders (NICRO).

14 University of the Witwatersrand, Historical Papers 1990c, AG 2679 F2, Women's Legal Status Committee, 'Memorandum – Rape Cases', Lieutenant Zulu, on behalf of the South African Police.

15 Ross (1993) argues that all the familiar sexist myths about rape have informed the legislation and policing of rape in South Africa.

16 Republic of South Africa, House of Assembly Debates, 1985, vol. 5, cols. 597–8. The numbers of incest cases which actually went to trial were far smaller still. Data was 'unavailable' for 1984; in 1983, 48 cases had gone to trial (col. 1001). Data was not supplied for the number of trials that produced a conviction. The experiences of hospitals, doctors and other organisations offering support to victims of child abuse suggested that numbers of incestuous child rapes would have been *substantially* higher (even in the absence of reliable and comprehensive national data).

17 The issue of how to regulate the practice and transaction of sexuality within African communities had long since been extremely vexed within the state, the site of conflicting logics of rule (see Posel (1995). In the case of Coloured communities, another set of stereotypes and myths kicked in, regarding the inherently 'criminogenic' and essentially unstable/violent nature of mixed-race communities. See e.g. Jensen (2003).

18 Read 'black' – arguably the appropriate referent here, given the huge intersection of race and class in the demography of apartheid, and the political squeamishness within the state in 1990 (with the beginning of the end of apartheid in sight) about using a more flat-footed discourse of race.

19 This fear, that the public identification of a child as the victim of a rape would produce the perception of 'devalued or damaged merchandise', is not unique to the South African case, and is part of the logic of secrecy about child abuse more globally (Lewis 1997).

20 The report of the SA Law Commission was duly noted, and its key recommendations were briefly summarised, but that was the end of it; no further commentary or discussion ensued.

21 The complexity of this mode of 'knowing' cannot be explored here. Suffice it to note at this point, as Cohen (2001) has argued, that secrecy involves a combination of knowing and not knowing: that which is secret

is hidden from public, but also often partially hidden from oneself, a symptom of the psychic and/or moral discomfort associated with that knowledge.

22 Under apartheid, a battery of censorship laws produced severe restrictions on the representation, display or discussion of pretty much anything to do with sex. So, while many countries in the West became thoroughly accustomed to the explicit depiction of sex, and to frequent public engagement with sexual issues, South Africans were subjected to a virtual black-out on the subject (Posel forthcoming).

23 *Christian Science Monitor*, 17 1998, 'Vigilante raises issues of Justice and Child Rape'.

24 *Sunday Times*, 4 April 1999, 'Child Rape: A Taboo within the AIDS Taboo'.

25 A full discussion of the issue of secrecy and sexual violence would need to grapple more comprehensively with these connections, and the orders of secrecy attached to AIDS. There is no space to do this within the scope of a single chapter. However, the centrality of AIDS re-emerges in part 4 of the paper.

26 *BBC News*, 27 November 2000, 'SA: Standing up to Rapists', http://news.bbc.co.uk/2hi/africa.

27 In Stanley Cohen's (1972, p. 7) words, 'Societies appear to be subject, every now and then, to periods of moral panic. A condition, episode, person or group of persons emerges to become defined as a threat to societal values and interests; its nature is presented in a stylized and stereotypical fashion by the mass media; the moral barricades are manned by editors, bishops, politicians and other right-thinking people; socially accredited experts pronounce their diagnoses and solutions; ways of coping are evolved or (more often) resorted to.'

28 Genetic tests subsequently exonerated them, but by then their identification as gang rapists was already complete in the public eye.

29 The rape of a 14-month-old baby by her two uncles in Tweeling, Free State, and another case of a three-year-old toddler raped by her grandfather, also alleged to have 'abused his own daughter, the injured child's mother, for years' (*The Star*, 1 November 2001, 'Shocking Statistics on Crimes against Children Unveiled'.

30 *The Star*, ibid.

31 *The Citizen*, 7 November 2001. 'Five More Child Rape Cases'; *The Citizen*, 12 November 2001, 'Child Rape Scourge Gets Worse'; *The Citizen*, 15 November 2001, 'KZN has the highest child abuse figures'; *Sowetan*,

23 November 2001, 'Boy (11) Arrested for Raping Sister'; CNN.com, 26 November 2001, 'SA Facing Child Rape Crisis'.
32 On 24 November 2002, the editor of the *Sunday Times*, Mathata Tsedu, wrote again of 'the horror of child rape', prompted by yet another child rape – a two-year-old girl sodomised to the point of near-death (*Sunday Times*, 24 November 2001, 'The Horror of Child Rape must incense us all into protest'.
33 CNN.com, 26 November 2001, 'SA Facing Child Rape Crisis'.
34 *Sowetan*, 12 November 2001, 'Outrage over Violence'.
35 http://allafrica.com/stories/200111260190/html: SA Men Protest Rape of Baby Girls, 26 November 2001.
36 *Sowetan*, 28 November 2001, 'Vigil to Highlight Child Abuse'.
37 The African Christian Democratic Party called for a return of the death penalty; the PAC proposed the chemical castration of offenders (Sowetan 15 November 2001, 'Gov to hold talks on moral values').
38 *The Citizen*, 15 November 2001, 'Parliament united in outrage at baby rape'.
39 Address by Deputy President Zuma to the Moral Regeneration Movement National Consultative Meeting, 23 November 2001, www.anc.org.za/ancdocs/history/zuma/2001.
40 *Saturday Star*, 8 December 2001. 'Healing our Moral Sickness'.
41 Address by Deputy President Zuma to the Moral Regeneration Movement National Consultative Meeting, 23 November 2001.
42 *Drum* magazine, 22 November 2001. 'Rape – Our National Shame'.
43 *Drum* magazine, 29 November 2001. 'You rape – you die!'.
44 *Sowetan*, 30 November 2001. 'Call on men and boys to fight against child abuse'.
45 *Saturday Star*, 13 April 2002, 'Restoring Respect for Family'
46 For example, *Sunday Independent*, 11 November 2001, 'Baby Rape highlights SA's shocking record of abuse'.
47 *Sunday Independent*, 11 November 2001. The offline readers included respondents interviewed at taxi ranks in Soweto, the Johannesburg CBD and East Rand townships.

48 For example, the November 2001 edition of *True Love* magazine carried a feature article on 'Raped – in the name of Love', including interviews with a series of women who 'broke their silence' on rape in marriage or relationships.

49 For example, *Saturday Star*, 13 April 2002, 'Restoring Respect for Family'.

50 For example, the Departmentt of Education's submission to the parliamentary Task Group on Sexual Abuse recognised that 'sexual abuse has been a constant feature of SA schools, as it has been of society at large. Unfortunately many of our schools have become violent and unsafe environments, particularly for the girl-child. It is also unfortunately a matter on which there has been a resounding silence from society' (not least the Department of Education itself)[www.gov.ac.za/reports/2002]

51 Quoted, for example, in *Peoples' Daily*, 27 November 2001, 'S. African President Disgusted by Child Abuse: Spokesman'.

52 *The Sunday Times*, 9 July 2000, 'Mbeki vs Leon: Dear Tony, 1 July 2000'.

53 'Castro Hlongwane, Caravans, Cats, Geese, Foot and Mouth and Statistics', a document with disputed authorship but allegedly closely associated with Mbeki, makes the case that politicising rape is racist, by ironic declamation: 'Yes, we, the men, abuse women and the girl-child with gay abandon! Yes, among us rape is endemic because of our culture!' (p. 88)

54 *The Citizen*, 26 June 2002, 'Child-Rape Film Furore'.

55 The coherence or not of this distinction is another matter. Indeed, when pushed, the distinction dissolves; after all, the parameters and substance of the 'private' domain was established in, and protected by, law – an essentially 'public' process. But for the purposes of this discussion, it is a conceptual device taken on its own terms.

56 The extent to which the powers of these norms have or have not changed is beyond the scope of this paper, and does not fundamentally affect the terms of the argument.

57 See Chapter 2 Bill of Rights, Section 12(1)C Freedom and Security of the Person, Constitution of the Republic of South Africa, Act 108 of 1996.

58 It should be noted, however, that there have been reports and studies of police responses to sexual violence which are not in line with the new norms established by the constitution. So the changes in question here remain somewhat uneven. But the point is that women – particularly those informed and assertive about their rights – have recourse to state protection where previously they did not.

59 See for example, Hacking (1995, ch. 4) and Hacking (2000, ch. 5).

60 See Vigarello (2001) for an account of this development in France and Hacking (1995) on the shift from a physical to psychological notion of trauma more generally.

61 For a fuller account of the AIDS controversy and Mbeki's interventions, see Posel (forthcoming).

62 *Thetha Nathi: Positive Lifestyle*, 2–6 September 2002, editorial; published by loveLife.

63 These arguments were presented by Charles Taylor in a public lecture at WISER, in June 2002.

64 For a more detailed account of the TRC, and fuller background to the argument made here see Posel and Simpson (2002).

64 The Eric Miyeni Show, SA Fm, 23 May 2003.

References

Andersson, N., Mhatre, S., Naidoo, S., Mayet, N., Mqotsi, M., Penderis, M., Onishi, J., Myburgh, M. and Merhi, N. (2000) *Beyond Victims and Villains: The Culture of Sexual Violence in South Africa.* Johannesburg. CIET-Africa.

Altman, D. (2001) *Global Sex.* (Chicago: The University of Chicago Press).

Arendt, Hannah. (1967) *The Origins of Totalitarianism.* (London: Allen & Unwin). Third edition.

Cohen, S. (1972) *Folk Devils and Moral Panics.* (Oxford: Martin Robertson).

Cohen, S. (2001) *States of Denial: Knowing about Atrocities and Suffering.* (Cambridge: Polity).

Delius, P. and Glaser, C. (2002) Sexual Socialisation in South Africa: An Historical Perspective. *African Studies*, 61, 1, 27–54.

Driver, E. and Droisen, A. (1989) *Child Sexual Abuse: Feminist Perspectives.* (Basingstoke and London: MacMillan).

Evans, D. (1993) *Sexual Citizenship: The Material Construction of Sexualities.* (London and New York: Routledge)

Gouws, A. and Kadalie, R. (1994) Women in the Struggle: Past and Future. (Liebenberg, I., Lortan, F., Nel, B. and Van der Westhuizen, G., 1994:216–232).

Green, D. (1999) *Gender Violence in Africa: African Women's Responses.* (Basingstoke and London: MacMillan)

Hacking, I. (1995) *Rewriting the Soul: Multiple Personality and the Sciences of Memory* (Princeton: Princeton University Press).

Hacking, I. (2000) *The Social Construction of What?* (Boston: Harvard University Press).

Hennessy, R. (2000) *Profit and Pleasure: Sexual Identities in Late Capitalism.* (New York and London: Routledge).

HSRC. (2002) Nelson Mandela/HSRC Study of HIV/AIDS, South African National HIV Prevalence, Behavioural Risks and Mass Media, Household Survey.

Ignatieff, M. (2003) *Empire Lite: Nation-Building in Bosnia, Kosovo and Afghanistan.* (London: Vintage).

Jensen, S. (2003) 'Claiming Community – Negotiating Crime: State Formation, Neighbourhood and Gangs in a Capetonian Township', PhD thesis, University of Roskilde.

Klug, H. (2000) *Constituting Democracy: Law, Globalism and South Africa's Political Reconstruction.* (Cambridge: Cambridge University Press).

Lewis, S. (1997) A cry that no-one hears. *ChildrenFIRST*, 2, 16.

Lewis, S. (1997) Theoretical and therapeutic aspects of extrafamilial child rape in the South African context: a preliminary exploration', Seminar no. 5, Centre for the Study of Violence and Reconciliation, Johannesburg, 28 May. http://www.csvr.org.za/papers/papchilr.htm

Liebenberg, I. et al, *The Long March.* (Pretoria: HSRC),

Lutya, T. (2001) Understanding the Social Context within which Violence against Women Occurs: An Exploratory Study in Johannesburg. MA research report, University of the Witwatersrand.

Marks, S. (2002) An epidemic waiting to happen. *African Studies*, 61, 1, 13–26.

McKendrick, B. and Hoffman, W. (eds.) (1990) *People and Violence in South Africa.* (Cape Town: Oxford University Press).

Posel, D. (forthcoming) Sex, death and the fate of the nation: reflections on the politicisation of sexuality in post-apartheid South Africa. *Africa*

Posel, D. (1995) State, power and gender: conflict over the registration of African customary marriage in South Africa, 1910–1970. *Journal of Historical Sociology*, 5, 3, 223–256

Posel, D. (2002) The TRC Report: What Kind of History? What Kind of Truth? (Posel and Simpson 2002)

Posel, D. and Simpson, G. (eds.) (2002). *Commissioning the Past: Understanding South Africa's Truth and Reconciliation Commission.* (Johannesburg: Witwatersrand University Press).

Republic of South Africa. Report of the Parliamentary Task Group on the Sexual Abuse of Children (2002)

Republic of South Africa. (2002) Joint Monitoring Committee on the Improvement of Quality of Life and Status of Women: Report on Violence against Women. (Pretoria: Government Printers).

Ross, K. (1993) *Women, Rape and Violence in South Africa: Two Preliminary Studies.* (Bellville: Community Law Centre, University of the Western Cape).

Russell, D. (1991) Rape and child sexual abuse in Soweto: an interview with community leader Mary Mabaso. *South African Sociological Review*, 3, 2, 62–83.

Russell, D. (1984) *Sexual Exploitation: Rape, Child Sexual Abuse and Workplace Harassment.* (Beverly Hills, London and New Delhi: Sage).

SA Law Commission. (1985) University of the Witwatersrand Library, Historical Papers, AG 2679, Women's Legal Status Committee, SA Law Commission, Project 45, 'Women and Sexual Offences in South Africa', April 1985.

Statistics South Africa. (2000) Quantitative Research Findings on Rape in South Africa. (Pretoria: Statistics South Africa).

Torpey, J. (ed.) (2003) *Politics and the Past: On Repairing Historical Injustices.* (Lanham: Rowman & Littlefield).

University of the Witwatersrand, Historical Papers (1990a). Carole Charlewood MP, Umbilo to The Honourable Minister of Law and Order, re 'Representation regarding Police Approach to Assaults on Women in the Home'. Wits Historical Papers, AG 2679 F 17, 5 June 1990. Women's Legal Status Committee.

University of the Witwatersrand, Historical Papers (1990b). AG 2679 F 17, M.W. Cronje, for Minister Adriaan Vlok to Mrs Charlewood re 'Representations regarding Police Approach to Assaults on Women in the Home', Wits Historical Papers, AG 2679 F 17, 21 August 1990.

University of the Witwatersrand, Historical Papers (1990c). AG 2679 F2, Women's Legal Status Committee, 'Memorandum – Rape Cases', Lieutenant Zulu, on behalf of the South African Police.

Vigarello, G. (2001) *A History of Rape: Sexual Violence in France from the 16th to the 20th Centuries.* (Cambridge: Polity).

Vogelman, L. (1990) *The Sexual Face of Violence: Rapists on Rape.* (Johannesburg: Ravan Press).

Wilson, R. (2001) *The Politics of Truth and Reconciliation in South Africa: Legitimizing the Post-Apartheid State.* (Cambridge: CUP).

Masculine domination in sexual violence: Interpreting accounts of three cases of rape in the South African Lowveld

Isak Niehaus

Introduction

In 1998, 49 280 cases of rape and attempted rape were reported to the South African Police Services. Though rape is still one of the most under-reported crimes in South Africa, these figures are among the highest for any country not at war (Human Rights Watch 1995). A particularly shocking aspect of these reported rapes is the young age of many victims. In 1998, 41 percent were below the age of seventeen.[1]

Despite its being a long-standing and serious problem, social scientists have begun to examine rape in South Africa systematically only over the past fifteen years. This analytic attention is closely related to moral panic about sexual violence in the post-apartheid era (Posel 2003). Existing studies generally endorse the view that rape is an act of power rather than of sexual gratification.[2] Vogelman (1990), Russel (1991, 1997), Varga (1997) and Jewkes & Abrahams (2002) point to the very substantial gender inequalities that exist across the South African social landscape. These authors see rape as both a manifestation and an assertion of male dominance over women. Sexual violence, they argue, occurs in contexts where male control of women and sexual entitlement feature strongly in constructions of masculinity. For example, young men use sexual violence when women are reluctant to enter into relationships with them (Wood & Jewkes 2001). Authors also blame the widespread use of violence in interpersonal conflict, abusive drinking, limited alternative arenas for men to achieve self-esteem and women's economic dependence, which renders them vulnerable to sexual abuse (Simpson 1991, Jewkes & Abrahams 2002).

This article reconsiders the relationship between masculine domination and rape from the perspectives of men, drawing on intermittent ethnographic fieldwork that I conducted from 1990 on in Impalahoek – a village of 20 000 people located in the Bushbuckridge area of the South African lowveld.[3]

Bushbuckridge has accommodated diverse groups of Northern Sotho and Tsonga-speaking (Shangaan) refugees from war since the mid-19th century, and was scheduled for exclusive African occupation in terms of the 1913 Land Act (Niehaus 2002a:559). A system of rent tenancy then emerged, whereby household heads paid taxes for residential, cultivation and stock-keeping rights (Ritchken 1995:96–98). The settlement pattern was one of scattered *metse* (singular *motse*). A *motse* comprised the homesteads, fields, and ancestral graves of a co-resident agnatic cluster. Its inhabitants were typically a father, his wives, his sons, his unmarried daughters, his daughters-in-law, and his grandchildren. Members of the motse co-operated in cultivating maize, sorghum and millet fields and in herding. Women planted, hoed, cut thatching grass and raised pigs and chickens. Men uprooted trees, ploughed, built homes, tended to goats and cattle, and migrated to work on the Pilgrim's Rest gold mines, in the Sabie forests and on the Witwatersrand. In a good year, during the 1930s, larger *metse* harvested up to ninety bags of maize plus thirty bags of sorghum, and kept herds in excess of 150 cattle. Smaller *metse* harvested twelve bags and kept fewer than twelve cattle (Niehaus 2001:20).

The male head of the *motse* commanded great authority and an ideology of common blood created loyalty between patrilineal descendants. Parents arranged the marriages of their children and assisted their sons to pay bride wealth. These payments were set at between ten and thirteen head of cattle. Though marriages were patri-virilocal, a wife still belonged to her father's descent group. The metaphors of the 'body' and 'head' expressed her ambiguous status. Bride wealth only signalled the transfer of a wife's body. Her head remained the property of her own kin. A wife could therefore always rely upon the protection of her agnates as a counterweight to spousal abuse (Stadler 1994:142). Only after all of the husband's older brothers had married could the couple set up their own independent household. Then the wife worked solely for her husband and received his remittances.

Under the apartheid policies of 1948, Bushbuckridge became a Native Reserve, administered by a white Assistant Native Commissioner. Agricultural production declined greatly as hundreds of African households relocated into the Reserve from the west and from nearby white-owned farms (Harries 1989:104). As men accepted longer migrant labour contracts, marital strife and separations became more pervasive. Divorced women were usually allocated homesteads on the outskirts of their fathers' *motse*. Here they lived with their children, cultivated their own fields and controlled their own sexuality.

In 1960 the Native Affairs Department implemented agricultural betterment schemes to accommodate the increased population. The department subdivided all land into residential settlements, arable fields and grazing camps, and relocated households onto the new residential stands. In 1968 ethnic 'homelands' were established, and Bushbuckridge was divided into two ethnic zones. Mapulaneng in the west became part of the Northern Sotho 'homeland', Lebowa, while Mhala in the east was incorporated into the Shangaan 'homeland', Gazankulu.

Under the 'homeland' system, households were entitled to keep only ten head of cattle, and gradually lost access to their fields. Given the smaller size of residential stands, large agnatic clusters were fragmented into smaller households, and parents and uterine brothers were allocated different stands. Sons now achieved independence from their fathers. They paid their own taxes and kept their cattle in separate kraals, while their wives cultivated different gardens. Whereas the members of the *motse* had previously worked together in agricultural pursuits, individual men now earned almost all income outside the group (Niehaus 2001:30). Marriage also changed. Sons now chose their own wives and paid their own bride wealth in cash. However, most men could only pay bride wealth in several instalments, over a length of time (Stadler 1994:150). Polygyny also greatly declined.

These ethnic structures persisted until South Africa's first democratic elections in 1994. Mapulaneng and Mhala again merged to be administered as a single municipality in the newly constituted Limpopo (formerly Northern) Province. But after a decade of democratic governance, few promises of prosperity have materialised. Bushbuckridge still exhibits many stereotypical features of a native reserve, such as high unemployment, welfare dependency, broken families, accusations of witchcraft, violence and suicide (see Kahn et al. 1999 and Niehaus 2001:156–182). Government has drastically improved social security payments (such as pensions and child support grants), constructed thousands of homes and introduced school feeding schemes, but villagers have had to cope with the devastating impacts of de-industrialisation and of the HIV/AIDS pandemic. Between 1993 and 1999 the number of labourers employed in South African gold mining decreased from 428 003 to 195 681; in coal mining from 51 267 to 21 155; in manufacturing from 1 409 977 to 1 286 694; and in construction from 355 114 to 219 797 (SAIRR 2001: 336–338). Current estimates place HIV prevalence in Limpopo at 17.5 percent (Gedye et al. 2004).

Working-class men are now more likely to be unemployed and unable to pay bride wealth, marry and support wives and children. During 1990 and 1991 I conducted a social survey of 85 households in Impalahoek. There were 164 men of working age, of whom 131 (80 percent) were wage earners, seven (4 percent) were self-employed and 107 (65 percent) were married; and 167 women of working age, of whom 47 (28 percent) were wage earners, twelve (7 percent) were self-employed and 103 (62 percent) were married. During 2003 and 2004 I revisited all previously surveyed households. There were now 223 men of working age, of whom only 103 (46 percent) were wage earners, thirteen (6 percent) were self-employed and 107 (48 percent) were married; and 259 women, of whom 86 (33 percent) were wage earners, thirteen (6 percent) were self-employed and 106 (41 percent) were married.

Poorer men were not only less likely to marry: they were also less likely to engage in casual sex. In Impalahoek, as elsewhere in South Africa, non-marital sexual liaisons have a large transactional component. Men are generally expected to provide their lovers and paramours with gifts and to purchase beer for the women they meet in drinking houses (Hunter 2002). Nearly all of the 15 men in Impalahoek who were alleged to have died from AIDS-related diseases were amongst the 'wealthier of the poor'. Only one man was unemployed when his sickness commenced. The others were migrant labourers, sales representatives, drivers, teachers and policemen. Fourteen of these men were married and only one was a divorcee.

Many respondents observed that through time rape had become an attack against individual women rather than against their entire *motse* or household, and they were adamant that rape had escalated dramatically over the past two decades. These impressions are coloured by the proverbial myth of the 'golden past', and are impossible to verify quantitatively. However, the relative ease with which I collected information about this sensitive topic in the 1990s seemed to substantiate these observations.[4]

During fieldwork I recorded details of 39 rapes in Impalahoek. While I was collecting the sexual biographies of young men, three informants described how they themselves had raped women, and seven told me of rapes they had witnessed. I learnt about an additional 12 cases from local Community Police Forum members and about another 17 cases from discussing newsworthy events that interrupted the usual flow of life (Malkki 1997) with informants I knew well. I sought to obtain 'experience near' accounts of these events by interviewing both male and female kin and acquaintances of the victims and perpetrators. My interviewees included only two rape victims.

Evidence suggests that we cannot see rape merely as an expression of masculine domination and entitlement, as this is apparent only in cases of sexual coercion by relatively privileged men. In the sections below, I suggest that during the era of de-industrialisation, marginal men who fell well short of meeting masculine ideals were more likely to perpetrate rape. I argue that rape can also be seen as a violent attempt to symbolically assert – and sometimes even to mimic – a dominant masculine persona. Through rape men demonstrate their heterosexual virility, humiliate economically successful women or enact an ideal of patriarchal rule within households.

Rape as an assertion of masculine domination

The rather bland description of rape as 'an expression of patriarchy' (Vogelman 1990:23) fails to distinguish between 'gender as it is constructed' and 'gender as it is lived'. As Moore (1994) argues, this distinction is vital for understanding sexual violence. She suggests that whilst discourses construct men as active, aggressive, trusting and powerful, these representations often have only the most tangential relations to the attributes of individual men. To acquire gender identities, individual men invest in certain of the diverse subject positions that these discourses provide (1994:61). Men fantasise about the powerful identities that are inscribed in gender hierarchies and commit themselves emotionally to these identities. But these investments are often thwarted. When men face contrary expectations, or when others refuse to take up certain subject positions vis-à-vis the men, a crisis of self-representation may ensue. In these contexts, Moore (1994) contends, violence 'reconfirms the nature of masculinity otherwise denied', and represents 'a struggle for the maintenance of certain fantasies of identity and power' (1994:70).

Today a vast discrepancy exists between 'constructed' and 'lived' masculinity in Impalahoek. Though the old social order of the *motse* has disappeared, a model of it continues to exists as a 'virtual reality', removed in time from the concrete social context in which it was originally produced (see Van Binsbergen 2001). Men are generally most committed to this model and often invoke images of the past to legitimise and claim masculine privilege. But men's ideas of success also include other reference points, drawn from contemporary consumer culture.

For men of Impalahoek the concept *monna na* ('man of men') captures the ideal masculine person. As a household head with access to a steady income, the *monna na* supports his wives and children, keeps lovers and always has the final say. He is also brave and decisive, and faces any problem head-on. The negative masculine countertypes are the idiot (*setlatla, setlayeha* or *sepokopoko*), the man without finesse (*mpara*), the coward (*lepshega* or *lekgwala*), who is controlled by women, and the bachelor (*kgope*) who lives by himself without progeny. When a bachelor dies, I was told, his kin would shove a burning log up the anus of his corpse to show their contempt for his status. (I am not aware of any case where this discursive idea was actually put into practice.)

This ideology of masculine domination assumes sexual entitlement and legitimises domestic violence. Indeed, some of my male informants said that in the past a chief could legitimately have sex with any unmarried woman in his chiefdom, and they referred to traditional arranged marriages in which wives had little say in the choice of their husbands. Even today, men claimed that no wife was allowed to refuse the sexual advances of her husband. Men regularly beat insubordinate wives and lovers (Jacobsen 2002) and I learnt of several gruelling episodes of domestic violence during my fieldwork.

Men who were both married and employed committed six (15 percent) of the 39 cases of rape that I recorded. In 1997 a local businessman, Aaron Mashile, was charged with raping his neighbour's twelve-year-old daughter. While her father was working as a migrant in Gauteng, the girl's stepmother allegedly sold her to Mashile for cash. Mashile raped the girl in her father's home and also in the storeroom of his café. Though her stepmother threatened to call Mashile to slit her throat if she spoke out, the girl did tell her teachers about these incidents. At the time Mashile had two wives and five children.

Because my research methodology was biased towards more visible and dramatic cases of rape, the proportion of rapes perpetrated by married men might well be higher than these figures suggest. Village gossip is generally more finely attuned to the sexual crimes of powerful men that occur outside the household (Niehaus 2002c) than to sexual crimes such as 'marital rape' (Russel 1990) that take place within households.

But it is also clear that numerous men failed to meet various 'masculine challenges' (Messerschmidt 2000) such as securing jobs, marrying, fathering children or establishing their own households. For these men who do not occupy secure positions within domestic structures, the 'performance of masculinity' (Herzveld 1985) is crucially important. As a violent performance, rape asserts the subjectivity and physical power of men whose status might otherwise be insecure, and humiliates the victim as object. The association of sex with masculine agency is apparent in the use of the Northern Sotho slang words *molamo* (knobkerrie) and *lerumo* (assegaai) for penis, and *go hloma* (to insert), *go ja* (eat), *go hlaba* (pierce) or *go kalama* (board) for sexual intercourse. However, the act of rape is orientated towards the present rather than the future. Whilst the fear of rape may well constrain women's behaviour in the long term, the act of rape does not redress the structural dilemma of marginal men. Frequently, men only mimic a dominant masculine persona.

In Impalahoek, the gendered concerns of men in general and of rapists in particular were profoundly structured by age. Eighteen rapists were younger than 25, 22 were adults between the ages of 26 and 50 years, and five rapists were elders. (As there had been six gang rapes, rapists exceed the numbers of rapes.) A foremost challenge for young men was to demonstrate their heterosexuality. In Bushbuckridge Northern Sotho-speaking boys from the age of 12 years are expected to spend a period of about six weeks at an initiation lodge in the bush. Here they are forcefully circumcised, compelled to undergo various other hardships, taught to respect elders and instructed in proper masculine conduct.[5] Medical doctors generally circumcise Shangaan boys. In either case the circumcision ritual severs boys from the comfortable domains of their mothers upon whom they rely for sustenance and love and inducts them into the hard realm of men. They now officially stand in a different relation to women and are expected to court girls outside the family. Young men's first sexual encounters are usually with girlfriends (*mothlabo* or *cheri*), whom they court with numerous proposals, gifts, displays of affection and persistent begging. In this process they build and test reputations amongst their peers. Many young rapists were insecure and unable to assert their masculinity by other means. Some were described to me as mentally retarded youngsters and cannabis (dagga) smokers who were undesired as lovers and suffered humiliating rejections during courtship. Others were simply said to be 'scared of girls'. Many young men are from poorer households and cannot count on their parents to support them financially. Some engage in housebreaking, shoplifting and game poaching as a means of survival and male bonding. Whilst participation in crime is not in itself inimical to successful masculinity (see Bourgois 1996), the young petty criminals of Impalahoek were seldom materially successful. However, as in the case of the *tsotsis* (Glaser 2000) and 'jackrollers' (Mokwena 1991) who have roamed the streets of South Africa's urban townships since the late 1930s, many forms of sexual coercion are related more to the oppositional lifestyle of local criminal youth than to social insecurity per se.

Marriage symbolises the boundary between youth and adulthood. Young adults are expected to pay bride wealth, to take wives, to father children and to establish their own homesteads. But each of these steps towards adult masculinity depends upon wage earning. The job losses that occurred in the 1990s affected young adults most severely. Only nine of the 22 adult rapists were employed: as businessmen, taxi drivers, radio announcers, telephone technicians or security guards. Most others were excluded from the labour market. One man, Enos Nyathi, was already in his fifties without ever having been married or holding a formal job. Enos had only done 'piece jobs' such as building fences and digging pit latrines. Though he had fathered four children, each by a different lover, he was unable to support any dependents. He drank exceptionally heavily. Other rapists were without girlfriends. For example, a friend of Noah Segodi, a 27-year-old man who had committed rape, told me, 'I've never noticed Noah with a woman … I don't think he'll ever get married. He shoplifts and stabs and is in jail too often.'

The ideal for an elderly man (*mokgalabje*) is to be the head of a large family. But whereas elderly men controlled vast resources in land and stock prior to villagisation, they exercise little authority in domestic and village settings today. Many had failed to secure a supportive network of kin and are vulnerable to abandonment in their old age. Only 229 (50 percent) of the 460 children in my social survey were affiliated to the households of their fathers.[6] Villagers regularly accuse neglected elderly men of using witchcraft to impose their authority (Stadler 1996). The three cases discussed below illustrate different aspects of the social situations of rapists, and capture some of the diverse meanings of rape.

The gang rape of Shelly Ngwenya

In 1997 Jackson Chiloane, an unemployed single man in his early twenties, visited his male cousin in the nearby township, Shatale. When Jackson arrived he found that his cousin and some friends were having a party. They had lots of beer, wine and spirits. While six men drank in the lounge, a youngster called Makandeni arrived with his girlfriend, Shelly, who was already drunk. Yet Makandeni grabbed a cask of wine from the fridge, and he and a friend took Shelly into one of the bedrooms.

> We heard many noises from the room. In a few minutes the girl had VO Bertrams [a brandy] mixed with wine. Shelly wanted to go outside to urinate, but the boys would not let her. One boy sent the other boy to fetch a bucket. They gave the bucket to the girl and she

started vomiting. They were afraid that she would flee if she got out of the room.

Makandeni then called my cousin to get into the room. Later, the boy came back and called another one of us. By eight o'clock all seven boys were inside. When I got into the room I saw the guys screwing Shelly – the one after the other. The boys were drunk and lay next to the bed. They would say, 'My turn.' It was all night long. One man said that he screwed her four times. Some visitors peeped through the window and laughed. When it was my turn my cousin tried to discourage me. He said that this could land me in trouble. But I argued with him. I was drunk and I had already taken off my pants.

She was unconscious when we screwed her. One man told us to depart because she is recovering. He took us home in his van. We did not want Shelly to know what happened and we left her to sleep with her boyfriend, Makandeni. When Sally awoke, we wanted her to believe that she had slept with him all night long.

The next morning someone woke me and told me that the police were looking for us in connection with last night's incident. He said that the police had already fetched some of the chaps. I was scared because I could see that the chaps were not there. I consoled myself by taking more beers. I said that I would drink myself out so I would not know anything when the police came. I was not enjoying it. Luckily the chaps returned and laughed. They were only joking. Nobody had reported the case to the police. I then returned to Impalahoek and I was relieved to know that I was a free man.

Jackson was sure that the young men had actually raped Shelly.

> Yes, she was raped. She did not complain. But even if she had complained, her complaints would have fallen on deaf ears. There was nothing that she could do. The boys gave her liquor so that she could not see what was happening. She would never have allowed them if she was sober-minded.
>
> One of the chaps later told me that he saw Shelly the next day and asked her, 'How was yesterday?' She replied that she enjoyed it and would bring along her friends next time. I do not believe this.

Maybe she enjoyed the liquor, not the screwing. Maybe she was scared. There were seven boys involved and if she laid a charge something could happen to her.

Gangs of young men perpetrated six of the rapes that I recorded. The Northern Sotho term for gang rape, *lepanta* ('belt'), evokes an image of a chain in which one rapist follows the other and also of a victim who is completely entrapped. Though victims suffer great trauma, the rapists' prime intension is not to punish or humiliate them.[7] Young women such as Shelly Ngwenya are 'incidental victims' who do not in any way threaten the social position of young men. Gang rape is essentially a kind of male bonding, in which young men who compete for women in everyday life collaborate and share the same woman as sexual object. For example, Jackson told me that Makandeni offered his girlfriend, Shelly, to his mates, because he was the youngest member of the group and wished to win their friendship:

> Makandeni is young and has no powers. He had no money with which to buy liquor and stuff. He always takes the advice of the other chaps because they buy him liquor. He does everything they tell him to do.

A second important feature of gang rapes is voyeurism and the opportunity it affords young men to publicly demonstrate their heterosexual virility to their peers (cf. Sanday 1990). Collective bonding and the contribution of each individual to the endeavours of the group, as symbolised by these acts of transgression, are important principles in the social organisation of male peer groups, such as criminal networks.

The misogyny of Solanka, a serial rapist

During the course of my research the arrest of a serial rapist called Solanka Khosa evoked much discussion. Solanka was born to Mozambican immigrants in 1959. He grew up in Mhala, became involved in serious crime and was imprisoned for six years on account of homicide. While he was in jail, his mother and sister came to live in Impalahoek. They reportedly wanted to start a new life where they were not stigmatised by his reputation. But in 1993 Solanka was released, located his mother and sister, and came to share their one-roomed house. They again fled from him and built a new house in Mloro. Since then, Solanka has held only one job. He worked at the Njaka dam as a security guard for a short while, but was dismissed. He was involved with two women. His first girlfriend left him immediately after she learnt that he was a convicted felon. His second lover stayed with him. She was a cripple who had had several miscarriages. Yet she received a disability grant and was the breadwinner at home.

In Impalahoek, Solanka lived a secret life of crime, stealing from other villages at night. He had acquired a legendary reputation as a housebreaker who could sneak into people's locked homes to steal their cellphones, revolvers and videocassette recorders while they slept. One of Solanka's neighbours described him to me as 'a very dangerous man' and joked, 'He can steal your underpants without taking off your trouser[s].' In 1999 Solanka was arrested for shoplifting, but he was released, only one week later. His neighbours also became aware that he was a rapist. Nana Maatsie recalled that Solanka once approached her at her field near the river:

> When I looked at him I could see that he was naked. He wore a shirt on top, but had nothing on the bottom. He called me, but I refused to come. I could see that his intension was to rape me. As I ran away he screamed at me, 'I propose to you, but you don't listen! Next time I meet you I'll rape you.'

In November 2001, Solanka was arrested on 13 counts of rape. Nearly all of his victims were financially successful women. They were teachers, a shopping centre supervisor's wife, a motel owner, a butcher, a telephone business owner, an ANC (African National Congress) leader, a wedding-dress maker and a bakery employee. Solanka carefully observed his victims and only attacked when they were alone at home. He broke into their homes wearing a stocking over his head, and stole their money and possessions before he raped them. Doris Nyathi, the dressmaker, told me how Solanka entered her bedroom at 2 a.m. At that time her husband was at work in Gauteng and her sister-in-law slept on a mattress on the floor beside her bed.

When I heard my bedroom door making a noise I got out of bed. That is when I saw him. He held a shining torch in one hand and a gun in the other. He first said, 'Sleep! Don't look at me. Give me your cellphone and money.' I said 'No. I don't have a phone, but you take the money.' Solanka then ransacked the whole house. Whenever he found money he would scream out the amount and say, 'I found so much.' After a while he told us, 'Lie down! Stretch your arms behind your head!' He then uncovered the blankets. He first undressed me, but because I menstruated he did not rape me. Instead, he raped my sister-in-law.

Solanka then demanded more money and threatened to kill us that side of Cottondale. He said, 'Get up. Give us money! This one refuses to give us money! Let's carry her away!' It was as if he spoke to someone else standing outside the house. He had taken R780 by himself and I gave him another R1 500. That makes it R2 280 in total. He only left at 4:30. When he ran away I saw that he was barefooted. But I could not tell if there was another man outside. The house was upside down – books, bags and everything. We summoned all the neighbours to show them what the house looked like and then phoned the police.

One month later, a municipal employee arrived at home to find Solanka raping his wife. Solanka did not wait to put on his clothes, and smashed the bedroom window to escape. That evening the police arrested him in a nearby tavern. Twelve different victims were called to identify him at the police station.

Like many other rapists, Solanka failed to meet the masculine challenges of his age cohort. Contrary to expectations that men should support their spouses, Solanka depended upon his wife's disability pension. The rapes Solanka perpetrated clearly differ from the gang rape of young women such as Shelly Ngwenya. Solanka's victims were not incidental, but were carefully selected and systematically degraded. At one level the status and wealth of Solanka's victims merely made theft worthwhile. At another level his attacks express misogynistic anger at the perceived feminisation of work and prosperity in the era of de-industrialisation. Solanka ritualistically deprived his victims of their money and even commanded the ANC leader to cook him food after he had raped her. (This perception is largely misplaced. Though women professionals are today more visible, we have seen that only a few more women are actually employed than was the case fifteen years ago.)

There are important similarities between Solanka's misogynistic rapes and those perpetrated by outlaws who live by themselves in the forest. These rapists prey upon girls using footpaths through the bush to go to school, teachers and nurses making their way to work, shoppers returning home with groceries and women collecting firewood. In June 2002, a man living in the bush raped two shop assistants and also stole their money, lunch boxes, cellphones and handbags. Such rapes were also exceptionally brutal. One outlaw shoved an old cloth down the throat of a 60-year-old woman, and he beat her so badly that she nearly suffocated from the blood in her mouth and the nose. Another rapist ran off with the clothes of his 50-year-old victim, leaving her completely naked.

Child rape as punishment

George Zandela, who was unemployed and single when I interviewed him, told me that the youngest woman with whom he ever had sex was merely 13 years old. In 1985, when in his twenties, George obtained work at a colliery in Witbank. From his earnings he paid bride wealth, married and supported a wife and child. However, in 1988, he learnt that another man had impregnated his wife and he separated from her. She later married a businessman. George's next serious relationship was with Lindiwe, a woman who lived in Witbank. She owned a house and a tavern and had two children from a previous marriage.

After George and Lindiwe had been together for some time he began to suspect that she, too, was cheating on him with other men. George once found her seated in her dining room with someone called Jacob and also saw them together eating ice cream at a Kentucky Fried Chicken outlet. George confronted Lindiwe about this and assaulted her. But only a month later, he saw Jacob and Thandi, Lindiwe's youngest child, carrying groceries at a taxi rank. George and two of his work mates tracked Jacob down at a beer hall and beat him so severely that he lost consciousness. George later heard rumours that Lindiwe still used Thandi to convey messages between her and Jacob.

I took care of Lindiwe's kids and bought her father food, but she cheated me with other men. I realised that the best way to punish her was to screw her daughter. Two months later I asked Lindiwe whether I could take Thandi to Johannesburg for a weekend to show her the city. Lindiwe said, 'No problem. I'll be happy if Thandi sees Johannesburg.' My main aim was to screw Thandi. We stayed at my brother's place in Soweto. On Friday and Saturday Thandi slept in a room with other girls.

On the Sunday I took Thandi to the city. I went to the Carlton Hotel. Ruben Masoko, who is my former classmate, worked there. He allowed us to watch a film for free. I told Ruben that I wanted to screw the girl, but I did not say that she was my stepdaughter. Then he would have refused. Ruben gave me keys for the maintenance room. There was no bed, only a sofa. I bought popcorn, Simba chips [crisps] and ice cream and Thandi went up and down in the lift. She had never seen a lift before.

We finally got into the room and sat on the sofa. Thandi asked me, 'Why are you waiting? Why are you locking the doors?' I said, 'We have no choice. All the taxis for Witbank had already left. She replied, 'No! Lets go!' I asked her, 'To where? We can't walk to Witbank. There are many *tsotsis* [thugs] on the way and they'll kill us.'

That evening Thandi confessed that her mother was in love with Jacob and with a Xhosa guy from the Transkei. I asked Thandi, 'Why did you not tell me from the word go? I buy you bread, meat and school clothes.' She said that her mother sent her [with messages to these men]. I then told her that because she listens to her mother and not to me, I would take revenge. I commanded her to undress, romanced her and touched her breasts. Then I put her on the sofa and screwed her. She had no choice. She thought that if she did not obey I would beat her. She was not screaming, but she cried all the time. There was blood on my penis. When I finished I gave her the popcorn, Simba chips and cold drinks. I screwed her a second time. Then she was no more crying. She was only scared.

At five o'clock I woke up, screwed her for the last time and gave Ruben the keys. Then we took the taxi to Witbank. Lindiwe was angry and asked me why I delayed. I lied and told her that there were no taxis. On Wednesday Lindiwe called me outside and told me that Thandi said I raped her. I said, 'Yes. I screwed Thandi because of you, because you always send Thandi to your boyfriends. I was worried about what you did to me. I wanted you to feel some of my pain.' I then said, 'Let the matter rest between you, Thandi and me. Tell no one else. This is very shameful.'

One year later, George was retrenched. He separated from Lindiwe and returned to Impalahoek. As Moore (1994) argues, men such as George Zandela, who cannot control the behaviour of the women in their lives, are unable to represent themselves as active and dominant in relation to femininity. They strike out at vulnerable women whom they can control and thereby reconfirm a masculinity otherwise denied. By raping his 'stepdaughter', George also asserted his dominance within the household. Moreover, George explicitly stated that his intension was to hurt Lindiwe, and he might have chosen this method of revenge to cause her maximum pain and to assert his dominance in the face of her actions that questioned his manliness.

This case is very similar to eight other cases in the sample, where elderly men raped girls between the ages of six and 19 years. Three men raped their own daughters, two men their granddaughters, one his niece, and two men the children of neighbours. These cases of incest occur despite a strict taboo against sexual intercourse between patrilineal relatives (Niehaus 2002b). However, as La Fontaine (1986) shows, incest is not the antithesis of kinship, but is rather an exaggeration of the patriarchal family structure, where men have power over women and children. Common knowledge of the guilty secret could also band the domestic unit together against the outside world.

In all these cases, rapists enacted a dominant masculine persona. Yet this performance of domination is orientated towards the present, and with the exception of the rape of sexual partners and of incest, rape does not establish routine social relations. In other words, the erotic allure of power seldom pays long-term dividends. Rape can also have devastating consequences for rapists themselves. Twenty of the 39 cases of rape that I recorded were reported to the police, 18 resulted in arrests and ten in prosecutions. The average sentence for rape was five years. Although these rates are drastically inflated by the visibility of many of the cases that I recorded and by the close proximity of Impalahoek to a major police station, one cannot ignore the risks that rapists take.

The present-day view of rape is illustrated by the case of Khazamula Mathebula, a 50-year-old man who raped and impregnated Bongi, the 15-year-old daughter of his neighbours. When Bongi's parents came to speak to him about the pregnancy, Khazamula was extremely rude and reportedly told them, 'Go and fuck yourself.' Three days later the police arrested Khazamula. He was so shaken that he tried to commit suicide by shooting himself in the charge office, but the bullet missed his heart by centimetres. Khazamula was hospitalised, handcuffed to his bed and guarded by police officers. One of my informants lay on the next bed. He recalled,

> Khazamula screamed all the time. He would shout, 'Give me a gun so I can kill myself! Give me poison to drink! Let me take off these handcuffs so that I can die! I want to grind bottles so that I can eat the glass and die. The gun missed, but the glass won't miss.' Once his family members visited him at ten o'clock in the morning. Khazamula told them, 'I am already dead. They will sentence me for life.' His relatives tried to comfort him and said, 'No. You're not dead.' He said, 'Yes. I'm dead. A lifetime sentence is worse than the grave. I won't see my relatives and friends anymore. Give me a gun, a knife or a bottle so that I can take a short cut to heaven.'

Conclusions

Evidence from Bushbuckridge supports the well-established theory that rape is not purely about sexual gratification, but is also an intensely political act that speaks about masculine domination. From the perspective of men who rape, the desire for sex is inseparable from the desire for power (Woodhull 1988). However, it is unhelpful to describe rape simply as expressing pre-existing patriarchal relations. The case material presented in this article shows that in many cases there was a significant disjuncture between masculine ideals and the real-life situation of rapists. Far from being 'men of men', men who rape often fail to meet conventional challenges of masculinity: many were young, unemployed, petty criminals, cheated by their wives and lovers, or marginal elders. Hence rape was as much an expression of sexual entitlement as a violent symbolic assertion of masculine domination, motivated by fantasies of power.

Evidence presented in this article also highlights the diverse meanings of rape. Rape was not simply a 'control mechanism, schooling women to confine their actions and attributes to within the parameters of acceptable gender role behaviour' (Vogelman 1990:23). This theory seems to describe more accurately the consequences of rape than the intentions of rapists. Men who rape are often more concerned about their own positions relative to other men and to women than about the status of their victims. As we have seen, young men participated in gang rapes as a means of male bonding and demonstrating their sexual and social worth, unemployed adults raped to degrade successful women, and elders to assert their dominance as fathers within domestic structures.

There are few grounds for seeing the high prevalence of rape as a feature of an emerging 'masculinity' in the economically marginal villages of South Africa's former 'homeland' areas. The search for a single model of masculinity often deflects attention from the multiple, contradictory and discordant discourses about gender that characterise these social settings. Moreover, the shared masculine ideals, the salience of images from the past, and the wide prevalence of violence are by no means exclusive to areas such as Impalahoek (see Morrell 2001a). Men's behaviour is not simply a response to internalised cultural patterns: it is also a response to the facts of their material life situations that contradict these cultural models. But there is, at the same time, little sense in trying to grasp rape in terms of a 'deficient masculinity' – as something that is finite, lost and won. (See Cornwall & Lindisfarne 1994 for a persuasive critique of this model.)

A more satisfying alternative for understanding the proliferation of rape in South Africa over the past two decades is to pay close attention to the diverse meanings of rape and to its association with masculine ideas and fantasies of power. Furthermore, we need to situate these local meanings in a framework of a changing broader political economy. There is definitely some merit to Posel's (2003) argument that the increased reports of rape are an index of the proliferation of discourses about sex since political liberation. She suggests that the secrecy and silence about sexual violence during the apartheid era has given way to moral panic in the post-apartheid era. Sexual violence is now at the forefront of public debate and the sexual abuse of women and children has become a national scandal. Posel argues that the recognition of sex as a site of human rights, AIDS awareness campaigns, and discourses of truth and reconciliation have all contributed to the undoing of sexual secrecy. But acts and discourses of sexual violence are not isolated from broader political economic changes, particularly from experiences of de-industrialisation. High job losses amongst men often stand at the centre of the disintegration of domestic units, the <u>disjuncture between men's ideals and actual life situations</u> and the prominence of criminal lifestyles. All these factors are related to violent assertions of masculine dominance.

In the struggle for gender equality, it is essential that we acknowledge the full effects of masculine domination, not only on women and children as its obvious victims, but also on men who are less visibly constrained by this ideology. We also need to emphasise that sexual violence and the maiming of women and children do not redress the structural dilemmas and social positions of marginal men.

Acknowledgements

This investigation was sponsored by a generous research grant from the Mellon Mentorship Programme, administered by the University of Pretoria. I thank my research assistants Mirinda Gillespie, Eliazaar Mohlala, Kally Shokane and Eric Thobela for their help. Erik Bähre, Rachel Jewkes, Robert Thornton, John Tosh, Charles van Onselen and Kate Wood all made useful suggestions. Given the nature of my topic, the usual disclaimers apply with special vigour. The information provided in this article is extremely sensitive, potentially harmful and even incriminating. Yet I believe that in a country afflicted by horrendous sexual violence, silence is a far more serious abuse of academic freedom than the exposure of secrets.

Notes

1. See Crime Information Analysis Centre, South African Police Services (Jewkes & Abrahams 2002:1232-8).
2. See Russel (1975), Sanday (1985, 1990), Gregor (1988), Winkler (1991), Olujic (1998), Woodhull (1998) and Helliwell (2000).
3. Throughout this article I use pseudonyms to disguise my field site and to conceal the identity of rapists and victims, even if their cases are well known in the village. Unless otherwise specified, all local terms are in Northern Sotho.
4. My research assistant, Mirinda Gillespie, unearthed only 20 cases of rape from the entire Bushbuckridge area that were heard in the Pilgrim's Rest circuit of the South African supreme court between 1918 and 1959.
5. See Hammond-Tooke's (1981) account of boys' initiation elsewhere in the South African lowveld.
6. Two hundred children lived with their mothers, 26 with their grandparents, and five with other maternal kin.
7. Gregor (1988:486) writes that Mehinalen men of Brazil gang-raped any woman who saw the sacred flutes in the men's house. In this sadistic form of punishment they exposed her genitals in public and contaminated her with semen.

References

Bond, G. and Ciekawy, D. (eds.) (2001) *Witchcraft Dialogues: Anthropological and Philosophical Exchanges*. (Athens, Ohio: Ohio University Press).

Bourgois, P. (1996) *In Search of Respect: Selling Crack in El Barrio*. (Cambridge: Cambridge University Press).

Cornwall, A. and Lindisfarne, N. (eds.) (1994) *Dislocating Masculinity: Comparative Ethnographies*. (London: Routledge).

Diamond, I. and Quinby, L. (eds.) (1988) *Feminism and Foucault: Reflections on Resistance*. (Boston: Northeastern University Press).

Gedye, L., James, C. and Lebea, M. (2004) Putting the government's HIV/AIDS plan to the test. *Mail & Guardian*, 26 November–2 December.

Glaser, C. (2000) *Bo-tsotsi: The Youth Gangs of Soweto, 1935–1976*. (London: Heinemann).

Gregor, T. (1988) Male Dominance and Sexual Coercion. (Stigler et al. 1988:477–95).

Gupta, A. and Ferguson, J. (eds.) (1997) *Anthropological Locations: Boundaries and Grounds of a Field Science*. (Berkeley and Los Angeles: University of California Press).

Hammond-Tooke, W.D. (1981) *Boundaries and Belief: The Structure of a Sotho Worldview*. (Johannesburg: Witwatersrand University Press).

Harries, P. (1989) Exclusion, classification and internal colonialism: the emergence of ethnicity among Tsonga-speakers of South Africa. In L. Vail (ed.) *The Creation of Tribalism in Southern Africa*. London: James Currey, 82–117.

Helliwell, C. (2000) 'It's only a penis': rape, feminism and difference. Signs: *Journal of Women in Culture and Society*, 25, 3, 789–816.

Herzfeld, M. (1985) *The Poetics of Manhood: Contest and Identity in a Cretan Mountain Village*. (Princeton: Princeton University Press).

Human Rights Watch/Africa. (1995) *Violence Against Women in South Africa: State Response to Domestic Violence and Rape*. (New York: Human Rights Watch).

Hunter, M. (2002) The materiality of everyday sex: thinking beyond prostitution. *African Studies*, 61, 1, 99–120.

Jacobsen, C. (2002) 'Loose Women' and 'Irresponsible Men': A Contextual Study of Domestic Violence, Marriage and Images of Tradition and the Modern in a South African Lowveld Village. MA dissertation, Aalborg University, Copenhagen.

Jewkes, R. and Abrahams, N. (2002) The epidemiology of rape and sexual coercion in South Africa: An Overview. *Social Science and Medicine*, 55, 1231–44.

Kahn, K., Tollman, S., Garenne, M. and Gear, J. (1999) Who dies from what? determining cause of death in South Africa's rural north-east. *Tropical Medicine and International Health*, 4, 6, 433–41.

La Fontaine, J. (1986) Child sexual abuse and the incest taboo: practical problems and theoretical issues. *Man* (n.s.), 23, 1, 1–18.

Malkki, L. (1997) News and culture: transitory phenomena and the fieldwork tradition. (Gupta and Ferguson 1997:86–101).

Messerschmidt, J. (2000) Becoming 'real men': adolescent masculinity challenges and sexual violence. *Men and Masculinities*, 2, 3, 286–307.

Mokwena, S. (1991) The Era of the Jackrollers: Contextualising the Rise of Youth Gangs in Soweto. Seminar no. 7. (Johannesburg: Centre for the Study of Violence and Reconciliation).

Moore, H. (1994) *A Passion for Difference: Essays in Anthropology and Gender.* (Bloomington: Indiana University Press).

Morrell, R. (2001a) The times of change: men and masculinity in South Africa. (Morrell 2001b: 317–36).

Morrell, R. (ed.) (2001b) *Changing Men in Southern Africa.* (Pietermaritzburg: University of Natal Press).

Niehaus, I. (2002a) Ethnicity and the boundaries of belonging: reconfiguring Shangaan identity in the South African Lowveld. *African Affairs*, 101, 3, 557–583.

Niehaus, I. (2002b) Bodies, heat and taboos: conceptualising 'modern personhood' in the South African Lowveld. *Ethnology*, 41, 3, 189–207

Niehaus, I. (2002c) Perversion of power: witchcraft and the sexuality of evil in the South African Lowveld. *Journal of Religion in Africa*, 32, 3, 269–99.

Niehaus, I. with E. Mohlala and K. Shokane (2001) Witchcraft, Power and Politics: *Exploring the Occult in the South African Lowveld.* (London: Pluto).

Olujic, M. (1998) Embodiment of terror: gendered violence in peacetime and wartime in Croatia and in Bosnia-Herzegovina. *Medical Anthropology Quarterly*, 12, 1, 31–50.

Posel, D. (2003) The scandal of manhood: unmaking secrets of sexual violence in post-apartheid South Africa. Unpublished paper presented at the Sex and Secrecy conference. (Johannesburg: Wits Institute for Social and Economic Research).

Ritchken, E. (1995) Leadership and Conflict in Bushbuckridge: Struggles to Define Moral Economies within the Context of Rapidly Transforming Political Economies. PhD thesis, University of the Witwatersrand.

Russel, D. (1975) *The Politics of Rape.* (New York: Stein and Day).

Russel, D (1990) *Rape in Marriage.* (Bloomington: Indiana University Press).

Russel, D. (1991) Rape and child sexual abuse in Soweto: an interview with community leader Mary Mabaso. *South African Sociological Review*, 3, 2, 62–83.

Russel, D. (1997) *Behind Closed Doors in White South Africa: Incest Survivors Tell their Stories.* (London: MacMillan Press).

Sanday, P. (1981) The socio-cultural context of rape: a cross-cultural study. *Journal of Social Issues*, 37, 4, 158–72.

Sanday, P. (1990) *Fraternity Gang Rape: Sex, Brotherhood and Privilege on Campus*. (New York: New York University Press).

Simpson, G. (1991) *Explaining Sexual Violence: Some Background Factors in the Current Socio-political Context*. (Johannesburg: Project for the Study of Violence.)

South African Institute of Race Relations. (2001) *South African Survey 2000/2001*. (Johannesburg: South African Institute of Race Relations)

Stadler, J. (1994) Generational Relationships in a Lowveld Village: Questions of Age, Household and Tradition. MA dissertation, University of the Witwatersrand.

Stadler, J. (1996) Witches and Witch-hunters: Witchcraft, Generational Relations and the Life Cycle in a Lowveld Village. *African Studies*, 55, 1, 87–110.

Stigler, J., Shweder, R., and Herdt, G. (eds.) (1988) *Cultural Psychology: Essays on Comparative Human Development*. (Cambridge: Cambridge University Press).

Van Binsbergen, W. (2001) Witchcraft in modern Africa as virtualised boundary conditions of the kinship order. (Bond & Ciekawy 2001:221–264).

Varga, C.A. (1997) Sexual decision-making and negotiations in the midst of AIDS: youth in KwaZulu-Natal, South Africa. *Health Transition Review*, 7, 3, 45–67.

Vogelman, L. (1990) *The Sexual Face of Violence: Rapists on Rape*. (Johannesburg: Ravan Press).

Winkler, C. (1991) Rape as social murder. *Anthropology Today*, 7, 3, 12–14.

Wood, K. and R. Jewkes (2001) 'Dangerous love': reflections on violence among Xhosa township youth. (Morrell 2001b:317–336).

Woodhull, W. (1988) Sexuality, Power and the Question of Rape. (Diamond & Quinby 1988:25–32).

4

Rules of engagement: Structuring sex and damage in men's prisons and beyond

Sasha Gear

Introduction

In South Africa, punitive popular attitudes to criminals refuse prisoners much public concern. Amidst high levels of violence and fear, society is tempted to conceive of prison as a black hole of nothingness into which criminals disappear forever. At the same time, what goes on in prison is regularly regarded as weird, perverse and fundamentally 'other' to the rest of society, more so where the taboo-laden issue of sex is concerned. A consideration of the rules and assumptions that operate in the dominant inmate culture to shape the circumstances of sex in prison points at once to the complex social world that prison environments in fact represent, and also to their connectedness to patterns played out beyond prison walls. New forms of identity and behaviour are demanded by the intricate codes and rulings to which inmates are subject, but these constructions and negotiations, while breaking with the outside, turn out to represent a precarious balancing of continuity with more broadly experienced norms and relationality to them.

A central site of cultural power and rule-making in prison lies in gangsterism, particularly among a collection of gangs known as 'the Numbers' (the 28s, 26s, 27s, Big 5s, and Airforce 3 and 4). Operating along quasi-military lines that mimic the colonial militarised institutions to which they emerged in resistance, the Numbers have been around for more than a century.[1] Each gang has specific objectives and its own code of conduct. The stated objective of the Airforce gangs, for example, is to escape from prison, while the Big 5s collaborate with the authorities to obtain food and other privileges, and the 28s protect and organise catamites, or *wyfies* as they are known, for sex. However, that actual gang practices diverge from the ideal codes is evident in the fact that all the Numbers gangs are apparently involved in the organisation of specific sexual interactions and relationships, even those where the formal codes expressly forbid it. Indeed, an investigation of sex in prison points to the multiple, sometimes contradictory layers of code and meaning employed in the organisation of particular sexual relations.

Rules, codes and meanings surrounding sexual practices in prison construct and police particular gendered identities. Gender and sex relations in prison, however, cannot be adequately explained by either the gang codes that seek to regulate prisoner behaviours, or by dominant processes in South African society to which they powerfully hark back. Rather, the identities and relations produced in prison are the work of an uneven confluence of discourses incorporated from the outside and others generated by the inmate culture on the inside (both of which represent complex and dynamic processes in themselves). In their negotiations of sex and gender, prisoners exaggerate, adapt and break the rules, sometimes more vehemently asserting oppressive power claims, and at other times subverting them. In the process, new configurations of identity and interaction emerge.

Carceral identities: imitation or rupture?

Approaches to the production of sexuality and gender in South African male prisons are usefully informed by perspectives in historical accounts of sexual practices amongst men who were housed in South African mine compounds. A central debate has emerged in the theorising of the relationship between sexual interactions and identity formation in South African 'carceral' (Dirsuweit 1999) institutions, namely mine compounds and, more recently, prisons. Subsequent to an initial break with the notion of these closed institutions as sealed off from processes in broader society,[2] scholars divided on the question of whether inmate identities and sexualities represent a smooth transitioning consistent with outside identities or whether a rupture (Achmat 1993) occurs between previously existing identities from the outside and those experienced during incarceration.

In their considerations of sex relationships amongst male migrant workers housed in mine compounds, Van Onselen (1984), Moodie

(1994) and Harries (1994) argue that the gendered identities forged around and central to relationships known as 'mine marriages' ultimately cohered with the miners' lives outside. Through a variety of cultural networks, the incorporation of home practices into the compound, and the performance of particular roles inside in the interests of achieving a status at home, compound identities were intimately tied to their home lives, and the miners' compound connected to spaces beyond it. These writers describe the particular moral economy of mine marriages that took place between older men and younger boys, the senior man assuming a masculinised role and taking the younger as his wife. In return for financial reward wives were required to take a passive sex role and to provide domestic services to their husbands. In these accounts, the norms of the marriages are traced to exchanges and identity structures operating in the miners' rural home communities, which were based on gerontocracy and patriarchy.

A 'natural' end to the marriage occurred when wives grew older and could claim a masculine status and the active sex role that went with it, taking wives of their own (Moodie 1994:127). This was a signal of status, and for a number of reasons the 'town women' were a less desirable sexual alternative. The danger of venereal disease and theft, fear of losing one's rural identity and acquiring additional responsibilities by becoming tied to women in the town apparently contributed to the preference for 'mine wives'. However, in mine wifehood too, masculine purposes were being achieved. Because the passive, feminised role was financially lucrative it enabled the young man to build his rural resources and pay bride wealth. 'Being a "wife" on the mine,' Moodie (1994:134) argues, 'for all its apparent gender reversals, eventually reinforced the potential for male hegemony at home.'

Achmat (1993) and Dirsuweit (1999, 2003) criticise this vein of analysis. Achmat (1993) argues that the sexual practices taking place in compounds could not be reduced to their relation to the rural communities and outside preoccupations, nor should we be intent on uncovering motivations for participation. Rather, he maintains that the compound 'partially freed the male body in its enslavement' (Achmat 1993:106), allowing 'a definitive change in the relations between the concepts of sexual pleasure and sexual reproduction' (Achmat 1993:108). The compound or prison is thus conceptualised as a 'rupture' that, by breaking with inhabitants' outside lives, presents possibilities for them to explore new configurations of desire and pleasure (Achmat 1993, Dirsuweit 1999, 2003).

Neither of these positions, ventures Dirsuweit (1999, 2003), adequately explains the sexual identities lived in carceral institutions. In her overview of the debate, she traces the different conceptions of the relationship between space and identity at play in these competing arguments. While the Van Onselen (1984) Moodie (1994) and Harries (1990, 1994) analyses suggest that identity remains constant through space and inscribes each new space with meaning, Achmat (1993) considers the compound/prison to have constituted a new space, discreet from traditional society, in which miners were able to recreate themselves (Dirsuweit 1999). Dirsuweit contributes an alternative conception of identity. Following Keith & Pile's (1993a) understanding of space and identity as a dynamic interaction, 'where both define each other in an unstable process which is constantly shifting and being renegotiated' (Dursuweit 1999:72), she argues that it is

> conceivable that the ... traditions of rural communities were carried into the mine ... while at the same time ... the entry into a new space free of the norms of tradition and custom allowed them to explore same-sex desire in relation to cultural codes of other spaces, and through renegotiations of the mine codes of conduct as their sexual identities shifted. (Dirsuweit 1999:72)

Dirsuweit's (1999, 2003) analysis of sexuality in South African women's prisons draws on Butler's (1990:141) notion of gender as performative and as constituted by a repetition of acts as opposed to an expression of a pre-existing identity (Butler 1990:141). She argues that the female inmates' construction and negotiations of sexual and gender identities, while 'based on norms of heterosexual interaction held in broader South African society', also fundamentally unsettle the discourses surrounding these norms in their shifting performances of gender (Dirsuweit 1999:82). 'Even if the roles ... mirror male-female gendered relationships, they still serve to question what basis there is for claims to male privilege' (Dirsuweit 1999:82). By identifying as men, asserting dominance over women and assuming an exclusively penetrative sex role, for example, 'butch' prisoners in female prisons endorse dominant gender relations, but at the same time hold up for parody the notion of gender as the natural and stable outcome of a particular sex. This is even more the case among those who do not restrict their enactment of gender to this singular 'masculine' identity. The threatened responses such inmates evoke in heterosexual prisoners and correctional staff, Dirsuweit argues, is testament to their subversive quality.

Dirsuweit's (2003) conception of the cultural environment is a valuable point of departure. This she presents as the particular but changing results of a complex interplay of discourses emanating from, and in interaction with, a range of spaces and power sources. In these interactions breaks are made, boundaries are pushed and shifts in understandings of self and others become possible.

> The carceral environment then can be approached as the intersection of different discursive structures which are not only based in state control, but also find their roots in prisoner based discourses and in the discourses of other institutions and cultural formations. In other words, the prisoner's subjectivity is produced outside of the carceral environment and in discursive formations within the prison which intersect with, but are not necessarily controlled by state authority. At the same time, carceral institutions present a rupture in established identity structures. (Dirsuweit 2003:64–65)

In exploring sexual practices and the production of gendered identities in South African mens' prisons I follow these theoretical conceptualisations of identity and the carceral environment. The goal is to open up questions of continuity and rupture in relation to the construction of gender, and propose a conception of rupture that is broader and more multi-natured than the existing work suggests. I argue that some of these breaks in fact occur because of continuities with outside norms. As a result, they also organise in contradictory unevenness between differently placed actors, and between levels of social organisation.

This chapter is based on data collected for a study done by the Centre for the Study of Violence and Reconciliation (CSVR),

Johannesburg. In-depth interviews and focus group discussions were held with 23 prisoners and ex-prisoners in Gauteng Province, South Africa.

Prison marriages & the sexual status quo: rules & roles

Male prison populations tend to be divided into people identified as 'men' and those identified as 'women'. 'Women' are seen primarily as the sexual property and servants of 'men' and are often forcibly taken as 'wives' (or *wyfies*) by other inmates in relationships known as 'marriages'.[3] They are required to take care of the 'home' space (cell) and to be sexually available to their partners. 'Men'/ 'husbands', on the other hand, provide materially for their 'wives' through activity in the 'business' of prison.[4] 'Marriage'-type interactions are reportedly the most common site of sex in men's prison and are accepted in the hegemonic inmate culture as the right place for sex to happen. As in accounts of sexual mores from the mine compounds (Moodie 1994) and women's prison's (Dirsuweit 1999, 2003) they arrange around a conflation of gender and sex role: 'men' penetrate and 'women' are penetrated.

Gang structures are intimately involved in the construction and regulation of 'women'. Members are divided between two ranking hierarchies: one of 'masculine' ranks and the other of 'feminine' ones. Each masculinised rank corresponds to a feminine one, determining which 'women' will be allocated as *wyfies* to which 'men'. Higher-ranking 'men' have the greatest entitlements to sex. Intricate rituals and regulations are in place to organise the maintenance of this sex and gender status quo. An ex-prisoner explained, for example, how *wyfies* in the Big 5s gang are schooled in their roles by the *wyfie* at the helm of the feminine hierarchy:

> The Star [is] ... the first [*wyfie*] in the Cabinet and all the [others] listen to her. He teaches them what ... we do not want in Big 5: ... 'If you stay with a person you have to treat him this way and not that way because if you do, you make him angry' ... They cannot tell us [men] that they do not like sex. The Star will tell them that they must not say things like that.

But fundamental to the controlling of 'women' and sex relations at the levels of individual partnerships, gangsterism and also beyond are the codes contained in public myths and discourses that have a grip on society more generally. These are behind the sexualised and inferior way in which 'women' are seen, the passivity expected of them, the entitlement of 'men' to sex from 'women', and the powerful perception that victims of forced sex in prison are, like those out of it, in some way to blame for what has happened to them (see for example Jewkes & Abrahams 2000, Zulu 2001, CIET International 2003). These meanings militate towards silence on the part of victims.[5] Sexual violence is constructed as a gendering experience that changes men into 'women', and 'real men' do not allow themselves to be raped. Respondents testify frequently to the potency of these public myths, for example, in their certainty that were the family of a prison 'wife' to find out what had happened to their relative in prison, his identity as a man and his role in the family would be demolished. 'His wife and children [will think], "You're nothing! After all, you've been raped; you are just as good as we women"... *Of course* he can't tell his family!!'

Making women, taking wives

The polarised gender categories that this moral economy requires demand that some inmates depart from the way they have understood themselves and been understood by others up until their incarceration. A range of rituals and methodologies are employed to bring about these breaks and to reallocate gender identities for the inside.

A typical path into being made a 'woman' and 'wife' is for a new offender to accept food, drugs or protection from another prisoner. Lacking prison 'suss', first-time offenders are especially vulnerable to the manipulation regularly employed by other inmates. They do not know that by accepting what is on offer an exchange is understood to have taken place, and a debt created. Later, the new offender will learn that he is expected to make good this debt by providing his 'provider' (the person from whom he accepted food, drugs, etc.) with sex. When trying to refuse, he will learn that there is no way out. Most marriages reportedly begin in this way, with the provider forcing sex with the person he subsequently takes as his 'wife'. Being sexually penetrated is understood to confirm 'womanhood'.

Accepting what is offered by another (who likely presents himself as a generous being in a sea of hostility) is to display naivety and trust, qualities that are understood to signal inferiority, weakness and 'woman-ness'. Poverty is also associated with femininity, and poor prisoners, frequently those who do not get visitors – a source of commodities and money – tend to be amongst those forced to join the ranks of 'women'. Physical weakness or unwillingness to use violence and also 'good looks' (apparently encompassing smooth-skinned youthfulness and plumpness) are said to make for likely targeting. But respondents emphasise that none of these characteristics are absolute prerequisites for being sexually subordinated and designated 'women'. Some people are targeted until submission, regardless of the way in which they conduct themselves. This is where overt violent rape is most often mentioned.

The rules in this one-sided game are therefore almost as changeable (on the part of the player) as they are hidden from those against whom the game is being played. Their hidden nature is central to the subordination strategies, but where these, despite the deception, do not produce the desired results they may be ditched for other less veiled ones. Nevertheless, the fact that they exist at all may be employed in justification of the acts (at other times dismissed as 'natural' entitlements).

> Obviously a prisoner's things are going to talk. I cannot give you a cigarette and then go [away and not bother you again]. So if you do not understand [stops short] ...
>
> In jail terms ... I cannot just give a person twenty rands and buy anything I want to buy him; and tomorrow he says that I have raped him.

Other explanations work to naturalise the establishment of the gender category that the acts bring into being, for example: 'You can never allow another man to come on top of you if you do not like it.'

Promotion from 'womanhood' to a masculine status is rare, and only available to those who are able to prove a claim to 'manhood', usually by performing a particular violent act. In addition to a preparedness to use violence and the ability to fight, markers of manhood reside in a portrayal of self-sufficiency, aggression and deviousness.

These assertions and pronouncements on gender strongly resonate with others experienced between men and women in South Africa. Amongst these are the notion of sex debt accruing on acceptance of money or gifts (Wood & Jewkes 2001, Vetten & Bhana 2001) and the wrapping up of violence with ideas of manhood (Wood & Jewkes 2001, CIET International 2003, Selikow et al. 2002).

Clear discontinuities with the outside are also presented. The possibility of being tricked into a state of 'womanhood', for instance, breaks with established gender enactments. At the same time, though, what targets are being tricked into is behaving in a way that can then be claimed to invoke more familiar assumptions about gender, based on its dominant construction into 'either/or' categories (where 'men' are providers and protectors, and 'women' are dependent and vulnerable). They are tricked into behaving in a way that is associated with 'woman-ness' or, the other side of the coin, accepting a show of 'man-ness' from another (which, in the way of binary oppositions, positions them as 'women'). This is one avenue through which the constructions are 'naturalised'.

Trickery, then, can be understood to effect a rupture with the outside that is necessary for the broader reproduction of 'heterosexuality' inside. (Unfamiliarity is exploited in the reconstruction of the familiar.) The break or rearrangement that is necessary is the creation of 'women' out of men. Moreover, trickery performs a related role of smoothing over these breaks in an attempt to render them invisible and stabilise, via reference to outside discourses and established gender assumptions, the 'women' identities it jolts into action.

With trickery being one of the cornerstones for the building and maintenance of the gendered sex system in prison, respondents emphasise the manipulation and deviousness which targets are up against:

> You have to be careful of what's happening around you in jail. You need tactics and you have to know your story ... Some people like sex ... They won't force you, they will manipulate you. They do it well. You can refuse and refuse, but you'll end up doing it because they will work on your mind.
>
> I lie to him ... I just twist his mind. After I have twisted his mind, he is going to ... give me [sex].

At the level of the gang, trickery and manipulation feature prominently in recruitment. Stories of sex may be directly implicated in gang members' engineering of increased fear levels in a bid to secure new recruits. A former Airforce 3 member explained how, in that gang, sex may be used as a topic of recruitment-speak. By cashing in on fear of forced sex and/or disapproval of male-on-male sex, new members are persuaded to join:

> I'll tell him that Airforce 3 do not indulge in prison activities like homosexuality ... He'll [think] ... 'If I can be one of these gangsters, I'll be in the right hands.'

Some of those for whom a prime motivation for joining may have been the belief that sex is not practised in that gang are subsequently made into 'wives' of other members.

That the meanings and identities surrounding sexual practices in prison cannot be reduced to their relation to norms of outside society, or explained as the particular creations of a disconnected prison space, is shown in this Airforce 3 member's recruitment strategy. While prison 'marriages' are organised so as to distance the sex that happens within them from notions of homosexuality, they may at the same time be referred to as just this, in order, paradoxically, to secure 'heterosexual' objects. A boundary between heterosexual and homosexual, key to the construction of hegemonic gendered sex relations, is thereby momentarily pushed, again with an act of trickery, so as to rearrange heterosexuality for the prison context.

Gang rituals of gender allocation[6]

In the Airforce 3 gang, a classifying ritual that reportedly allocates gender to new members also depends on hidden codes. The ritual is performed by an official known as the 'Blacksmith'.

> [The new guy] knows that homosexuality is not being practised [in the Airforce] but ... once you are in the office[7] of this guy called Blacksmith ... he is going to trick you into having sex ... He must classify you ... whether you are a young man ['woman'] or ... a full soldier ['man']: 'Look, ... there is the camp of full soldiers and the

camp of young soldiers ... [To] be a full soldier, ... you've got to know that you'll be working with blood ... We give you a knife and say, "Go and stab so-and-so" or "go and stab a warder."' Now the young man will ... think about the beating up that he'll get from committing such a crime ... He already has this tattoo and has been told that ... if he takes it out ... he's going to die ... He must choose to stab or he must choose to be a young man ... Once he says he falls into this camp of young soldiers ... then the blacksmith will say *Ungigcwalisele* ('make me believe you' ... [that] you can be a young soldier ... He'll say, 'Okay' ... [without having] any idea of how he must convince this guy. But ... the Blacksmith has the intelligence of speaking ... of scaring him ... [so that] he must be compliant ... 'Come'. Maybe they go to the shower ... (soldiers are standing guard outside ... keeping watch for the warders). 'Take off your trousers' ... [The Blacksmith's tone] has changed now. The young man will see, 'Aish! I haven't got a chance ... I must agree with everything that this man says.' Maybe he'll say, 'Ay man, I don't like this thing.' [The Blacksmith] will say, 'No! ... you've already taken my tattoo and you want to tell me stories!'

According to this respondent, a literal sex act (usually rape) follows for those who do not commit to proving their capacity for violence. But both the meaning of what a 'young soldier' role entails and the centrality of violence to retaining a claim to 'manhood' are not available to the new recruit.

Another account of a gender classification ritual in the Big 5s gang powerfully elucidates the resolve to establish gender identity as a natural and biologically determined fact. New members are sent to an official known as the 'Medical Doctor', who is responsible for classifying them as either 'soldiers' (men) or 'free Moscows' (women).[8] The Doctor performs a ritual of listening to the pulse of the recruit. Depending on the number of *kloks* (beats) that he 'hears' flowing in the blood, the recruit is designated as either *wyfie* ('free Moscow') or 'soldier'.

He must put your hand like this [he holds it at the wrist] and he says *Jou bloed klok 25 male getalle van vier.* ['Your blood beats 25 times 4.'] 'Times 4' means you are Section 4, which means you are a free Moscow. If you are a big man I say [that] your blood beats 25 times 5. That means your blood is full, [that] you are a soldier. The medical doctor ... must hear how many times your blood *kloks*.

The pulse rate detected by the Doctor, explained the respondent, will be determined by how the recruit has come across to the Doctor in a preceding conversation. The Doctor will be assessing, 'Can [I] see that this guy is a small guy [i.e. woman]? Yes he is a small guy.' Putting the new recruit through the ritual quite often appears to represent the rubberstamping of a decision already made elsewhere – in the regular auditioning and testing of unknowing subjects for gendered parts.

For all the ritual's apparent strangeness, multiple discourses and processes that have their roots beyond prison walls are put to work in the naturalisation of gender construction. Key is a discourse that situates the medical fraternity as holders of irrefutable truths about the body, and as Butler (1990) and Foucault (1992) have shown, medical discourses have regularly been drawn upon in the construction of cultural norms around gender. Via the 'Medical Doctor' the discourse that has medical knowledge equated with natural truth is incorporated, and a sense of the fact-full-ness of gender classification sought. In the absence of recourse to sex as the 'source' of gender, the Doctor's ritual of listening to the pulse makes a medical pronouncement rest on a reconstituted body where the truth of gender lies resident in blood flow.

Deconstructing masculinity: un-man-ness, a state of prison woman-ness

Overall, the processes and languages through which the dominant construction of gender occurs in prison can at once be understood as breaking with those on the outside (the newcomer's unfamiliarity with them is regularly central to the process) and fundamentally connected to them. Starkly evident is the imperative to ensure the reproduction of what Butler (1990:35) conceives of as the 'heterosexual matrix' where subjects are categorised into stable genders expressing stable sexes that are 'oppositionally and hierarchically defined through the compulsory practice of heterosexuality' (Butler 1990:151). In this context, the requirement for opposite stable sexes is translated into the requirement for oppositional stable sex roles (active penetration or passive receiving).

It is precisely the drive to re-establish this outside arrangement that is simultaneously behind the sudden and decisive break from existing identity structures which some prisoners experience in the forcible reconstruction of them as 'women'. The mightiness of this break follows from the oppositional and hierarchical construction of gender where one category is brought into being by its difference to the other, and in this way (hegemonic) masculinity is 'precariously achieved' by the insistence of total (superior) opposite-ness to femininity (and homosexuality) (Weeks 1985:190). The individual is inserted into the position that up until then defined what he was not. He is situated as his erstwhile 'other'. At the broader level, however, the status of 'compulsory heterosexuality' is affirmed.

But the break effected at the individual level through the loss of the 'script' of masculinity is not clean or total, nor is the transition into a 'woman' role smooth. More often it seems to be characterised by the vying of competing oppositional identity constructs. This is the experience of much more than the contradictory and tenuous nature of different identity positions – 'our irreducible scrappiness' (Hernstein Smith, cited in Gutterman 2001:57) that constitutes all subjects.

The part of very direct initial force in the imposition of the 'woman' script as opposed to the more subtle workings of general discourse power leads to a markedly conscious enactment of that gendered role: the 'woman' submits to appease others and prevent consequences of not going along with the performance. However, this enactment of 'woman-ness' (even if it is more conscious) and the demands of dominant gender discourses throw his sense of his 'man-ness' into question.[9]

Prison 'womanhood' is distinguishable from the dominant 'womanhoods' of broader society, in large part because of the demolished 'man-ness' it is understood to involve. As such, it is thoroughly shaped by a previous outside identity. The extent to which this is so provides exaggerated illustration of the inevitable inclusion in emerging normativities, of existing dominant discourses: the former are expressed in relation to the latter (Butler 1990, Gutterman 2001, Dirsuweit 2003). As one respondent viewed it, 'They will hate themselves so much for having lowered themselves, for having not been man enough to stand [up] against other men.'

Another, in his explanation of the shame and silence typically surrounding the forced enactment of prison 'womanhood', pointed to a difference he perceived in the responses to sexual violation between 'women' inside, and their outside counterparts:

> Men are controlled by pride, they are so secretive about bad things that happen ... They will never go for counselling, they will keep quiet ... Men are not like women. Women ... come up with things like [the concept of] 'rape survivors'. Men will never.

Dominant prison culture, in its emphatic enactment of heterosexuality, insists on the stability of genders, and unlike on the mines, where a coming-of-age saw a gender reorganisation, for prison *wyfies* there is no 'natural' end to their feminised status. Immediately available routes whereby the status could be incorporated into the achievement of a broader 'masculinity' are not forthcoming. In addition, as suggested by the ex-prisoner cited above, they likely lack tools for the integration of their sexual violation that would potentially be available to them were they 'outside' women. New processes in identity formation, distinct from those outside, are therefore brought into being in moments of gender positioning in prison, while they are the productive work of the same discourses that structure gender in broader South African society.

Transgressive ruptures

The breaks with existing identity formations outlined above are a far cry from the ruptures that Achmat (1993) had in mind when he called for the abandonment of heteronormative readings of prison sex, an acknowledgement of pleasure and desire in explanations of prison sexual practices, and a recognition of the freedom to explore these that could come in the removed spaces of prison environments. In contrast, the ruptures focused upon here, which many prison *wyfies* experience, depart from Achmat's readings both in their brutal nature and in the very direct links to (mimicking of) the dominant discourses that have a grip on society more generally. Indeed, it is through the enactment of the demands of some of the most oppressive of these dominant discourses that dramatic change is forced.

At the same time, the reconstruction of heterosexist relations in prison exposes a notion of a fixed and essential gender identity to be, quite literally, the result of tricks. The typical relations that surround the widespread practice of gender production – the breaking-in of prison 'wives' – show up the performativity of identity. Having unknowingly been auditioned for gendered parts, *wyfie* candidates are forced into performances of 'womanhood', and the 'regulatory fiction of heterosexual coherence' (Butler 1990:136) (which has fixed gender following fixed sex) loses its footing. However, Butler's contention that 'parody [of gender-sex coherence] by itself is not subversive' (1990:139) is invoked when the relations produced in the process seem for the most part to exaggerate and intensify tenets of patriarchal and heterosexist oppression. But this is not the whole story. While the workings of gangs as the explicit guardians of inmate culture are concerned with the strict regulation of sex in prison, and with closing the spaces in which alternative modes of relating can be negotiated, these are not total, stable, or fully successful.

Ushintsha ipondo is one type of interaction that transgresses the rules of prison sex, is treated as deviant and is officially outlawed by the gangs. Even so, it is reportedly the most common type of sexual interaction after the 'marriage'-style variety. Literally meaning 'to exchange a pound', it is defined in terms of how the sexual interaction takes place: as an equal exchange of sex for sex. In this type of sex, both the power dynamics and the related rules of interaction associated with 'marriage'-type sex are undermined. It is marked by its consensual nature and often articulated as 'doing each other favours' or 'taking turns to be the man'. Participants, neither of whom is considered inferior or superior, take turns to penetrate and receive. And herein lies its subversiveness: by both penetrating and receiving they are disrupting the system that allocates a gender identity on the basis of a restricted sex role (where penetrators are 'men' and penetrated are 'women'). This blurring of gender roles also results in an association of the practice with notions of homosexuality. To participate in the practice is reportedly to invite punishment or extortion to keep it quiet.

Indeed, gangs claim exclusive rights to sex in prison (despite considerable contestations around sex within the gangs). Members police the 'who' of sex interactions ('one-ones' or *mphatas* as non-gang members are known, are not supposed to be involved) and also attempt to rule on types of interaction. In relation to the practice of *ushintsha ipondo*, respondents explain,

> That is not allowed at all by gangsterism. Those people are just taking their chances; they make sure they're not caught.
>
> They've got to be very careful and very secretive because once they are seen ... it's a very serious matter.

Or, some suggest, it may involve negotiations and discretion rather than instant punishment. While respondents unite in reports that partaking in *ushintsha ipondo* is dangerous, levels of conditional tolerance would appear to vary, depending on intensity of gangster presence, for instance – or on others seeking benefits from contraventions of sex rules, and the individuals involved. Participants are commonly young prisoners who are simultaneously the 'wives' of other inmates. Some respondents suggest that where such participants might get away if they use discretion, the older and more 'masculinised' the participants, the more heinous is considered the crime and the threat to the status quo.

> I've seen [older men doing it as well] but it's more scandalous than that of the younger people ... No officer of a gang can do that. His gang, hey! They can – ay, ay, ay, ay!!

The uneven turning of a blind eye may find its roots beyond prison walls in relatively strong expectations in some South African communities of sexual experimentation amongst pre-initiated youth (Wood & Jewkes 2001, Glaser 1998, Mager 1998 cited in Wood & Jewkes 2001). In contrast, the involvement by senior masculine-identified participants poses a far greater threat. Such individuals are at the centre of the sex-gender power structures, and as Gutterman (2001:68) puts it: 'The more central an element is to a system in power – and the more fundamental that system is in the grander scheme of structures of cultural order – the more the "deviant" identification or behaviour will be contested and ostracized.'

Out of widespread oppressive relations then, other configurations emerge that challenge the assumptions of both inmate codes and the broader norms on which these are based. In the case of *ushintsha ipondo* the disruption comes with a refusal to solidify and make stable the gender categories brought into being, on which the system relies. It could be argued that these emergent but transgressive behaviours are the productions not only of the partial freeing of the male body 'through its enslavement' by the prison regime as Achmat (1993:106) claims, but that at the next level down of enslavement, in the 'marriage', a form of partial freeing may also occur. Having been brutally initiated into the myth-fulness of stable-gender as expression of stable-sex, some *wyfies*, in seeking out pleasure, then play with the roles enforced on them, and refuse the demand to stabilise them. (As such, *ushintsha ipondo* could also represent an expression of some measure of integration around a 'not man, not woman' status.)

More generally, while the dynamics surrounding two of the reportedly most common modes of sexual interaction have been broadly sketched here ('marriage' and *ushintsha ipondo*), a potentially vast range of circumstances surround prison sex, which is negotiated by numerous and diverse individuals and takes place in varied contexts. The unstable nature of gang identity and influence must also be emphasised. As already mentioned, gang rules are regularly internally inconsistent and shifting. Moreover, their memberships are differently tied to the meanings that make sense of these, some being embedded in them and others largely ignorant; and while respondents speak of what 'the gangs' do, they are also far from homogenous. Within gangs, sex and sexual violence specifically are contested issues.

In addition to marriage mode and *ushintsha ipondo*, another category of sex interaction – contained in relationships defined by the 'love' feelings existing between participants – makes a brief appearance in some interviewee accounts. Alternative modes of relating may also be negotiated in the little pockets of privacy that prisoners create for themselves, even when they ostensibly resemble particular 'types' of interaction. The nature of interactions also changes through time. In the process, diverse negotiations of sexuality and gender will be enacted. Many more of these require attention.

Conclusion

New forms of identity and behaviour are demanded by the intricate codes and rulings to which inmates are subject, but these emerge as neither wholly 'new' and confined to the 'inside' or pre-existing and traceable to the 'outside'. Rather, constructions and negotiations of sex in prison represent a subtle balancing of adaptation, continuity and rupture with more broadly experienced norms.

Paradoxically, in the male prison, it is precisely the mimicking of the 'outside' arrangement that conflates sex and gender that sees, for some inmates, defining breaks with their lives outside. The break comes as *wyfies* are positioned as the very difference (woman-ness) that has up until that point defined what they are not – the 'other': hegemonic 'masculinity' is maintained by the insistence of total and superior opposite-ness to femininity (and homosexuality). While there is need to guard against blanket assumptions in relation to the state of prison 'wifedom', at an individual level, for many a *wyfie* dramatic discontinuity is wrought as they are catapulted from one end of the gender hierarchy to the despised other. But, at the level of the framing paradigm, patriarchal heterosexuality is 'compulsively' (Dirsuweit 2003:76) maintained.

The ruptures and rapid generation of hybridised versions of self are multi-natured at the same time as they are characterised by unevenness amongst actors. While the requirements of 'manhood' in prison may be particularly exaggerated, those who continue to achieve enough of it (to maintain a 'man' status) will not experience a comparable break in the sense they make of their gendered selves to that experienced by 'women'. Different types of discontinuity or rupture are also distinguished. In contrast to that affected by the repositioning of men as 'women', transgressive ruptures are brought about as prisoners break and push the gender-sex rules dictated by both inmate codes and patriarchal heterosexuality, thereby deconstructing the assumptions on which they rely.

Acknowledgments

Thanks to Teresa Dirsuweit for supervision support, to Kindiza Ngubeni for his co-researching, and to the CHS reviewers for their comments. I am grateful to Amanda Dissel, Mona Saungweme, Ebrahim Fakir, John Gear and David Bruce for commenting on early drafts, and to Liz Walker, Penny Ploughman, Graeme Reid, Bilkees and Irshaad Vawda, Fraser Gear and Rishy Singh for their support. Thanks to Ireland Aid (now Development Cooperation Ireland) for making the research possible.

Notes

1 According to Van Onselen (1984) these gangs originated outside of prison. See also Haysom (1981).
2 Van Onselen highlights the extent to which imprisonment in South Africa has historically been intertwined with the migrant system, with the 'pass laws ensuring a constant flow of men into and out of prisons' and causing constant articulation between 'prison, mine compound and black township alike' (Van Onselen 1984:23).
3 Other terms that refer to prison 'women' are 'small boy', 'young man', 'madam' and 'girlfriend'. In this article, 'wife', *'wyfie'* and 'women' are used for ease of reference.
4 Participation in smuggling networks is a key activity.
5 This is bolstered by other pressures, ranging from death threats to the dictates of prevalent inmate culture concerning interaction with authorities.
6 We did not interview long-standing members of the 28s, the gang most often associated with taking *wyfies*, but our most detailed insights into the relationships of gangsterism and sex come from members of other gangs, which is suggestive of the extent to which specific sex relations are institutionalised in inmate culture. Also note that the detail of the rituals outlined here was provided in the individual testimonies of specific long-standing members.
7 'It's an imaginary office in a cell somewhere,' he explains. In addition, 'office' refers to the position of the official.
8 The 'free Moscow' category consists of the most junior 'women' in the gang.

9   The extent to which the two competing scripts of gender enforced onto many a *wyfie* subject and dictated by the discourses of hegemonic heterosexuality are irreconcilable perhaps constitutes a point of 'trauma' from a performativity theory perspective.

References

Achmat, Z. (1993) 'Apostles of civilised vice': 'immoral practices' and 'unnatural vice' in South African prisons and compounds, 1890–1920. *Social Dynamics* 19, 2, 92–110.

Butler, J. (1990) *Gender Trouble: Feminism and the Subversion of Identity*. (London: Routledge).

CIET International. (2003) Beyond victims and villains: the culture of sexual violence in south Johannesburg. Http://www.ciet.org/www/image/country/safrica_victims.html

Dirsuweit, T. (1999) Carceral spaces in South Africa: a case study of institutional power, sexuality and transgression in a women's prison. Geoforum, 30, 71–83.

Dirsuweit, T. (2003) Geographies of Carceral Institutions: A Case Study of a South African Women's Prison, PhD thesis, University of the Witwatersrand.

Foucault, M. (1992) *The History of Sexuality. Volume 2: The Use of Pleasure*. (London: Penguin).

Glaser, C. (1988) Swines, hazels and the dirty dozen: masculinity, territoriality and the youth gangs of Soweto, 1960–1976. *Journal of Southern African Studies*, 24, 4.

Gutterman, D. (2001) Postmodernism and the interrogation of masculinity. (Whitehead & Barrett 56–71).

Harries, P. (1990). Symbols and sexuality: culture and identity on the early Witwatersrand gold mines. *Gender and History*, 2, 318–336.

Harries, P. (1994) *Work, Culture and Identity: Migrant Labourers in Mozambique and South Africa, c. 1860–1910*. (Johannesburg: Witwatersrand University Press).

Haysom, N. (1981). Towards an understanding of prison gangs. (Cape Town: Institute of Criminology, University of Cape Town).

Jewkes, R. and Abrahams, N. (2000) Violence against women in South Africa: rape and sexual coercion. (Pretoria: Women's Health Research Unit, Medical Research Council).

Keith, M. and Pile, S. (1993a). Introduction. (Keith & Pile 1993b 1–40).

Keith, M. and Pile, S. (eds.) (1993b). *Place and the Politics of Identity* (London: Routledge).

Moodie, T.D., with Ndatshe, V. (1994) *Going for Gold*. (Johannesburg: Witwatersrand University Press).

Morrell, R. (ed.) *Changing Men in Southern Africa* (Pietermaritzburg: University of Natal Press, and London: Zed Books).

Selikow, T., Zulu, B., and Cedras, E. (2002) The *ingagara*, the *regte* and the cherry: HIV/AIDS and youth culture in urban contemporary townships. *Agenda*, 53, 22–31.

Van Onselen, C. (1984) *The Small Matter of a Horse: The Life of 'Nongoloza' Mathebula, 1867–1948*. (Johannesburg: Ravan Press).

Vetten, L. and Bhana, K. (2001) Violence, Vengeance and Gender: A Preliminary Investigation into the Links between Violence against Women and HIV/AIDS in South Africa. (Johannesburg: Centre for the Study of Violence and Reconciliation).

Weeks, J. (1985) *Sexuality and its Discontents: Meanings, Myths and Modern Sexualities*. (London: Routledge & Kegan Paul).

Whitehead, S. and Barrett, F. (eds.) *The Masculinities Reader*. (Cambridge: Polity Press).

Wood, K. and Jewkes, R. (2001) 'Dangerous' love: reflections on violence among Xhosa township youth. (Morrell 2001:317–336).

Zulu, B. (2001) Sexual violence and coercion: Zojazem learners' (mis)perceptions. (Johannesburg: Centre for the Study of Violence and Reconciliation).

5

'You have to change and you don't know how!': Contesting what it means to be a man in a rural area of South Africa

Tina Sideris

Introduction

In a remote corner of South Africa a group of men are negotiating more caring and equal relationships with their wives and children.[1] It is not remarkable that there are caring men in Nkomazi, where they live. What is notable is that these individuals are mindful of their intimate relationships and define themselves as different to other men. They are concerned about how they treat women and children, reflect on their roles in family life, consciously attempt to create more equal ways of sharing domestic tasks and decisions, and explicitly reject violent methods of resolving conflicts. Yet they live in a social context where traditional notions of the family hold sway. According to these ideas, gender and age hierarchies dictate the rights, duties and obligations of men, women and children in the family. Biology and 'God's will' are invoked to justify these structures of hierarchy and in this way they are presented as the *natural* order of family relations. And popular ideas about gender permit the use of violence to maintain male authority.

The endeavour to understand men who quite explicitly cast themselves as different to the norm has a practical purpose. South Africa is plagued by alarmingly high levels of domestic violence, and ideas, values, and social and institutional practices that affirm gender inequalities still hold currency, despite the political endorsement of equal constitutional rights for men and women. In this context the most obvious question that arises is what we might learn from examining the lives of these men about factors that discourage violent conventions and promote greater equality in intimate relationships.

This chapter examines individual men who, in the private arenas of their lives, are engaged in redefining and reworking their practices. Against the background of prevailing gender norms and dominant views of family relations in a rural area, their stories of difference are unpacked in relation to domestic violence and particular components of the household economy.

Apart from the immediate practical significance of understanding the efforts that men make to alter conventional habits and routines, there are questions of broader social and theoretical interest. By examining the practices of men who transgress norms, and their debates about 'what it means to be a man' in a historically specific context, the chapter provides some insight into the structural and subjective dimensions of change. As these men negotiate changes in practices that underpin the exercise of power in domestic relations, they are confronted by the fragile foundations on which their identities are constructed.

A discourse of human rights combined with Christian principles provides the moral framework within which the men who are the focus of this study locate their changing practices. But the framework they employ does not provide them with an adequate foundation on which to reformulate the positions of authority they occupy as heads of their families. While they draw on a discourse of human rights to reframe particular practices in the domestic sphere, they call on culture to help explain their ambiguous investment in the authority which being the head of the family implies.

Thus the tension between change and permanence in gender relations is expressed as a debate between rights and culture.[2] These men's references to culture suggest a living set of meanings and practices that shape social life. A portrayal of 'culture' as a set of moral codes that have a strong, albeit not unchanging, continuity with the past, perhaps more accurately termed 'tradition', reflects their need to preserve a sense of social identity (Nhlapo 2000). But in this context cultural prescriptions of the way family relations should be ordered imply the secondary status of women, and thus the appeal to culture entails a defense of privilege (Chanock 2000). Evidence presented below indicates that other men in Nkomazi, who more decisively aspire to dominant masculine ideals, appeal to tradition, as a fixed set of principles, to legitimise their authority as men.

However, for men who are grappling to embrace change, there appears to be an additional factor, a psychological dynamic, at play. Redefining family relations on the basis of gender equality very quickly leads to confronting the domination of women. As will be shown below, in Nkomazi, the authority of the head of a family is a key symbol of what it means to be a man. Disputing this position calls into question one of the foundations on which men's identities as men are based; thus men experience the critique of domination as a threat to difference, and they display the anxiety associated with not knowing how to validate their sense of themselves as men (Connell 1995, Segal 1990).

In the absence of role models and with little social support for constructing different practices, appealing to culture may represent as much an avoidance of anxiety as a defense of privilege. Cultural constructions of what it means to be a man not only legitimise male authority, they also provide men with a set of regulations that spell out the rights, duties and obligations that accompany paternal authority. Reverting to this framework is one way of escaping the personal uncertainty that change induces.

The following section of the chapter introduces the research participants. A degree of social and economic stability allows them greater space to manoeuvre in redefining their roles in family life. The demands of survival must play a role in restraining the degree to which working-class or unemployed men and women may reconstruct the household economy even if they have the will and desire to do so (Segal 1990). In addition to relative economic stability, their levels of education and past political activism likely contribute to a capacity to reflect on their lives and relationships.

There is a growing body of literature on men in contemporary South Africa. The second section of this chapter briefly discusses some of this scholarship and considers theoretical concepts that throw light on the subject of this study. In particular, this section suggests the complexity of understanding how the subjective experience of gender identity and gendered relations of power interpenetrate.

In the third section the background against which these men reflect on and redefine their practices is examined. Gender struggles as they are elaborated by locally specific meanings and broader social and political forces are discussed, as are cultural dialogues on appropriate social positions and personal conduct for men and women.

The final sections of the chapter are devoted to a detailed description and discussion of how individual men in a rural area reflect on and reformulate their practices. In its concluding section the chapter suggests the limitations of dominant political discourses, which tend to mask the power that structures gender relations and to neglect the tensions that change induces.

'Non-violent' men in violent communities – the research participants and the methods of data collection

This chapter draws on fieldwork and clinical work conducted over the past eight years on the types and intensity of gender violence that occur in the Nkomazi region, a sliver of land and congested villages that straddles the Mozambican and Swaziland borders in the south-east corner of Mpumalanga province.

The testimony presented is drawn from in-depth interviews with seven men, a focus group discussion in which they participated, and interviews with the women with whom they are currently involved. All of these interviews were conducted through a local community-based organisation, Masisukumeni Women's Crisis Centre. This organisation was established nine years ago to assist survivors of rape, domestic violence and sexual assault on children. Staff at the centre provide counselling and medico-legal advice, and help survivors to pursue their legal rights. In the year 2003, 1500 individuals consulted centre staff. The large majority of these (over 60 percent) sought help in relation to complaints of domestic violence, including physical beating, sexual abuse and financial deprivation.

The following case, reported to Masisukumeni, is a typical example of the kind of violence that shapes the lives of women:

> As you know there has been no water in Block A. It was late when I arrived home, about 8 o'clock, but I decided to go and fetch water at the river. On the way I met my husband. He was with another woman. I have known about this woman. He asked me where I was going and why I did not stay in the house that he built for me. He asked me why I was spying on him. In front of that woman he beat

me and beat me. I have just come from the hospital. I do not want to lay a charge of assault against him because in October my daughter was raped and we need him to help us with her case. For the sake of my daughter I won't put him in jail. (Personal communication, February 2003)

The extent and banality of the violence perpetrated against women and children in the villages of Nkomazi highlights the practical significance of understanding how men can, in the face of powerful pressures to the contrary, behave in ways that undermine gender-related violence and the inequalities that underpin abuse.

The seven men whose experiences are the focus of this chapter range in age from 30 to 45 years old. All are involved in long-term relationships with women, and are either already married or in the process of planning marriage. They all have at least one child with their current partners. Religion plays an important part in the personal and family lives of all of the men except one. The others are active members of Christian churches and regard their participation in the church and their religious beliefs as important sources of stability. But for these men, as for the large majority of people living in Nkomazi, holding Christian beliefs accommodates and intertwines with engaging in indigenous religious ceremonies and customary rituals.

To varying degrees they uphold tradition by observing its dictates in their daily lives and in celebrating major life crises. For example, not without question and with differing amounts of enthusiasm, all have engaged in the rituals and requirements of *lobola* (bridewealth) to cement the duties and obligations of kinship with the families of their current partners.

The members of this group of men have completed or partly completed tertiary education. Although most of them are currently managing to maintain a degree of financial and social stability, getting there has not been easy. Poverty defined their childhood and all experienced the absence of at least one parent, who migrated to towns to find work. With deep emotion, some of them describe being left by both parents to the care of older siblings or relatives; and all relate experiences of domestic violence. Not surprisingly, adolescence was a turbulent time, during which they engaged in personal and political struggles to achieve more fulfilling lives, and simultaneously acted out their frustration at individuals who failed them, and at a social system that violated them.

Without question they welcome the transition to political democracy. But they live in a context where, for the large majority of people, unemployment, poverty and violence make the social and material conditions of life harsh. In contrast, the wealth of a small elite, who have profited from access to government jobs and new commercial opportunities, is displayed in conspicuous consumption. Under these conditions, and because they were keenly aware of the urgent need for social justice and equity in economic transformation, concern about the development of their communities led these men to participate in this study.

The seven men participating in the research constitute a purposive sample, in the sense that they were invited to take part because they were known openly to reject violence against women and children. They came to join this study in different ways. Two of them initially made contact with Masisukumeni Women's Centre around assistance to abused women. One of the other men referred a young girl, who he suspected was a victim of incest, to the centre for help. A short time after he sent her for help the child's uncle tracked him down and physically assaulted him for interfering in their family affairs. Two of the group had frequently visited the centre to have photocopies made. They engaged staff in discussion about the services offered and the kinds of questions they asked reflected a concern about the way women are treated. One of these men, in a separate discussion with members of the centre's staff, expressed his frustration about the attitudes of men around him.

When these men were approached and asked to share their life histories in order to contribute to a study on the practices of men they were enthusiastic. The sample size is convenient, small enough to allow for a detailed case study, but it in no way suggests they are the only men in Nkomazi who aspire to relational care and equality in their intimate relationships. How unusual the research participants are in Nkomazi has not been empirically evaluated.

A wider set of interviews with perpetrators of sexual violence and a series of interviews with men who hold leadership positions in

Nkomazi provide contextual detail and a means of locating the experiences of the men who are the focus of this chapter in relation to dominant notions of manhood and the dynamics of power that structure gender relations.[3]

The ingredients that contribute to high levels of violence in intimate relations are readily found in Nkomazi, which was part of the former KaNgwane homeland and still bears the scars of the underdevelopment that was a result of apartheid's separate development policies. The assumption that men rightfully dominate women and children, extreme poverty, a high rate of unemployment, an increasingly visible gap in wealth between an emerging elite and the rest of the population, and general levels of violence, together make up a potent recipe for gender-related violence (Segal 1990).

The dilemmas of change

A growing body of literature in South Africa details transformations in the meanings attributed to manhood and changes in the practices of men. A collection of papers edited by Morrell (2001) brings together research that explores the varying expressions of masculinity that have been fashioned by South Africa's complex and violent racial and sexual politics. Without discounting the historical challenges that social, economic and political forces have posed for different sectors of men and the ongoing transformation of ideas that define masculinity in South Africa, recent scholarship identifies the transition to political democracy as a moment of significant challenge to men (Morrell 2001, Posel 2003, Walker 2003).

The structures that secure men's power in the state, the economy and the realm of private relations have not been dismantled by political transformation. Nor has the widely held view that men should be in dominant positions – over women and children and over other men – been dislodged. But social and political changes in post-apartheid South Africa have sharpened the tensions that characterise gender relations. Women's equal right to the entitlements of citizenship, legislation that defends the integrity of women, and the human rights discourse pose challenges to the legitimacy of men's privileged status over women. Scholarship shows that constitutional change and a growing public acknowledgement of social crises, in particular the AIDS epidemic and sexual violence, have generated a contestation of the norms and conventions that assert male authority in sexual practice (see Posel 2003).

Responses to these challenges are diverse. Mediated by race and class, men's practices and the meanings given to gender identity are being contested, defended and redefined, in institutions, in interpersonal relationships and by individual men and women. For some men, particularly young men disillusioned with their marginal status, sexuality has become the principal focus of manhood and many assert their dominance in violent ways (Wood & Jewkes 1998). But importantly, literature on men also shows that the requirements of new behavioural standards resulting from social and political challenges have opened a space for reflection amongst men and even criticism of past models of manhood (Hunter 2003, Posel 2003, Walker 2003).

In a paper that analyses the changing politics of sexual violence, Posel (2003) tracks the emergence of public scrutiny of sexual violence in media reports. She argues that it was the rape of infants that 'focused the spotlight of shame squarely on men' and evoked a sense of moral panic (2003:16). But public expressions of anger included protests from various groupings of men who called for activism to combat violence against children and women (2003:16).

Walker examines young men, perpetrators of abuse, who have joined an organisation that provides support and counselling to men who want to change. Her analysis of their testimony reveals their struggle to remake themselves in contrast to past versions of manhood which they interpret as oppressive (2003:23). Careful to avoid rigid and premature categorisation of the efforts these men make to come to terms with the process of change, Walker (2003) nevertheless suggests the rise of new notions of masculinity.

The alarm surrounding the AIDS epidemic and discourses of safe sex that expound the dangers of having multiple sexual partners provide one explanation for the negative redefinition of the *isoka* manhood that celebrates 'multiple concurrent sexual partners' identified in Hunter's research (2003:2). Locating his analysis in the historically changing conditions of marriage for men living in a town on the KwaZulu-Natal coast, Hunter shows that while growing criticism, by both men and women, of having many sexual partners is diminishing the dominance of the *isoka* ideal, alternative models of successful masculinity have not emerged (Hunter 2003:25)

Two themes run through this scholarship on men in contemporary South Africa. Firstly this work demonstrates the fluid and contradictory nature of men's responses to the major social changes that are taking place. Of particular relevance for the subject of this chapter is that while there are encouraging signs in the moves that individual and groups of men are making towards considering less authoritarian and violent practices, the literature reveals that fully formed alternative models have not materialised and that emerging forms are indeterminate (Hunter 2003, Walker 2003).

A second theme that is evident in work on men and masculinity is that post-transition challenges have put men under pressure. Research evidence makes it clear that social, economic and political forces put different sectors of men under varying degrees of strain. One of the questions that arises is how we conceptualise the pressures confronting men, and their responses. Drawing on local research and international literature, Walker (2003) refers to the 'crisis in masculinity'. She argues for consideration of the limitations of the 'crisis' theory, in particular when understood from within a gender paradigm, including its homogenising tendencies, its neglect of power and the scant attention given to the effects of sexuality. But she suggests that the role confusion and experiences of uncertainty around identity, sexuality and work that characterise the 'crisis in masculinity' have parallels in South Africa, and that the adoption of the Constitution, public discourses of human rights and the transition to democracy have brought the crisis into sharp focus (2003:3).

Appropriated for conservative use, the 'crisis' theory tends towards blaming women for the anxieties of men and finds a home in a variety of men's groups and organisations that have as a central concern male bonding and the reanimation of male privilege (Faludi 2000, Segal 1999). In South Africa a clear example of this is the South African Association of Men, formed by white middle-class men to restore conventional masculine icons and fight against the perceived feminist attack on masculinity (see Morrell 2001:26). Equally worrying are the simplistic associations between men's beleaguered status and their violent behaviour that emanate from such quarters.

A second concern is that, by translating individual or group experiences of confusion, vulnerability and insecurity into a 'crisis in masculinity', the political dimensions of gender relations are neglected and what men do to maintain power is de-emphasised (Connell 2000, McMahon 1993, Segal 1999). The 'crisis' theory encourages a focus on psychological distress and thereby shifts attention from sexual politics (McMahon 1993). Segal (1999) suggests that a different light is thrown on men's sense of failure when it is viewed against the widely held assumption that men should dominate. Arguing against the reduction of gender relations to individual psychic phenomena, Segal emphasises that the 'dilemmas of masculinity' can only be understood by locating the psychology of men in the context of wider social relations and changing gender relations that unsettle male domination (1990:103).

Similarly, Connell (1995) argues against the 'crisis of masculinity' in favour of looking at changes in masculinity in relation to tensions in the order of gender relations:

> [A]s a theoretical term 'crisis' presupposes a coherent system of some kind, which is destroyed or restored by the outcome of the crisis. Masculinity is not a system in that sense. It is rather a configuration of practice within a system of gender relations ... and we can speak of a crisis of a gender order as a whole, and of its tendencies towards crisis. Such tendencies will always implicate masculinities though not necessarily by disrupting them. Crisis tendencies may, for instance, provoke attempts to restore dominant masculinity. (1995:84)

From this perspective, understanding changes in men's practices needs to take into account struggles around the exercise of power in gender relations. Posel (1991) provides a particularly useful theoretical framework for understanding the negotiation of power relations in the household. She draws a distinction between power and authority, where authority is power of the type that is 'publicly and formally represented as legitimate' (1991:12). In this conception relations of authority may be contested but carry the threat of sanction if seriously threatened (1991:12). Thus, Posel argues, in patriarchal societies, where men have the monopoly of authority, women may extend their power in domestic struggles without challenging the legitimacy of men's power (1991:15). Struggles that contest men's right to authority constitute a threat to patriarchal norms (1991:15).

But an examination of changes in men's practices must simultaneously take into account that gender is a subjective experience. If power is a key to understanding the structure of gender relations, difference is a register of gender identity. Even accepting that sexual difference (gender identity) is socially constructed does not detract from the intensity with which it is felt as constitutive of personal identity. Aronowitz (1995:317) makes a strong case for the power of sexual difference by arguing that culture as a series of material practices 'plants deep roots'.

Change and continuity in gender relations

In the rural areas of South Africa where labour migrancy and proletarianisation generated a crisis in gender relations, tradition, articulated through ethnic ideologies, took on special significance in mediating struggles around relations of power and authority. In the homelands the effectiveness of the hold of tradition and its appeal for controlling women was in no small measure dependent on the created institutions of chiefs and customary law.

But tradition is more than ideology. The power of tradition lies in its selection of past meanings that connect to the present as a living system of meanings and values regulating attitudes and social relations (Williams 1977). In this sense tradition 'plants deep roots' (Aronowitz 1995:317) and because it is so closely tied to the practices of everyday life, plays an important role in elaborating gender and the variable boundaries hierarchy of sexual difference. It is not surprising, then, to find that contemporary gender struggles are expressed as a conflict between tradition and rights. Nor is it unexpected that men who confront the precariousness nature of gender categories appeal to tradition to deal with their confusion.

Morrell (1998) makes the point that the homelands were spheres in which social relations and customary practices displayed continuity with earlier social systems. Male power was legitimised by a system in which the chief, his headmen and elders sat in a descending order of authority with exclusive rights to communal land, echoing precolonial arrangements. In this system women were absent from the public world of men and had few rights, but occupying particular positions in the family gave some women a relative degree of power, particularly over other women. This gender order suggests what Brod calls personal patriarchal power, in which male dominance is enforced through power exercised by individual patriarchs.

History transformed 'traditional African' social arrangements. Through racial oppression and proletarianisation men experienced the transition to forms of patriarchy in which power is exercised collectively and men themselves are dominated by collective patriarchal power (Brod 1990:132). For migrant workers with strong ties to the rural areas, the vision of the individual patriarch as head of the household, whose power is expressed in control over women's domestic labour and sexuality, remained an ideal, and, some have argued, a way of making sense of life in the city (Morrell 1998:628). Threatened as they were by signs of independence and growing power exercised amongst women in rural areas, visions of the patriarch offered men the promise of maintaining control over their wives and children.

The force of this ideal is still evident in Nkomazi. It is widely held by men and women that the status of manhood is conferred by having a wife and child, and establishing a home separate to that of one's parents. In others words, boyhood aspirations to manhood incorporate the fantasy of becoming the head of a family, at which point life as a man, *indvodza*, starts:

> To be considered a man you must have a woman. If you are not married you can't go to the places where men are discussing problems. Without a wife and a child you are still a boy. (Personal communication, 2001)

Duties and obligations accompany paternal authority, including the responsibility to provide for the needs of the family, the task of protecting the family unit against external threats, and the obligation to maintain the family's reputation in the wider community. Violent forms of control, though sanctioned, are regulated. Below, a local headman describes the mechanisms that are used to deal with conflicts that arise when women transgress their expected submission:

> The community does not accept that violence. What is acceptable is that a woman must submit. Nowadays there are laws. Before, there were *indunas* and they put him at the *ibandla* (court). If he is wrong they penalise him. You cannot beat your wife for anything. After you have undergone certain stages of disciplining and they don't work, then you can beat her. (Personal communication, 2001)

The legacy of forced removals, the effects of poverty and unemployment, and more recently the HIV/AIDS epidemic, have eroded men's capacity to provide and protect and have spawned a wide variety of family arrangements. Changing family structures usually involve women assuming increasing responsibility for the provision of the family's needs; and in assuming these responsibilities, women, in practice, have encroached on men's power to regulate family affairs.

In the face of the challenges posed to gender relations and the conditions of male authority by socioeconomic conditions, 'tradition' is evoked to restore the dominant ideal. Williams argues that the process of constructing a version of the past that connects with and ratifies the contemporary orders is 'radically selective' and 'within a particular hegemony, this selection is usually presented and successfully passed off as "the tradition"' (1977:115). There are several examples in contemporary South Africa of the rediscovery of tradition in response to social crises. One of these is the recent revival of virginity testing as a response to the HIV/AIDS epidemic, which has been represented as a mechanism for protecting girl children but might also be interpreted as a tactic for controlling female sexuality (Scorgie 2002).

In Nkomazi, where the material foundations necessary to fulfilling the role of the head of a family have been stripped away, and women have gathered power by managing the household economy, it is the authority to exercise control over the family that has come to actively shape beliefs about what constitutes being a man. Fashioned and enforced by particular interpretations of the past, the headship of the family is a key symbol of what it means to be man.

There still are a variety of institutions that can be called on to legitimate and reinforce this authority. A local municipal counsellor emphasises his authority and describes the support that local institutions provide in asserting it:

> If there is a disagreement, the man must have the final decision. If she goes against that, as Africans, it's a case. I will report to the *indunas* and my relatives. They will call her and her family and will counsel her to learn to obey. She will be sent to her parents three times. If she doesn't change, my family will decide to chase her [away]. (Personal communication, 2001)

But the increasing social regulation of gender relations through the courts and welfare mechanisms present more fundamental tests of male authority (Brod 1990:132) and significantly alter the terms of negotiating power. Welfare regulations, such as those that order men to pay maintenance, transform the personal obligations of the patriarch to provide for his family into a legal duty. And the growing willingness women and children show to protect themselves against violence by pursuing their legal rights shifts the balance of power in interpersonal relationships. Thus, although in Nkomazi the ideology that legitimises men's power remains strong, these social and legal changes increasingly demand a redefinition of the boundaries of male authority.

Changing practices in Nkomazi

Viewed against the prevailing ideology and the high incidence of domestic violence in this area, men who explicitly reject violent ways of resolving conflict and talk about equality at home are unusual. Motivated in large part by a desire to remedy the damage done by the violence of their parents, they attempt to create families that incorporate relational care. Something in the language of human rights and the public acknowledgement of domestic violence as a violation of rights resonates with their own experience, and herein lies some potential for fostering change in everyday practices in the home.

Domestic violence is not a recent phenomenon in South Africa. While current analyses debate the influence that the insecurities of political transition have had on the incidence and forms of domestic violence, there is no doubt that political change has focused our attention on neglected issues. One of the more striking aspects of the life histories of the men who have been interviewed is the violence that patterned their childhood.

At our first meeting, Mr S. became emotional when he recalled his mother and how she had been treated by his father. He described his father as

> [an] animal, a non-living somebody. Nothing he can point out he did or bought for us. We struggled. I struggled to complete Std 10 ... He was a fighting type, beating her severely. As children we used to try and come to the rescue of our mother and ourselves be beaten.

He was nine years old in 1972 when his parents left him to go and seek work. He recalls the material deprivation he endured:

> We stayed alone. Our parents were in Gauteng. My mother went to stay with my father. He was abusing money so she went there to control him and get some of his salary ... There were younger children. I was looking after those. I was the second-born. My elder brother was five years older, looking after us younger ones ... School was not good. I had a lack of proper clothing. No school uniform. One shirt and one pants for the whole year. No school funds. I never went on a school trip. No books. I was tempted to steal books from the staff room in order to learn. Sometimes you would go home for breakfast and lunch. You go because others are going, meanwhile you know there is nothing at home.

When he was asked to define domestic violence, he included economic abuse:

> I want to formulate my own definition, not that one that I'm used to in the book. I can say it's a mishandling, of uh, directed to, males and females and children. A mishandling of the man, the women and the children by anybody in that family. I mean that you can mishandle by not providing for the financial needs. I know that leads us to the official definition.

In response to a request for more examples he included, 'Insults, stalking, sexual harassment, like something you call someone it's a prostitute or it's a hoer [whore].' To these examples he added a heartrending description of the brutality his mother suffered. He recalled the scars on her arm, a result of being thrown against a coal stove by her husband. And he concluded about domestic violence: 'It's more than the beating.'

The recollections of violence and the interpretations of domestic violence presented above are typical of those presented in the interviews of the men participating in the research. They use the language of human rights as one framework with which to reflect on what they went through as children, and to connect their experiences to a wider project. And their interpretations resonate with the definition contained in the Domestic Violence Act of 1999, which implies a continuum of violence made up of a range of physical and non-physical forms of abuse.

Shifting the balance of power in the home

By extending the definition of domestic violence to include non-physical forms of abuse, such as economic deprivation and verbal aggression, these men open the door to disrupting some of the practices that are constituted by and reconstitute men's control over their spouses and children. They reflect on their changing practices in two areas – the domestic division of labour and the distribution of the family income.

Division of labour

Mr H. associates the ease with which he takes on tasks usually reserved for women with the personal and interpersonal relations that made up his childhood. Social circumstances and individual personalities combined in his family to produce atypical gender conventions. He identifies strongly with his father, who, faced with an alcoholic wife, assumed the major responsibilities for the domestic duties:

> My father was a cool man. She [his mother] was drinking on the weekends. She was working in the kitchens, so during the week no drinking ... Even when she was not drinking she was *kwaai* [hot-tempered]. Some days my father was cooking for us and we find my mother was not present.
>
> We are equal. Anybody can cook. I enjoy cooking. And the washing I can do it, there is no problem for me. But we have employed someone to do it.

In general, these men take tentative steps towards crossing the rigid boundaries that distinguish men's and women's tasks in the domestic sphere and relinquishing the benefits they derive from women's domestic labour and emotional care. They are willing to step in under unusual circumstances, to help their wives or fiancées if they are busy or if they are sick. Mr S. explains:

If I see she is busy I prepare food. Even in the morning I say to her, 'Sleep!' If I prepare food I prepare enough for her also. Even her parents know this man does things for himself. I say to the children, 'Did you eat?'

Distribution of the family income

Ultimate control over resources is one of the pillars upon which male power in the household rests. In Nkomazi, historically shaped conceptions that define family relations in terms of economic exchange combine with the demands of poverty to make the generation and distribution of income a common cause of conflict and abuse. Traditional constructions of family order authorise paternal control over financial resources. In the words of a local government councillor: 'As Africans it is not allowed for a women to keep her money.'

In this light the willingness of some men to consider sharing financial decisions, let alone make real efforts to do so, is a positive response:

I don't make myself superior to her. I don't want her to look down on herself as if I am the husband. I involve her as much as I can. She knows everything ... One other thing – the Christian way of life. I want to live a life that makes the other happy. We are equal partners. Sometimes she has this tendency, women have got this tendency, of looking down on themselves. She would ask me for permission. I stopped her. I took my bank card and gave it to her so she could go and decide what to buy (Mr K.).

When sharing financial decisions is more deliberately linked to wider structures of oppression, a challenge is made to the prevailing values. Motivated in part by a desire for harmony, equality in decision making is a principle that Mr H. extends to other relationships:

> Some men at work, they don't discuss with their wives. Your wife will be angry. Two must discuss and make a planning when you have got a wife ... We are equal, I am not above her. I don't like to oppress another person, even here at work I like to be equal. I don't use my promotion to oppress.

These men negotiate from positions of power and relative privilege. They reserve the right to decide when to share tasks. That they have jobs, and indeed, that there is income over which to negotiate, gives them more space to reflect on and manoeuvre around decision making than is available to unemployed men, for example. And they benefit from the labour and care of their spouses, who continue to carry the major responsiblity for child care and domestic duties. Nevertheless, performing tasks usually reserved for women and engaging in joint decision making admits the prospect for redefining rigid gender roles and for levelling the balance of power in domestic relations.

The sensitivity to the needs of the other, on which these changes are in part based, can disrupt men's preoccupation with domination (Connell 1995). Replacing gender and age as the organising principles of a family with equality, and accessing care by negotiation rather than entitlement, bring relational needs, intimacy and commitment into focus (Giddens 1999b). To the extent that practice creates reality, reworking these elements of domestic relations contributes, albeit in small ways, to redefining the meaning of being a man.

The negotiation of more equal ways of relating and simultaneously upholding the legitimacy of men's power described above is mirrored in the accounts of the men's wives. These women describe a degree of control over the daily management of the household that is testimony to how women exercise power that defies cultural prescriptions of male and female positions. Yet their testimony clearly shows how women reinforce male authority by deferring to paternal dominance and by buttressing difference through the household tasks they assign to children. They weave together concessions to the authority of men with the considerable power they exercise in certain realms (see Posel 1991). But this cannot be understood as simply a conscious set of tactics. The values and meanings that fortify male authority are lived – 'constitutive and constituting – which as they are experienced as practices appear as reciprocally confirming' (Williams 1977:110). For example, Ms S., who was raised without the support of a father and financed her own education to qualify as a nursing sister, describes her control over the domestic finances and command of the household. Despite her achievements and the power over family affairs she exercises in daily life she affirms her husband's status as head of the family. Her inability to provide any material foundation for her affirmation of his status attests to the internalisation of the ideas and values that assert male authority.

> Ms S.: We are almost equal.
> Interviewer: 'Almost', what do you mean 'almost'?
> Ms S.: I suppose he is a man. In our culture a man is the head of the house. I don't know how to put it that in our culture a man is a man. But he (Mr S.) doesn't practice it in the way of abusing us ... Because the way we were brought up, the father is the father ... The man is the man.

But feminist scholarship has also shown that when women reflect they recognise the contradiction between lived experience and received wisdom. If the political transition in South Africa created a space for men to reflect on their practices, it also authorised women to question accepted conventions more openly. When asked to contemplate gender equality in the abstract – outside the complexities of intimate relations where values are enacted and compromises are struck in the interest of affection, shared desires and protecting domains of power – Ms S. commented in the following way:

> More equality, yes, because we are all contributing to that home ... I think it's the way they were brought up and the way they look upon us as females. They look upon us as being inferior ... Now we are working, both of us. We do take care of children, both of us. Maybe I am even better than him. So I don't know.

Negotiating sexual difference

The ambivalence that questioning male authority in intimate relationships makes women feel is more akin to disorientation in men, when these questions challenge their assumptions about what it means to be a man. In contrast to the relative candour with which they were able to engage in discussion on the division of labour and shared decision making, questions about their views on being the head of the family evoked ambiguity and tension. Their tones, gestures and nervous laughs suggested varying degrees of discomfort and their less decisive verbal responses were indicative of their confusion.

It is interesting that it is in a group context, in the focus group discussions, where men confronted each other with the challenge of relinquishing positions of authority, that the tension was most palpable and the most vehement defenses of male authority were expressed. For men in a group confronting the fundamentals of their gender interests, domination and difference, it is surprising that the tension was largely contained.

The following extract from the focus group discussion captures the debates:

> Mr N.: I was trying to see what it is that a male does in order to be the head of the family in today's life. Apart from being a breadwinner and so forth, we have already said that a woman can have a family and do these things. So what is it that makes us the head?
> Mr S.: You know, I as a head, I take a girl, make her my wife and have children and give them a home. That home has my surname. I am the head of that particular family.
> Mr N.: What if your fiancée or wife builds the house and brings the food for the house and the love is there?
> Mr M.: When you propose you pay lobola.
> Mr N.: And that *lobola* makes me the head?
> Mr M.: It does, yes. Yes!
> Mr N.: I'm a bit puzzled here. I'm still trying to see what makes us the heads.
> Mr K.: According to the Bible, who was created first? Right, a man, and then women after.
> Mr S.: That is that.
> Mr N.: OK, you see we have a few things now. We've got our current times; we've got our culture and now comes the Bible. I agree, culturally we are heads. But what about current times now? Like in the constitution we have equal right throughout, even in the family. And what about if one doesn't pay *lobola*?

> Mr M.: Listen, Mr N.! In general we are superior. In our culture I can take two wives, but she can only take one [husband]. In our culture I can propose but she cannot. We pay *lobola*. Another thing, Mr N., if she wants to do something she must ask me first. If I say no, I say no!

In general the interviews and focus group discussions were characterised by attempts to open discussion, punctuated by boisterous banter, a not uncharacteristic medium for expressing unease and anxiety.

There are accounts that indicate an ability to interrogate male authority without manifesting the same degree of vulnerability. For example, Mr H. appeared to be more at ease in his rejection of the concept of the head of the household.

It is important to consider that he associates his views with those of his father, who crossed the boundaries of conventional gender roles by assuming caretaking responsibilities in the family, and who resisted the aggressive behaviours through which domination is expressed:

> I told you my mother was a problem while we were growing up ... She is a woman who is violent. She likes assaults to the children. Shouting ... She is a heavy drinker ... It is very painful to think about this, very painful. My father was quiet ... My father taught me not to assault the wife. He was that kind of a person not liking conflict and force. He was not allowing me even to assault another child. He used to stop me.
>
> Gone are those days when a man must exercise his power. If you treat someone equally that person is not afraid of you ... This is in 'tradition', the father is the head. It means you are above. At home you are a controller. So the wife is under you. This *nhloko* (head), I don't like it. I am not *nhloko* at home. If I was, my wife would not be free, even my children. I can put it aside ... You know, I have learnt something, especially in the working environment. This thing of *nhloko*, he even applies it at work. You find then as a manager your staff is afraid of you. You don't give them a chance. Even in the working environment they apply this. I have experienced this oppression.

Unlike Mr H., most of these men found it difficult to consider disassociating being a man from being the head of a family. If this link encapsulates the idea of sexual difference, then elaborate descriptions of the differences between men and women made in order to justify men's entitlement to this position become more understandable.

Mr K., who argues that he accepts the principle of equality in relation to his wife, submits differences between men and women to explain why he believes men should be heads of their families:

> This head of household – it has a correct meaning but people misunderstand and misuse it. This thing I think it is 'culture' and biblical. Because I take the wife, the wife does not take me. It's difficult for a girl to approach a boy and ask for marriage. The one who begins this is regarded as the head. The other is the helper. They are going to build a home together. If they deadlock, the woman will say, 'No, father, decide on how to do this.' The mother is able to say, 'I have done everything I can about this, so now you decide.' It's where I take it the father is the head. Other men take a woman as not even a servant but as a slave. I have seen the suffering. You become a head for good things – to develop your family. Being a head means more responsibility.

Though Mr S. considers *de-gendering* the category 'head', his reflections are infused with uncertainty. Given that he comes from a family in which his mother took by far the greatest responsibility, he is able to conceive that women can perform the functions attached to the head. But the depth of his ambivalence is reflected in his reconstruction of sexual polarity, which he does by conceding financial control to his wife:

> In fact to be head is to protect your family against any violent situation, you support them financially, you are caring for them …
>
> I am Thabo [the President] and you're Zuma [the Deputy President]. If I am away you can take over.
>
> But in fact it's the mothers in most cases who are the heads … I mean 50-50, it means that we are both heads, because females are excelling.

> But myself, my money must work differently than my wife. I cannot take her money. She must enjoy her money. As a man I feel my money must go to the needs of the family. I feel she can use her money as she wants.

These accounts illustrate the tension the men experience when they confront the contradiction between embracing rights in the domestic arena and the widely held views that associate manhood with domination over women and children in the family. In Nkomazi their confusion is amplified because the formal endorsement of customary law, which asserts rigid gender and age hierarchies, stands side by side with calls for the right to equality. In the words of one of the men participating in this study:

You have to change and you don't know how. The government is confusing things. They say let's go back to our culture and then they say let's go forth. Meanwhile they are legalising polygamy, [yet] they say women have equal rights.

Their narratives are compelling for showing how difficult it is for them to consider simply giving up the idea of being a head. Instead they employ the strategy of reworking the notion of head, or seek reasons to explain why they earn the position. Their testimony reflects the anxiety induced by discovering the fragile foundations on which their sense of sexual difference is based.

Conclusion

The accounts of difference that are reflected through the voices of these ordinary men living in Nkomazi can be described as 'strongly individualised', 'personal quests' to undo the damage of their own childhoods by creating more stable and harmonious family lives for their children (Connell 1995:118). But rejecting violence, performing 'women's work', and surrendering exclusive control over family income do not just stabilise the family. They recompose family relations. Viewed in context, these changes are substantial. Their friends and colleagues in Nkomazi consider them at best mad or bewitched, and at worst, a threat.

It is not surprising that these men are considered deviant. While the changes they are making do not constitute a material threat to male authority, by embracing a discourse of rights to negotiate the balance of power in domestic relationships they are representative of the challenges posed to conventional modes of male authority by recent constitutional and legal changes. In Nkomazi the predominant response to the crisis in the order of gender relations generated by political transition is an historical one – the appeal to tradition to reassert the legitimacy of male authority and maintain control over women and children. And for the moment, institutions are available to support these attempts.

Such appeals to 'the tradition' represent a resistance to change, a retreat to a fixed set of principles by which to organise behaviours and relationships, that admit neither interrogation nor alternative customs. This kind of assertion of tradition bears the danger of *fundamentalism* and, for women, holds the peril of their being denied the full entitlements of citizenship (Giddens 1999a, Mama 2003, McFadden 2001).

The more marginal response to fissures in gender relations, that is, to adopt a code of rights, evokes considerable personal confusion and anxiety. Rights discourses, cast in terms of individual autonomy and directed at individual change, do not address how relations between men and women are coupled to a wider system of power relations. Neither do these discourses confront the ways in which difference is specified as part of a hierarchy, a relation of domination and subordination (Connell 1995, Frosh 1994). Yet for men who embark on the journey of change, being exposed to these dimensions of their intimate relationships is a primary source of their unease.

Moves toward sharing domestic tasks and decision making and relinquishing the power that the threat of violence bestows on them force men to engage more directly with the inconsistencies between received gender constructions and lived relations. They are confronted with the capacity of significant women in their lives to assume the responsibilities associated with paternal authority. And they are faced with the contradiction between the will to equality and the domination and benefits that being the head of family implies. The unease, uncertainty and anxiety they experience as a consequence are less a result of confusion about role expectations and styles of being men, and are more fundamentally linked to glimpsing the instability of the positions of power that define their identity as men and their difference from women.

Without other options for resolving these dilemmas they turn to familiar meanings and values. The narrative accounts suggest that in reverting to tradition some of these men are seeking ways to rework the notion of 'head of the family' by reinventing the care and responsibility it implies and downplaying the control that it contains. Recent work on masculinity in South Africa raises similar questions about whether the elements of personal discipline, responsibility and reciprocity contained in African conceptions of manhood and family relations represent a set of values that men can draw on to construct a more positive sense of gender identity (Morrell 2003).

Other men participating in this study are posing different questions about how to redefine their intimate relationships. These men are more ambivalent about the dictates of tradition. For example, they express doubts about the value of seeking lobola for their daughters. Perhaps the questions these men are asking reflect the domestic realm as a site of struggle between tradition and modern styles of relating (Giddens 1999b) and signal the emergence in Nkomazi of a struggle against tradition that coincides with the legal regulation of intimate relations.

In a country where violence against women is so frequently a display of power and control, the individual narratives presented in this chapter are hopeful. Testimony to the argument that men are able to change and are changing (Segal 1990), these men's discourse demonstrates openness to new ways of thinking and a commitment to trying to find ways of relating that are not oppressive. But caution needs to be applied in research that examines men's more positive responses to changing gender relations in South Africa. In this kind of work, which focuses on the details of personal relationships between men and women, there is a danger of celebrating the creative force of human agency, whilst ignoring the power of deeper psychological anxieties and wider social structures that sustain relations of domination and subordination. For men who experience the contradictions between received interpretations of gender and lived relations the challenge lies in shifting the discussion from the private to making the links between personal and relational struggles and wider structures of privilege.

Notes

1. Thanks to colleagues at WISER for their critical insights. The support of the Mellon Foundation is gratefully acknowledged. Masisukumeni Women's Crisis Centre, the Foundation for Human Rights and AUSAID made the fieldwork possible.
2. It is important to note that 'culture' and 'tradition' are used interchangeably by the people whose views form the subject of this chapter.
3. The interviews with perpetrators of violence and community leaders were all conducted during 2001 as part of a different project. In this chapter these interviews are referenced as 'personal communication, 2001'.

References

Aronowitz, S. (1995) My masculinity. (Berger et al. 306–19).

Berger, M., Wallis, B. and Watson, S. (eds.) *Constructing Masculinity*. (London: Routledge).

Brod, H. (1990) Pornography and the alienation of male sexuality. (Hearn et al. 124–139).

Chanock, M. (2000) Culture and human rights: orientalising, occidentalising and authenticity. (Mamdani 2000:15–36).

Connell, R.W. (1995) *Masculinities*. (Cambridge: Polity).

Connell, R.W. (2000) *The Men and the Boys*. (Cambridge: Polity).

Faludi, S. (2000) *Stiffed. The Betrayal of Modern Man*. (London: Vintage).

Frosh, S. (1994) *Sexual Difference, Masculinity and Psychoanalysis*. (London: Routledge).

Giddens, A. (1999a) *Tradition. Lecture 3*. Reith Lecture Series. (London: BBC).

Giddens, A. (1999b) *Family. Lecture 4*. Reith Lecture Series. (London: BBC).

Hearn, J. and Morgan, D. (eds.) *Men, Masculinities and Social Theory*. (London: Unwin Hyman).

Hunter, M. (2003) Masculinities and multiple sexual partners in KwaZulu-Natal: the making and unmaking of *isoka*. Paper presented at the *Sex and Secrecy* conference, University of the Witwatersrand, Johannesburg, 22–25 June.

Mama, A. (2003) Challenging subjects: gender, power and identity in African contexts. (2003/06/12http:/web.uct.ac.za/org/agi/papers/challeng.html).

Mamdani, M. (2000) (ed.) *Beyond Rights Talk and Culture Talk. Comparative Essays on the Politics of Rights and Culture*. (Cape Town: David Philip).

McFadden, P. (2001) Political power: the challenges of sexuality, patriarchy and globalisation in Africa. Paper presented at a seminar hosted by the Mauritius Women's Movement (MLF) and the Workers' Education Association (LPT), Port Louis, Mauritius.

McMahon, A. (1993) Male readings of feminist theory: the psychologization of sexual politics in the masculinity literature. *Theory and Society*, 22, 675–695.

Morrell, R. (1998) Of boys and men: masculinity and gender in southern African studies. *Journal of Southern African Studies*, 24, 4, 605–630.

Morrell, R. (2001) (ed.). *Changing Men in Southern Africa*. (London: Zed Books).

Morrell, R. (2003) Politics, theory and research: postcolonial masculinities and schooling in South Africa. Paper presented at the *Congress of the Social Sciences and Humanities*, 28 May–5 June, Nova Scotia, Canada.

Nhlapo, T. (2000) The African customary law of marriage and the rights conundrum. (Mamdani 2000:136–148).

Posel, D. (1991) Women's powers, men's authority: rethinking patriarchy. Paper presented at the *Conference on Women and Gender in Southern Africa*, 30 January–2 February, University of Natal, Durban.

Posel, D. (2003) The scandal of manhood: 'unmaking' secrets of sexual violence in post-apartheid South Africa and beyond. Paper presented at the *Sex and Secrecy* conference, University of the Witwatersrand, Johannesburg, 22–25 June.

Scorgie, F. (2002) Virginity testing and the politics of sexual responsibility: implications for AIDS interventions. *African Studies*, 61, 1, 55–76.

Segal, L. (1990) *Slow Motion. Changing Masculinities. Changing Men.* (London: Virago).

Segal, L. (1999) *Why Feminism? Gender, Psychology, Politics.* (Cambridge: Polity).

Walker, L. (2003) Men behaving differently: South African men since 1994. Paper presented at the *Sex and Secrecy* conference, University of the Witwatersrand, Johannesburg, 22–25 June.

Williams, R. (1977) *Marxism and Literature*. (Oxford: Oxford University Press).

Wood, K. and Jewkes, R. (1998) *'Love is a Dangerous Thing': Micro-dynamics of Violence in Sexual Relationships of Young People in Umtata.* (Pretoria: Medical Research Council).

6

Cultural politics and masculinities: Multiple-partners in historical perspective in KwaZulu-Natal

Mark Hunter

Introduction

Seventy percent of the total number of HIV-positive people worldwide – 28.5 million people – live in sub-Saharan Africa. Unlike North America and Europe, where HIV/AIDS is predominantly found among men who have sex with men and injecting drug users, in Africa most transmissions take place through heterosexual sex (UNAIDS 2004). Although there is now considerable agreement that gender is central to any understanding of male–female transmission, the social values surrounding manhood have been less often examined (Mane & Aggleton 2001). Yet studies have shown the benefits of such an approach. In South Africa, for instance, scholars have noted how dominant masculinities can shape men's sometimes violent control over women, the demand for 'flesh to flesh' sex, and the celebration of multiple partners (Campbell 1997, Wood & Jewkes 2001, Hunter 2002).

From a somewhat different perspective, an important recent theme in HIV/AIDS research is that of 'sexual networking'. Epidemiologists have argued that multiple-partnered relations may play an important part in driving the HIV pandemic: having the same number of overall partners within concurrent rather than serial relationships leads to a considerably more rapid advance of sexually transmitted diseases (Morris & Kretzschmar 1997; see also Legarde et al. 2001). Positioning multiple-partnered relations as one element of what they call a 'distinct and internally coherent African system of sexuality', the influential demographers Pat and John Caldwell and their collaborators have stressed the prevalence of such relationship patterns within African society and their embeddedness within its underlying social structure

(Caldwell et al. 1989:187). Drawing (somewhat uncritically) on early ethnographies, they view such relations in the context of African wives' sexual unavailability for long periods because of both high fertility rates and long periods of post-partum abstinence. I will attempt to show that this approach is fundamentally flawed since it ultimately leaves little room for tracing how sexual networking has emerged and changed over time. Moreover, unlike the masculinities framework, it fails to explore adequately how men's 'tradition' of having multiple partners both results from and shapes male power.[1]

This paper is situated geographically in KwaZulu-Natal (KZN), a province where one person in three is thought to be HIV-positive (Department of Health 2002). Showing how masculinities emerge out of changing material conditions, it is influenced by the work of the Italian Marxist Antonio Gramsci, who devoted his short life (he died in an Italian fascist prison cell in 1937 at the age of 46) to interpreting and challenging the dominant political and cultural forces that shape a society's 'common sense' (see for instance Gramsci 1971). Bob Connell's (1987, 1995) seminal writings on masculinities draw strongly on this Gramscian tradition, stressing how women and men, the gay and the straight, contest and produce a plurality of masculinities. Applied to Zulu society, this conception of culture rejects the search for some kind of static logic to Zulu sexuality that public-health workers can easily 'map' and then 'modify', perhaps through 'education'. Instead it posits an understanding of Zulu-ness as being constructed through contestations in everyday life where material and cultural change are inseparable and co-determining and where 'education' is but one of a number of shapers of 'culture'.[2]

To contextualise and historicise masculinities is especially important because the frightening reality of HIV/AIDS causes much research to gravitate towards the present day.[3] Additionally, popular discourse tends to characterise African people as inherently 'diseased' and 'promiscuous', making it imperative to problematise representations of static African masculinities (see Vaughan 1991 and McClintock 1995). At a time when gender is now correctly a taken-for-granted concept in the study of AIDS, there is value in stepping back and considering how male power has been assembled over time. What gendered battles took place to produce today's taken-for-granted traditions? How are men's social and ideological strengths maintained and what contradictions do they face?

Following a brief methodological note, this paper charts the rise and fall of the *isoka*, broadly a man with 'multiple sexual partners', a powerful though fluid concept in *isiZulu*. The importance of the notion of the *isoka* has been noted in KwaZulu-Natal (see for example Varga 1997), but the concept has not been historicised. This paper argues that colonial rule and capitalist penetration significantly altered paths to manhood and reworked the meanings and practices surrounding multiple partners. Evidence suggests that in 19th-century Natal and Zululand having multiple partners was not solely the prerogative of men and that unmarried women could also enjoy limited sexual relations with more than one boyfriend. In contrast, by the 1940s and 1950s, the earliest period recalled by my informants, most oral testimonies suggest that *umthetho* (the law) allowed only men to have multiple sexual partners. An *isoka* was juxtaposed to and sharply contrasted with an *isifebe*, a 'loose' woman engaging in several relations. Men, however, did not enjoy unlimited freedom. If an unmarried man 'played' with multiple girls whom he had no intention of marrying he could be castigated as being *isoka lamanyala* (literally a dirty *isoka*). Men among men were expected to marry, establish an independent household, and enlarge this domestic unit by fathering children.

This paper draws particular attention to the period from the 1980s when most informants recount tremendous difficulty in securing affordable housing and stable employment, if any. Consequently, most young men today are unable to marry because of the high cost of *ilobolo* (bridewealth), and find it difficult to establish an independent *umuzi* (homestead or home) and become *abanumzana* (heads of homesteads). The expansion of women's work opportunities in the last 50 years has also disrupted men's position as the sole 'provider', although many women face harsh poverty, particularly as unemployment has increased since the 1990s. In this context, securing multiple partners, once celebrated as a youthful pastime, has taken on an exaggerated significance for men and, indeed, for some women desperate to secure money or gifts. The article ends by noting the rising doubts that men now harbour around the *isoka* masculinity in the era of AIDS.

Context and method
The analysis that follows combines ethnographic, archival and secondary sources collected for my doctoral dissertation, which concerned Mandeni, a municipality 120 km north of Durban, on the north coast of KwaZulu-Natal. The principal data that this paper draws from is approximately 300 interviews with informants aged between 16 and 80 (all of the names of people appearing in this paper are pseudonyms). Interviews were semi-structured and geared towards understanding informants' life histories, with a special emphasis on relationships. Some informants were questioned as many as five times. These interviews, alongside 15 meetings with same-sex groups of three to four young people, were mined for clues as to how sexuality has transformed from the 1940s. Virtually all interviews were conducted and transcribed in isiZulu (the Zulu language). Useful supplementary sources include the Zulu newspapers *Ilanga* and *Isolezwe* and the radio station Ukhozi FM.

These sources were interpreted in conjunction with numerous informal conversations and observations. Beginning with a four-month stay in 2000, I have lived in Mandeni for a year and a half in total, staying with the Dlamini family in Isithebe informal settlement. The contradictions inherent in my own position as a white male born in the UK and studying in the USA of course need to be acknowledged. Just a stone's throw away from the informal settlement where I stayed in the Dlamini family's large *umuzi* is Isithebe Industrial Park; driving from the informal settlement on the dirt, often mud, roads, past the many *imijondolo* (rented one-room 'shacks') and into the adjacent factory complex quickly repositioned me as a probable factory manager with power over hundreds of lives. This is just one example of the power dynamics involved in conducting research in a country where the 'racial becomes the spatial' (Pred 2000:98) so starkly.

Nineteenth-century masculinities: the homestead economy and women with multiple partners
Zulu society emerged from a period of military warfare at the turn of the 20th century, and bravery and fighting skills were important attributes associated with manliness. The central economic focus for isiZulu speakers, however, was the *umuzi* (the homestead) and, in turn, the

physical and symbolical centre of this institution was the *isibaya* (cattle kraal). Big men accumulated many cattle, took several wives, and thus built a successful homestead; the more wives a man had, the more labour he was able to control and the richer and more esteemed an *umnumzana* (household head) he became (see Carton 2000 on masculinities at the turn of the century among isiZulu speakers). The commencement of courting was thus a significant step towards marriage and manhood and this is suggested by the fact that one meaning of the word *isoka* was 'unmarried man'. More fully, Colenso's (1861) dictionary gives the 19th-century meaning of the noun *isoka* as: 'Unmarried man; handsome young man; sweetheart; accepted lover; a young man liked by the girls'. With the emphasis of its meaning in this era on the courting stage it is perhaps not surprising that the noun *isoka* bears close similarity to the verb *ukusoka* (circumcision), a rite of passage from boyhood abolished by Shaka in the early 19th century. As is evident from the above definition, an *isoka* was also seen as a man popular with girls.

Controlling fertility was paramount in pre-colonial society since an *umuzi* could grow only through childbirth or the acquisition of additional wives (see Guy 1987). Nevertheless, sexual practices that avoided childbirth were relatively freely permitted. Evidence from court cases, oral testimonies collected by the colonial official and historian James Stuart at the turn of the 20th century, and early ethnographies all suggest that non-penetrative forms of sex (*ukusoma*, or thigh sex) were widely practiced among unmarried persons.[4] Somewhat surprisingly in light of future attitudes, records also indicate a certain level of acceptance of women having more than one soma partner, although it is true that those overstepping the mark could be chastised as being *izifebe* (pl. of *isifebe*, a loose woman). Monica Hunter [Wilson] (1936), writing in the 1930s about the Mpondo, a group less exposed to Western institutions although closely related to isiZulu speakers, describes the attitude of unmarried women having multiple boyfriends as 'the more skulls the better'. Extra-marital affairs also appear to have been quite well accepted in Southern Africa well before the onset of migrant labour (see Delius & Glaser 2003). Indeed, before the introduction of Christian notions of 'the body as the temple of God' the essence of *ukugana* (a verb translated sometimes too readily as 'to marry') was childbirth and building an *umuzi* and not sexual fidelity for its own sake. Such relatively open attitudes around certain forms of sexuality at certain times should not, however, be drawn upon to suggest that African society was in any way 'promiscuous'. Virginity-testing ceremonies institutionalised the enormous value placed on premarital virginity for young women, and a chaste demeanour was essential if a woman was to be seen as marriageable. In certain respects, especially where fertility was involved, African society could be extremely sexually conservative.

Multiple partners in rural areas in the 1940s and 1950s: men being *amasoka*, women behaving badly

If 19th-century Zulu society was structured around largely self-sufficient homesteads, by the 1950s most rural areas were dependent on migrant labour. Drawn first to the diamond and gold mines in the late 19th century, in the 20th century men increasingly found work in the mushrooming industries of large towns such as Johannesburg and Durban. A greater number of women too began to build livelihoods in urban areas, often as domestic workers or by engaging in informal activities such as the brewing of beer. Wage labour gave men new powers but it also meant that there were fresh expectations of them; in assuming the position of 'breadwinners' men took on primary responsibility for supporting the *umuzi* (Silberschmidt 2001).

Interviews with elderly informants in rural areas suggest that, against this transforming terrain, accepted thinking on having multiple sexual partners in the 1940s and '50s had transmuted significantly from the 19th century: notably, men and women's rights to have multiple partners had diverged sharply. Transformations are most evident in premarital sexuality where, in contrast to the 19th century, all informants are adamant that *umthetho* (the law) only allowed women to have a single lover; having multiple partners was the prerogative of *amasoka* (pl. of *isoka*) alone. That a growing asymmetry emerged between men and women's rights to have multiple partners is suggested by an apparent change in the meaning of *isoka*. Doke et al.'s dictionary, compiled in the 1940s and 1950s, differentiates between an 'original meaning' of *isoka* as 'a man old enough to commence courting' and later meanings that encompass a 'young man popular among girls'. Vilakazi (1962:47) describes in powerful terms the Don Juan or Casanova status of the *isoka* in the mid-century, a strong theme in testimonies:

> Courting behaviour among traditional young men is a very important part of their education; for a young man must achieve the distinction of being an *isoka*, i.e. a Don Juan or a Casanova.

According to informants, being an *isoka* and having several girlfriends was countered to the ignominy of life as an *isishimane*, a man too scared to talk with girls and without a single girlfriend. As a symbolic substitute for polygamy, the *isoka* concept was widely circulated, and at times challenged, in everyday discourse, as demonstrated by its prominent position in *izibongo* (oral praise poems) (Koopman 1987, Gunner & Gwala 1991, Turner 1999). If the archetypal *isoka* figure in the 1950s was a single young man famous for his prowess in courting several women, the *isoka* masculinity had a much wider ambit, one example being its bolstering of husbands' position that they alone should enjoy extramarital liaisons, especially important at a time when polygamy had become extremely rare.

This *isoka* masculinity was dominant but not universal. Christianity sanctioned a single, monogamous, moral code that was endorsed, if not always strictly followed, by male *amakholwa* (Christians/believers). Schooling and Christianity certainly seem to have influenced a more seditious attitude among women to their husband's extra-marital affairs (see Longmore 1959, Wilson & Mafeje 1963). The existence of same-sex relations also suggested a further challenge to heterosexual norms, the Zulu words for a homosexual man being *isitabane* or *ingqingili* (see also Epprecht 1998 on same-sex relations in Zimbabwe). Moreover, being an *isoka*, even in the 1950s, could lead to embarrassing illnesses. Especially for urban men, penetrative sex (as opposed to ukusoma) had become a mark of manliness, and yet the embarrassing symptoms of STIs such as syphilis reminded men of the hazards of a masculinity that celebrated multiple sexual conquests.[5] The harsh reality of migrant labour also meant that, although women's sexuality was jealously guarded in some circumstances, a number of women did have extramarital affairs with a certain level of implicit approval: many of my older female informants smiled wryly when relating how a secondary lover was dubbed *isidikiselo*, the top of a pot, while the first man, the *ibhodwe*, was the main pot; these metaphors are closely linked to women's need for sexual relations, and sometimes support, when their husbands were working in the towns.

Moreover, the *isoka* masculinity faced restrictions precisely because other paths to manhood were ultimately more valued. While an *isoka* could *soma* (engage in thigh sex) with several partners, in order to become a respected *umnumzana* he had to have a wife and build an *umuzi*. The phrase *isoka lamanyala* (*amanyala* means 'dirt' or 'a disgraceful act'), used to rebuke men with too many girlfriends, signified an unseemly masculinity, a masculinity gone too far. Though some men did recall a certain status associated with being *isoka lamanyala*, for most it was a reproach. Men with more than one girlfriend, including married men partaking in extramarital relations, could be called to account for their intention to marry their girlfriends particularly by parents with a heavy stake in their daughter's future *ilobolo*. Indeed, most informants were adamant that an *isoka*'s ability to attract women was heavily dependent on his control over cattle and other resources necessary for marriage; hence in the 1940s and 1950s, despite the bravado around the language of *isoka*, men who had not yet secured work found it difficult to be *qoma'd* (chosen) by even a single woman.

In the mid-century, what forces consolidated this *isoka* masculinity and, in contrast to the 19th century, frowned on women who had multiple partners? A persistent theme in writings on colonial Africa is how African men and the colonial state looked towards 'customary law' to solidify patriarchal 'traditions'. (On the detrimental effects of customary law on women in Natal, see Simons 1968 and Horrel 1968.) The control of women, and women's sexuality, was especially important given the expansion of opportunities for women in towns. It was mentioned above that Christianity could facilitate greater female assertion, but church morals also placed enormous pressure on women to act with 'purity'. Christian Africans played a significant role in reasserting 'traditions' that could stem women's revolt (Gaitskell 1982, Marks 1989). The apparent new tradition that limited women, particularly the unmarried, to only one boyfriend seemed to have emerged out of this subtle blend of 'Zulu' and Christian values. Demonstrating this, while most informants said that a woman's restriction to only one boyfriend was part of a timeless Zulu *umthetho* (law), tellingly some sourced the rule as coming from God. Yet these struggles over tradition did not take place in a social or geographical vacuum. They were underpinned by shifts in bargaining power as a consequence of migrant labour and the erosion of agricultural capacity in rural society. Instead of being dependent on their fathers for bridewealth, young migrant workers, now able to save *ilobolo* themselves, were in a strong position to demand that their girlfriends adopt a chaste demeanour and refrain from having secondary partners.

Though some women, of course, did develop intimate relations with more than one man, those doing so, especially the unmarried, were chastised as being *izifebe*. So severe was this insult that it could result in a claim of defamation.[6] Indeed, in the eyes of many men the *ihlazo* (disgrace) of having a child before marriage or being seen as *izifebe* positioned women as lacking *inhlonipho* (respect) and therefore undesirable to marry – condemned to a low status in society or forced to escape derision by moving to towns. Young girls' chaste living was further supervised by *amaqhikiza* (girls who had already selected a boyfriend) and elder women who periodically tested girls' virginity. While parents set firm limits, notably against pregnancy, they were rarely involved in the day-to-day socialisation of young men or women's sexuality. (On changing forms of sexual socialisation see Delius & Glaser 2002.)

As is common in the telling of oral histories, many respondents tended to remember the 1940s and 1950s with nostalgia – as a period of stability, opulence, and convention. The *umnumzana* figure that I have drawn attention to sometimes figured in these accounts as a marker of a static and romanticised manhood. Certainly, one can easily underestimate the extent to which aspiring to manhood in the mid-century placed men in an extremely ambiguous position; building a rural home and family forced men to work in towns and yet the consequences of the separation from their families often undermined the very institution men sought to construct. A final important point of ambiguity results from the need to see sexuality as closely connected to broader gendered patterns. Parents in particular could position their daughters as being *izifebe* – or 'loose' women – in order to deny them the opportunity to worship or to attend school, both practices associated with possible desertion to the towns and the loss of labour and *ilobolo*. Sexuality, as Weeks (1985:16) points out, is 'a transmission belt for wider social anxieties' – contestations over sexuality are about much more than simply sex. Put another way, the cultural politics of having multiple partners overlapped with parallel contestations over the roles and duties of women in society.

In conclusion, the evidence suggests that having multiple partners was the subject of ongoing change and contestation in the 1950s. Tradition, rather than being simply passed down or lost, faced intense contestation at every point. Although both men and women were engaging in multiple-partnered relations, compared to the 19th century, women, particularly unmarried women, faced much more public censure for doing so; the notion of the *isoka* saw to it that this right was coded as a male right only, pivoting on the 'tradition' of polygamy. The section that follows explores contestations over multiple-partnered relations in the contemporary period.

Multiple-partnered relations in the era of democracy and unemployment

A persistent theme in oral accounts is the long and arduous investments men made in order to become *abanumzana* (heads of homesteads). In the colonial and apartheid era this was never an easy project. Indeed, as the 20th century progressed, men became progressively dependent on wage labour to provide *ilobolo* (bridewealth). At work, in particular, African men faced the humiliation of being positioned as 'boys'. Today, however, arguably two further forces threaten South African men's path to *umnumzana* status: the difficulty that they face in marrying and setting up an independent household and the greater participation of women in the labour market and thus their independence from men.

Population census data suggests that marital rates began to drop from the 1960s. This was probably in response to increased cohabiting in towns, more educated women gaining new work opportunities, and migrant labour biting deeper into the ability of men and women to form long-term relationships. From the 1970s, however, technological developments, slow growth, population rises, and, since 1994, tariff reductions, prompted a dramatic increase in unemployment and a greater casualisation of work. Unemployment estimates today range from 30–42 percent, depending on the methodology used (Altman 2003). Though some African people have taken advantage of the post-apartheid deracialisation of schooling and employment, for the great majority the prospects of steady work are very slim. As marriage is now so dependent on employment, weddings in many South African communities are infrequent events. In KwaZulu-Natal, the common *ilobolo* figure of ten cows (plus one beast, the *ingquthu*, for the mother) was set as a maximum payment by the colonial administration in 1869 and later incorporated in the Natal Code of Native Law (Welsh 1971). Today in KZN, the paying of 11 cows is ironically seen as one of the most timeless of all African 'traditions' (although not in other provinces where, unlike in Natal, customary law was not codified). Certainly marriage has always been a process rather than an event and the institution is demonstrating flexibility – most families today utilise generous cattle–cash exchange rates. Nonetheless, wedlock continues to remain outside the scope of most young men's financial capacity. According to the most recent population census, less than 30 percent of African men and women over 15 years of age in South Africa were in marital relations in 2001. Interlinked changes in women's status and roles also serve to undermine men's position as *abanumzana*. Many men are no longer the sole provider and some are even dependent on women for survival. This is the context in which marriage becomes not only undesirable but unnecessary from the perspective of women.

The seismic changes to the institution of African marriage in the 20th century have long been noted in published work. Especially in urban areas, increased numbers of 'illegitimate' children, extramarital relations, and 'prostitution' were seen as evidence for societal breakdown over half a century ago (see Krige 1936, Hellman 1948, Longmore 1959). Yet, although urban areas undoubtedly did rework sexuality, it must be recognised that urban growth also fashioned the emergence of an alternative urban masculinity. Throughout the colonial and apartheid eras, elements in the state and society debated the extent to which African urban dwellers should be 'stabilised'. In the 1950s and 1960s, although influx controls were severely tightened, formal township housing programmes expanded at their fastest rate for those with urban residential rights. According to Posel (1995:237),

'This stabilisation strategy included, at its very core, efforts to "build" stable African family units.' The advertisement below (fig. 1), appearing in the Zulu-language newspaper *Ilanga laseNatal* in the 1950s, draws on the imagery of a modern urban *umnumzana*, a man who aspired to Western standards of education and fashion. The important point to stress is that urbanisation, often seen as a process that led to immorality, could also lead to new notions of manhood, ones in which notions of marriage and 'building a home' still played a central part.

Figure 1: Griffiths Motsieloa, a well-known musician in the 1940s, advertises C to C cigarettes, markers of 'urban life'. The newspaper *Ilanga*, from which this advert is sourced, was widely read in rural and urban areas by educated men and it helped to foster a modern image of the *umnumzana* (household head) – a man confidently in control of his destiny and firmly at the helm of a domestic household. (*Ilanga laseNatal*, 18 March 1950, Killie Campbell Africana Library)

Silberschmidt (2001) has argued that in East Africa, high unemployment and low incomes created a context in which men's self-esteem could be bolstered through multiple-partnered relations and violence against women. South African society is perhaps even more divided than East African in terms of wealth and poverty both between and within 'races'. At the bottom of the social hierarchy many unemployed or poorly paid women are forced to engage in 'transactional sex' with men, often multiple men (see Hunter 2002). Another significant trend is the dependence of some less successful men on women. Further, some poor men complain bitterly that they cannot secure any girlfriends. The inability of many men to achieve *umnumzana* status, I would argue, is an important context in which expressions of manliness that celebrate numerous sexual conquests must be understood. This situation is underpinned by high unemployment rates and the tremendous cost of housing in urban areas, particularly in comparison to the period when the first township houses were built. Seventeen-year-old township resident Sipho describes the way some men position their quest for women: 'If he has six, I want seven, then he wants to have eight.' The numbers are very often much higher than the one or two girlfriends mentioned by the elder generation, and penetrative sex is invariably taken for granted: many youths, especially in urban areas, are unaware that the practice of *ukusoma* (thigh sex) ever existed.

Despite the diverse history of the *isoka* masculinity noted here, men generally present being an *isoka* as a part of a seamless Zulu custom. Zandi, a 22-year-old township woman, describes how men conflate polygamy with having multiple partners, to justify the latter: 'They say that it is their culture to have more than one girl. They say my grandfather had six wives, I want to be like him.' To denote an unacceptable side of the *isoka* masculinity, young men and women, like their grandparents, still speak of *isoka lamanyala* (dirty *isoka*), although today the concept has been partially delinked from marriage. It is no longer common to hear of men being lambasted with the term *isoka* lamanyala for having many girlfriends and showing no intention of marrying any of them. A more likely usage of *isoka lamanyala* might be to describe a man who cheats on his girlfriend with her best friend, or a man who spreads HIV.

Certainly, AIDS is bearing heavily down on the *isoka* masculinity. HIV/AIDS-related illnesses transform some of the most virile and popular bodies into barely living skeletons, shunned by friends and neighbours. Outwardly confident about being *amasoka*, at times men betray their inner doubt. The contradictions of being amasoka in the era of HIV/AIDS are perhaps most tragically played out at the many funerals in the area; previous 'players' are buried by their friends who were once envious of their ability to attract women. Consequently, men and masculinities are under intense scrutiny and critique, even if women are still commonly blamed for 'promiscuity' and AIDS. Men's own self-doubt is further propelled by women's often aggressive critique of irresponsible men infecting women with HIV. One 29-year-old woman told me that many women no longer use the 'traditional' concept of *isoka lamanyala* to criticise men: 'the young, they just call [bad men] *izinja* (dogs)'.

There is some evidence in South Africa that male doubt is being institutionalised in groups such as Men for Change, noted by Liz Walker (2003) in Alexandra township. These groups can counter the risk-taking and bravado implicit in dominant masculinities. Certainly, in my last three years of working in Mandeni, interviews documented rising doubt among young men over the celebration of multiple partners. Nonetheless, sexuality is so deeply embedded within a broader cultural politics that its transformation takes place through contradictory tugs rather than unidirectional movements. Women seeking education and other opportunities have long been scorned as *izifebe* ('loose' women) and today the disciplining of rebellious women as 'loose' still serves to bolster male power. One only has to spend a short time in many homes in South Africa's townships or rural areas to observe that women shoulder huge burdens of domestic responsibility. The insult of *isifebe* hovers over women who challenge taken-for-granted attributes of gender in the home and elsewhere. With this in mind, it is easier to see how men can adhere to differential claims about multiple-partnered relations embodied in concepts such as *isoka/isifebe* that, while threatening to their lives if enacted in multiple-partnered relations, reiterate gendered power in broader spheres of everyday life. These binary categories also, of course, help to reiterate the normative heterosexuality of dominant masculinities.

But it is too simplistic to suggest that masculinities are simply defended by most men and challenged by women. Women's efforts to secure livelihoods in harsh socioeconomic circumstances can also serve to reproduce dominant masculinities. Many women are themselves quick to see the benefits of securing multiple partners, living in an environment where the prospect of work and marriage is slim, and where they are often aware of their own boyfriends' unfaithfulness, and conscious that relationships can end quickly in violence. As one young man recently put it: 'now [the post-apartheid period] women say that it is 50/50 – if we have other girlfriends, they have other boyfriends'; a sentiment with a long history, of course. The pleasure of sex is openly celebrated, but these liaisons can also be brazenly about money, especially relationships with 'sugar daddies'. Although some unemployed men or schoolboys complain that they find it difficult to secure a single girlfriend, 'sugar daddies' are usually said to work at well-paying firms in Mandeni. The type of acquired dispositions (Bourdieu 1990) that women would invest in the 1940s, such as being seen to be chaste, *khuthele* (hard-working), and respectful, are much less important today as it is a sexy demeanour that can secure men and money in contemporary South Africa.

Figures 2, 3: A postcard given away in July 2003 with the popular magazine *Drum*. Oscar is a successful South African music personality. With a condom attached, the postcard speaks to young men through the word *baba* (father). *Baba*, a term historically used by older men, has been appropriated by young township men today as an informal, yet respectful, greeting. Youth AIDS thus doubly appropriates it in an attempt to bestow responsibility on youth to engage in safe sex.

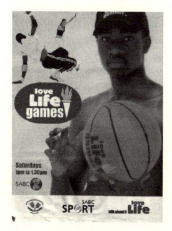

Fig. 4: loveLife, South Africa's largest intervention campaign, portrays itself as a new lifestyle brand, competing with consumer icons such as Nike and Coke. In an era when *umnumzana* (head of household) status is denied to many men, sports are promoted as a fashionable alternative expression of manliness (source: S'camtoPrint, Issue 53, 17 August 2003).

Facing these circumstances, intervention messages are highly contradictory, often unable to reconcile themselves with the material realities of life for the majority in post-apartheid South Africa. At least publicly, churches tend to forcefully promote abstinence before marriage though the message seems hollow when betrothal is such a rarity. In KwaZulu-Natal, the pandemic has led to attempts to revive the practice of virginity testing (see Scorgie 2002). In Mandeni's township, a local church now annually organises a virginity-testing ceremony, an intervention not without irony, given the historical role of churches in railing against heathen traditions.[7]

One theme running through the narratives of youth interventions in South Africa is the need to treat young people, particularly women, with 'respect'. Young peoples' 'rights' are championed and the category of 'youth' is symbolically reworked to place young people on a more even footing with adults. The postcard advert from Youth AIDS (figures 2, 3) is suggestive of this theme, appropriating as it does the word *baba* (father) in its text: 'If you are going to have sex, use a condom *baba*.' Many young male readers will indeed be fathers, yet the postcard blends trendy youth images with a word usually reserved for older men, though now part of township lingo. It bestows on youth the duties of responsibility associated with manhood, in exchange for elevated male respect – respect being redefined away from 'traditional' practices pivoting on gender and generational hierarchies. Such strategies of creating alternative values around manhood are also attempted by the highest-profile AIDS institution in South Africa, loveLife, a large NGO established to reduce teenage pregnancies and HIV infections through media campaigns, telephone advice lines, and youth centres. The loveLife poster (fig. 4) encourages men to achieve respect through a healthy body, positioning sport as a desirable expression of manhood.

It is easy to see how these and other 'groovy' intervention messages promoting choice, independence, and self-respect can appeal to those who envisage bright prospects in the new South Africa. Certainly there is a growing African middle class in South Africa and most South Africa whites have relatively good prospects of work. However, for the majority of poorer, predominantly African, South Africans (the principal subject of this paper), the resonances between 'choice', 'positive living' and the lived experiences of poor schooling and unemployment are more muted. Notwithstanding these comments, it has perhaps become too easy to dismiss campaigns such as loveLife's out of hand. A more balanced assessment must also recognise how deeply *any* interventions to rework masculinities, and more broadly sexuality, are hampered by the extreme poverty in many areas of the country. Creating a new lifestyle brand, as loveLife has attempted to do, certainly does open up spaces for contestation by all South Africans, rich and poor, and this must be seen as a positive development. At the moment, however, it seems that it is middle-class, urban-based youth who have the strongest base from which to employ such symbols to challenge dominant expressions of sexuality. This is where the grassroots activism of groups such as the Treatment Action Campaign (TAC) is so important in South Africa: dominated by poor, HIV-positive women, TAC draws from modern rights-based discourses to argue for more equitable access to AIDS medication in South Africa and, ultimately, for a shift in health and intervention priorities towards the poorest members of South African society.

Viewing masculinities and notions of respect through a historical lens also makes it possible to see why one of the key slogans of loveLife, 'Talk about it' – promoting parent–child dialogue on sex – is so controversial in South Africa. Sexual socialisation historically took place through age-sets; talking about sex across generations could be seen as highly impertinent and counter to notions of *inhlonipho* (respect). Thus, opposition to new notions of mutual respect and universal 'rights' may have more to do with attempts to preserve gendered and generational hierarchies than any kind of blanket African 'taboo' on talking about sex, as some suggest. Supporters and critics of campaigns such as loveLife all arguably tend to focus too narrowly on sexuality rather then exploring its embeddedness within a multiplicity of gendered struggles and practices in everyday life.

Disaggregating male power and foregrounding cultural politics

The notion of cultural politics captures the way that men and women, the young and the old, the gay and the straight, contest everyday cultural beliefs, ones that have real material consequences. The practice of having multiple partners has never been static in South African history and is contested within the ebb and flow of changing material livelihoods. Gender is more than simply the one-dimensional expression of male power but, as historical analysis of the *isoka* masculinity demonstrates, it is embodied in male vulnerabilities and weaknesses. It is the coming together of male power in some ideological and material domains with men's weakness in others, including the difficulties they experience in achieving full manhood through building an *umuzi* (home), that can create the violence and risky masculinities so often tragically noted in the era of HIV/AIDS. Historically rooted analysis – rarely featuring in HIV/AIDS debates – has an important role to play in replacing stereotypes of static 'African masculinities' or 'culture' with accounts that recognise complex, contested, processes of cultural change.

Acknowledgements

Many thanks to Ben Carton, Robert Morrell and the anonymous reviewers of the present collection for comments on previous versions of this paper. Gratitude is due to the Dlamini family for hosting me in Isithebe. I also wish to thank the many residents of Mandeni whom I interviewed. Philisiwe Mabunda facilitated and transcribed most of the interviews upon which this article is based with great skill and commitment. This research was funded by fellowships from the Wenner-Gren Foundation for Anthropological Research and the International Dissertation Field Research Fellowship Program of the Social Science Research Council with funds provided by the Andrew W. Mellon foundation.

Notes

1 See also Heald (1995) for this critique of the Caldwells' work.
2 See Morrell (1996) and also Hamilton (1998) for important historical writings on 'Zulu-ness'.
3 Particularly important exceptions combining contemporary ethnography with historical analysis are Schoepf (1988) and Setel (1999).
4 Ndukwana in a long and complex testimony to James Stuart at the turn of the century makes several references to unmarried women being allowed to have a number of *soma* partners, as long as she *soma'd* with only one per month so that pregnancy could be accounted for (testimony

of Ndukwana in Webb & Wright 1986:300, 353). Accounts of courting contained in evidence for criminal court cases from this period also suggest that unmarried women had a significant degree of sexual freedom: see RSC II/1/42 Rex v Gumakwake (85/1887) and RSC II/1/44 Rex v Ulusawana (45/1888).

5 Describing the effect of STIs on masculinity, a doctor's assistant practising in the area in the 1960s remembers the embarrassment attached to syphilis and suggests that, like AIDS, it could provide a check on masculinity, although its curability of course contrasts strongly with AIDS today.

6 Most of the small number of defamation cases that I have seen from this period resulted because a women had been called *isifebe* – a great offence to both Christian and non-Christian women. See Majozi v Khuzwayo (1/ESH uncatalogued civil case, 65/63) for a rural setting and Buthelezi v Ntuli (1/ESH uncatalogued civil case, 66/66) for a more urban setting.

7 And again, somewhat paradoxically, in 2002 the church hired a DJ and a loud music system to sustain the interests of youth amidst their enactment of 'traditional' songs and dances.

References

Altman, M. (2003) The state of employment and unemployment in South Africa. (Daniel et al. 2003).

Bourdieu, P. (1990) *The Logic of Practice*. (Stanford: Stanford University Press).

Caldwell, J., Caldwell, O., and Quiggin, P. (1989) The social context of AIDS in sub-Saharan Africa. *Population Development Review*, 15, 185–234.

Campbell, C. (1997) Migrancy, masculine identities and AIDS: the psychosocial context of HIV transmission on the South African gold mines. *Social Science and Medicine*, 45, 2, 273–81.

Carton, B. (2000) *Blood from Your Children: The Colonial Origins of Generational Conflict in South Africa* (Pietermaritzburg: University of Natal Press).

Colenso, J.W. (1861) *Zulu–English Dictionary*. (Pietermaritzburg: Davis).

Connell, R. (1987) *Gender and Power*. (Cambridge: Polity).

Connell, R. (1995) *Masculinities*. (Berkeley: University of California Press).

Daniel, J., Habib, A. and Southall, R. (2003) *State of the Nation: South Africa 2003–2004*. (Cape Town: HSRC).

Delius, P. and Glaser, C. (2002) Sexual socialisation in South Africa: a historical perspective. *African Studies*, 61, 1, 27–54.

Delius, P. and Glaser, C. (2003) The myth of polygamy: a history of extra-marital and multi-partnership sex in South Africa. Paper presented to the *Sex and Secrecy* Conference, University of the Witwatersrand, 22–25 June 2003.

Department of Health. (2002) National HIV and syphilis sero-prevalence survey in South Africa, 2001. < http://www.doh.gov.za/aids/index.html>

Doke, C., Malcolm, D., Sikakana, J. and Vilikazi, B. (1990) *English–Zulu Zulu–English Dictionary*. (Johannesburg: Witwatersrand University Press).

Epprecht, M. (1998) 'Good God almighty, what's this!': homosexual crime in early colonial Zimbabwe. (Murray & Roscoe 1998:197–221).

Gaitskell, D. (1982) 'Wailing for Purity': prayer unions, African mothers and adolescent daughters, 1912–1940. (Marks & Rathbone 1982:338–357).

Gramsci, A. (1971) *Selection from the Prison Notebooks*. Edited and translated by Q. Hoare & G. Nowell Smith. (New York: International Publishers).

Gunner, E. and Gwala, M. (1994) *Musho: Zulu Popular Praises*. (Johannesburg: Witwatersrand University Press).

Guy, J. (1987) Analysing pre-capitalist societies in Southern Africa. *Journal of Southern African Studies*, 14, 1, 18–37.

Hamilton, C. (1998) *Terrific Majesty: The Powers of Shaka Zulu and the Limits of Historical Invention*. (Cambridge, Massachusetts: Harvard University Press).

Heald, S. (1995) The power of sex: some reflections on the Caldwells' 'African sexuality' thesis. *Africa*, 65, 4, 489–505.

Hellmann, E. (1948) *Rooiyard: A Sociological Survey of an Urban Slum Yard*. (Manchester: Manchester University Press).

Horrell, M. (1968) *The Rights of African Women: Some Suggested Reforms*. (Johannesburg: Institute of Race Relations).

Hunter, Monica. (1936) *Reaction to Conquest: Effects of Contact with Europeans on the Pondo of South Africa*. (London: Oxford University Press).

Hunter, Mark. (2002) The materiality of everyday sex: thinking beyond 'prostitution'. *African Studies*, 61, 1, 99–120.

Koopman, A. (1987) The praises of young Zulu men. *Theoria*, 70, 41–54.

Krige, E. (1936) Changing conditions in marital relations and parental duties among urbanized natives. *Africa*, 1, 1–23.

Legarde, E. et al. (2001). Concurrent sexual partnerships and HIV prevalence in five urban communities of sub-Saharan Africa. *AIDS*, 15, 877–884.

Longmore, L. (1959) *The Dispossessed: A Study of the Sex-life of Bantu Women in Urban Areas around Johannesburg*. (London: Jonathan Cape).

Mane, P. and Aggleton, P. (2001) Gender and HIV/AIDS: what do men have to do with it? *Current Sociology*, 49, 6, 23–37.

Marks, S. (1989) Patriotism, patriarchy and purity: Natal and the politics of Zulu ethnic consciousness. (Vail 1989).

Marks, S. and Rathbone, R. (eds.) (1982) *Industrialisation and Social Change in South Africa*. (Essex: Longman).

McClintock, A. (1995) *Imperial Leather: Race, Gender and Sexuality in the Colonial Conquest*. (New York and London: Routledge).

Morrell, R. (ed.) (1996) *Political Economy and Identities in KwaZulu-Natal: Historical and Social Perspectives*. (Durban: Indicator Press).

Morrell, R. (ed.) (2001) *Changing Men in Southern Africa*. (Pietermaritzburg: University of Natal Press).

Morris, M. and Kretzschmar, M. Concurrent partnerships and the spread of HIV. *AIDS*, 11, 641–648.

Murray, S. and Roscoe, W. (eds.) (1998) *Boy-Wives and Female Husbands: Studies of African Homosexualities*. (New York: St Martin's Press).

Posel, D. (1995) State, power and gender: conflict over the registration of African customary marriage in South Africa c. 1910–1970. *Journal of Historical Sociology*, 8, 3, 223–256.

Pred, A. (2000) *Even in Sweden: Racisms, Racialized Spaces and the Popular Geographical Imagination*. (Berkeley: University of California Press).

Schoepf, B. (1988) Women, AIDS and economic crisis in Central Africa. *Canadian Journal of African Studies*, 22, 3, 625–44.

Scorgie, F. (2002) Virginity testing and the politics of sexual responsibility: implications for AIDS intervention. *African Studies*, 61, 1, 55–75.

Setel, P. (1999) *Plague of Paradoxes*. (Chicago: University of Chicago Press).

Silberschmidt, M. (2001) Disempowerment of men in rural and urban East Africa: implications for male identity and sexual behaviour. *World Development*. 29, 4, 657–671.

Simons, J. (1968) *African Women: Their Legal Status in South Africa*. (London: C. Hurst & Co.).

Turner, N.S. (1999) Representations of masculinity in the contemporary oral praise poetry of Zulu men. *South African Journal of African Languages*, 19, 3, 196–203.

UNAIDS. (2004) AIDS Epidemic Update 2004. <unaids.org.za>

Vail, L. (ed.) (1989) *The Creation of Tribalism in Southern Africa*. (Berkeley: University of California Press).

Varga, C. (1997) Sexual decision making and negotiation in the midst of AIDS: youth in KwaZulu-Natal, South Africa. *Health Transition Review*, 7, supplement 3, 45–67.

Vaughan, M. (1991) *Curing their Ills: Colonial Power and African Illness*. (Oxford: Basil Blackwell).

Vilakazi, A. (1962) *Zulu Transformations. A Study of the Dynamics of Social Change*. (Pietermaritzburg: University of Natal Press).

Walker, L (2003) Men behaving differently: South African men since 1994. Paper presented at the *Sex and Secrecy* Conference, University of the Witwatersrand, 22–25 June 2003.

Webb, C., and Wright, J. (1986) *The James Stuart Archive of Recorded Evidence Relating to the History of the Zulu and Neighbouring Peoples. Volume 4*. (Pietermaritzburg: University of Natal Press).

Weeks, J. (1985) *Sexuality and its Discontents: Meaning, Myths and Modern Sexualities*. (London: Routledge).

Welsh, D. (1971) *The Roots of Segregation: Native Policy in Colonial Natal, 1845–1910*. (Cape Town: Oxford University Press).

Wilson, M., and Mafeje, A. (1963) *Langa. A Study of Social Groups in an African Township*. (Cape Town: Oxford University Press).

Wood, K., and Jewkes, R. (2001) 'Dangerous love': reflections on violence among Xhosa township youth. (Morrell 2001:317–336).

Natal Archives, Durban

Civil Cases, Eshowe District (1/Esh). Majozi v Khuzwayo (uncatalogued civil case, 65/63); Buthelezi v Ntuli (uncatalogued civil case, 66/66).

Criminal cases, Natal: RSC II/1/42 Rex v Gumakwake (85/1887) and RSC II/1/44 Rex v Ulusawana (45/1888).

7
Negotiating the boundaries of masculinity in post-apartheid South Africa

Liz Walker

Introduction

In contemporary South Africa, traditional versions and expressions of masculinity[1] and male sexuality have been disturbed and destabilised. Figures of manhood and masculine identity represented in the 1996 Constitution and Bill of Rights derive from, but also break with, the past. The Constitution's implicit understanding of sexuality is premised on a figure of manhood which is as liberal as the Constitution itself. However, the transitions in gender/power relations embodied in the Constitution have exacerbated a crisis of masculinity, which has taken different forms. The responses of some men to the shifts in gender/power relations have been violent, ruthless and reactionary, yet the responses of others have been embracing. While 'constitutional sexuality' seems to have shut some doors for men by shrinking the 'patriarchal dividend' (at least at the level of legislation), it has simultaneously opened up spaces and created opportunities for men to construct new masculinities. The discussion which follows draws on in-depth interviews conducted over the past year with young men in Alexandra township, north of Johannesburg.[2] It argues that contemporary expressions of masculinity are embryonic, ambivalent and characterised by the struggle between traditional/conventional male practices and the desire to be a modern, respectable, responsible man.

Situating South Africa's 'crisis of masculinity' in context

In recent years, scholars working in the fields of gender, sexuality and health studies have pointed to a 'crisis in masculinity' characterised by instability and uncertainty 'over social role and identity, sexuality, work and personal relationships' (Frosh et al. 2002:1). Men are perceived to be in trouble collectively (Dowsett 2002). Frosh et al. (2002:1) argue that, if indeed such a crisis exists, it has its roots in a number of social phenomena,

> includ[ing] the collapse of traditional men's work, the growth of a technological culture which cannot be 'passed on' in any recognisable way between the generations, the rise of feminist consciousness amongst women, and, more abstractly, challenges to the dominance of the forms of rationality with which masculinity has been identified, at least in the West.

Underpinning this is the assumption that men's traditional dominant role, guaranteed through patriarchy, has significantly changed or has in some way been unseated.

Whitehead (2002) argues that this male crisis discourse has assumed common-sense proportions. This, he argues, is most evident in Europe and North America in politics and various public policies. He suggests that male crisis discourse informs public policy in the areas of education, health and crime. Men's health, for example, has become a growing area of public (and social science) concern. The recognition that macho masculinity is bad for men's health has focused attention on the issues of heart disease, suicide, body image, eating disorders and male mortality rates. This discourse presupposes that the failures of men are due to the successes of women, which potentially disrupt the social/gender order. Internationally, men's responses to feminism echo this: some men, reacting angrily, have fought to maintain and increase their power and privilege (Faludi 1991, Dworkin 1997), while others have welcomed opportunities for change, as is reflected in the growing numbers of men's movements working for gender justice (Connell 1995).

In South Africa, there are important parallels to be drawn (and differences to be noted) which could be usefully situated in relation to the following set of questions: What is the nature of the crisis of masculinity in contemporary South Africa? How do masculine identities constituted in the past resonate with contemporary figures of manhood? How have men reacted to the crisis in masculinity and in what ways are they also the victims of it?

South Africa's contemporary crisis of masculinity and male sexuality has been brought into sharp focus by the transition to democracy (especially gender transformation), the adoption of the Constitution and the public discourses of a human rights culture. Being a man in post-apartheid South Africa is of necessity different, yet the present does not represent a complete rupture with the past. Rather, current models and practices of manhood are historically embedded. The 'crisis of masculinity' in contemporary South Africa may therefore be different, but it is certainly not new.[3]

Constitutional sexuality

Vocal and sustained lobbying by the women's movement in the early 1990s, coupled with a strong public commitment to end women's oppression, ensured that gender equity was high on the priority list of the democratically elected government in 1994. South Africa has the most progressive constitution in the world. The founding provisions of the Constitution include four sets of values upon which the democratic state of South Africa is founded. Non-racism and non-sexism take their place alongside the achievement of equality and the advancement of human rights and freedoms. The 'equality clause' in the Bill of Rights states:

> The state may not unfairly discriminate directly or indirectly against anyone on one or more grounds, including race, gender, sex, pregnancy, marital status, ethnic or social origin, colour, sexual orientation, age, disability, religion, conscience, belief, culture, language and birth.

State institutions, such as the Commission for Gender Equality, have been established in order to strengthen constitutional democracy in South Africa.

There have been substantial legislative changes that address the subordinate position of women in South Africa. Women comprise 30 percent of members of parliament; marital rape is now a recognised offence; domestic violence is subject to new and tougher sentencing; people (mainly men) who defy child maintenance court orders are liable to prosecution; companies are obliged to appoint women in terms of labour legislation; women have to be paid the same as men for equivalent work; and, in education, the interests of female children have been identified as needing special efforts (Morrell 2002:5). Additionally, South African abortion legislation is amongst the most liberal in the world. Women may access abortion on demand in the first trimester of pregnancy and under certain conditions in the second trimester. While encouraged to inform their parents, minors do not need their permission to have an abortion, and partner consent is also not required.

The legal and social position of some women has undoubtedly altered through these measures. There has been a shift (at least at the level of perception) in gender/power relations since 1994. Hassim (1999) argues that women have acquired citizenship through these processes, and their situation has been transformed from one of presence to one of power. But women's gains should not be overstated, as more women than men continue to live in poverty, greater numbers of women are unemployed, and generally women have a lower education status than men.

In addition to legislative measures, the liberal understanding of sexuality embedded in the Constitution is evident in many other ways. Indeed, the public profiling of sex and sexuality 'marks the post-apartheid landscape' (Posel 2003a:6). Reid & Dirsuweit (2002) argue that gay people had never been as visible in South Africa as they have been in the period of democratic transformation. Access to previously unavailable books, films, and magazines (including pornographic material) and the rapid growth in 'adult sex shops' accompanied the period of democratic transition. In some ways, sexual freedom was ushered in by political freedom (Marks 2002). The Constitution is 'impeccably liberal' (Posel 2003a), and nowhere is this more evident than with respect to gender equality. Yet the very liberal version of 'constitutional sexuality' does not speak to many masculinities of the past. Those masculinities, steeped in violence and authoritarianism, are anathema to the 'gender equality' prescribed by the Constitution and the battery of policies and laws which have been written in its wake. The ideal South African man in this framework is one who is non-violent, a good father and husband, employed and able to provide for his family.

Moreover, the social and sexual context of political transition has been (and remains) a hostile one. The HIV/AIDS epidemic[4] and deepening poverty form the backdrop to the implementation of 'constitutional sexuality'. The social and economic context of political transition was at worst unresponsive to changes in the gender order, and at best a highly contested and fraught set of circumstances in which men and women were being called upon to renegotiate and rearticulate their gender identity and sexuality.

Consequences of constitutional sexuality

It is ironic but not surprising that the liberalisation of sexuality appears to have been accompanied by an increase in gender violence. Violent masculinities of the past have, if anything, become more violent in the present. Some local scholars writing in the fields of criminality, youth and masculinity map old masculinities onto new ones by showing how ex-members of self-defence units have turned to crime. Xaba (2001:7) argues:

> The heroic struggle masculinity of the 1980s has been delegitimized and, without the prospects of jobs and having lost the political status they formerly had, these young men have gone on the rampage, robbing, killing and raping.

Constitutional, legislative and ideological efforts to reconstruct and reward less violent and less patriarchal masculinities in the period of transition have had the unintended consequence of lifting the lid on sexual violence and destabilising old masculinities.

In the last seven years, domestic violence and rape have increased. As many as 50 percent of women in South Africa report experiencing domestic violence, be it physical, emotional, or financial. In 1998, South Africa had the highest per capita rate of reported rape in the world – 115.6 cases per year for every 100 000 of the population. The controversial assumption often made is that only one out of every twenty rapes is reported. If this is the case, then approximately one million rapes occur in South Africa annually (Johnson & Budlender 2002:9). There has also been an increase in child and infant rape, sparking huge public outcry and condemnation. Between January and

December 2000, 13 540 children under the age of 17 were raped, of whom 7899 were under the age of 11 (Smith 2001:328).

Sexual violence against women is only one form of gender-based violence which is on the increase. According to Reid & Dirsuweit (2002:21), homophobic violence is also rising, increasingly involving sexual assault and rape. These authors argue that the increased visibility of homosexuality is partly to blame:

> A more public homosexual landscape has been enabled through the post-apartheid constitution which subverts the heterosexual landscape of Johannesburg. Gay men and lesbians are victimised in response to this subversion.

However, increased sexual violence, coupled with the prominent attention it receives (in the media, from women's organisations and from AIDS organisations), cannot be read as a direct response to gender transformation. The histories of sexual violence and the links between them and current forms of sexual abuse are highly complex and are mediated by many social and psychological factors. But increased sexual violence could usefully be understood as one indicator of South Africa's crisis of sex post-1994 – more specifically as a barometer of the 'crisis of masculinity' and the extent to which masculinities are in disarray. Posel (2003b:12–13) argues:

> The post-apartheid constitution has created the spaces for moral and cultural alternatives in the midst of – rather than by displacing – the taboos of old, as well as provoking new sources of anger and discomfort. The new visibility of sexuality coexists with a combination of angry outbursts and stern objections on the one hand, and resistant silences, denials and refusals, on the other.

Negotiating the boundaries of masculinity post-1994

The research I conducted with young men in Alexandra Township was concerned to understand the ways in which they have made sense of their crises of masculinity, and, in particular, what brought them to an organisation such as Men for Change (MFC). MFC is one of a number of non-governmental organisations established in post-apartheid

South Africa. Its stated objectives are (1) to educate men on the negatives of gender socialisation and raise men's awareness of community-based organisations; (2) to provide counselling and support for men who have been violent and are prepared to change; and (3) to train men in leadership positions in schools and organisations on gender sensitivity. Established in 1999, MFC is a gender advocacy group and embraces competing gender discourses. On the one hand, men (as reflected in many interviews) speak in repentant and confessional terms, yet on the other hand they are seizing opportunities for change in recognising the bankruptcy of 'old ways of being men'. For MFC, if men are going to make it in contemporary South Africa, then they need to adapt to the 'new gender order'.

Operating from a small office in a community centre in Alexandra, MFC has given counselling to 1770 men over the past five years. Men are referred there by many different sources, including anti-domestic violence groups and churches. Often it is abused women who turn to the organisation for help. 'Women come forward for help and we try to talk to their men' (interview, 13 June 2003). This study was not an organisational one, though. Rather, MFC provided an avenue through which I could begin to research alternative and different masculinities, specifically the following questions: How have men navigated the new gender order, how have they forged new masculinities and of what do these new masculinities consist?

A methodological note

Together with a research assistant (male, black), I conducted 17 formal interviews with men involved in MFC. All the men interviewed were black, lived in Alexandra and were between the ages of 22 and 35. I also held numerous informal discussions with men who worked for the organisation as lay counsellors. I conducted five interviews with social workers, nurses and psychologists located at the Centre for the Study of Violence and Reconciliation Trauma Clinic specifically on their experiences of counselling male victims and perpetrators of violence. Perhaps surprisingly, the race and gender of the interviewers had minimal influence on the interaction with the men. It would not be possible to identify from the written transcripts of the interviews whether they were conducted by myself or by the research assistant. In fact, the social distance between me as a white, middle-class woman and the respondents seemed to facilitate the discussion rather than restrict it. My being an outsider created a non-threatening space in which to converse.

Perceptions of constitutional sexuality

If one of the consequences of constitutional sexuality was to lift the lid on sexual violence, another was to add to men's anxieties about the changing position of women. In interviews, some men commented that they feel threatened by women's improved status and their perception that women have attained equality. They stated (in a manner that projected confusion and alarm) that men's dominant, privileged position has in some way been unseated and undermined as a consequence. Vusi[5] commented thus:

> We are seen as the enemy now. Women are advancing in education, economically. Men feel threatened. I see a lot of women who have gained a lot of confidence in who they are. I know women who provide for themselves now and that threat is actually what may be evoking a lot of violence. It is that strength, it is that threat of knowing that I can no longer hold onto that same position I held, or my father or my brother held. I suppose you could say I feel weaker. I'm not saying the rape is a new thing but it's playing itself out in why men are being more violent. (Interview, 25 April 2002)

Women were thus seen to be usurping roles previously allocated to men, creating uncertainty, insecurity and anxiety. Some men felt redundant. This perception was reinforced by the most recent census data, which indicated that it is African women who have been the greatest beneficiaries of affirmative action in the last five years. Tumi stated:

> You know, the biggest problem facing men today is women. Women are emancipated now. They are much more self-sufficient, they are able to do things for themselves. They don't need us men to survive. You don't even need a man anymore to have children. You need a sperm, yes, but at the end of the day women can survive without men. (Interview, 25 April 2002)

The men's views suggest that life for men post-1994 has changed, and some hold the government firmly responsible. James revealed the ambivalence and ambiguity embedded in many of the narratives: a clear recognition of the need for men to change, but the reluctance to part with male power:

> The challenge is to accept that things are changing, that is for sure. Men say, there is a voice for women, what about us? Some believe that the government is treating women much better … that the government is overdoing it … when women shout the government listens. Change to men is like taking away their privileges. When things change they fear it, I fear it, because they don't know what will be happening. (Interview, 11 June 2002)

Searching for emotional order: seeking to reject violence

Without exception, the men interviewed spoke of the psychological, social and political disorder which is dominating their lives: of being overwhelmed and overtaken by life events, of wanting to make something of themselves in this period of 'new opportunities', and of the tremendous difficulties this entailed.

Their narratives reflected very different crises. Some of the men interviewed were still abusing their partners, while others had been involved in sexual, criminal and gang violence in the past. Some men came to MFC because they were the victims of violence – they were violated by their fathers or witnessed violence against their mothers or siblings. One young man had been sexually harassed by his male employer. All were searching for help, to undo the damage of these experiences.

Eight of the 17 men interviewed had abused their female partners.[6] They spoke openly of beating their girlfriends. Mandla describes his violent relationship with his girlfriend, who had recently laid a charge against him with the police, which she later withdrew:

> There are many things [that brought me to MFC]. I was involved in women abuse. It's not even four weeks since I have been to court. And then my girlfriend is pregnant and I abuse her still. I was under

the influence of liquor. It was on New Year's Day. But we have talked and she withdrew the case. Right now I think I have changed, that I want to change. I am no longer a drunkard. I drink but not too much. I have changed because I realised that this thing is not good. (Interview, 18 March 2003)

Mandla described his experiences in gangs, which he said dominated his life for many years. His involvement ceased because he said he realised the dangers 'of this life', the physical and emotional implications of gang life, and returned to school as a young adult. His narrative reflected conflicting pressures and indeed conflicting masculinities: violence, prowess, having a place in the gang, having many girlfriends – these are behaviours which are all valorised and bring substantial material rewards, but at a cost which he now acknowledges.

I was involved going round and committing crime. I used to carry unlicensed firearms. I am from the gangsters. They call me Bra ['brother'] X. I became a womaniser, but I stopped that because I realised that that was wrong. But as a human being you have to tell yourself that where am I going to end up if I am doing this thing. Then I did manage to matriculate and I stopped being involved with gangsters. I worked for the government. As a human being you have to change. (Interview, 18 March 2003)

Sbu spoke of 'beating girls', but described this as part of a gender order that did not condemn violence. In his experience violating girls was normal; it was a means of gaining and maintaining respect. Like Mandla, Sbu now describes his behaviour as 'wrong':

There was this other girl who confronted me and said there is a group called MFC. You know I used to beat girls, so she was concerned as to why I liked beating girls. But I would say no, she disrespects me, that's why I beat her. But even myself, I never knew what it meant when I said she disrespects me. I did not realise that what I was doing was wrong, that it was a form of violence that I was doing. (Interview, 25 March 2003)

Sam reflected on his relationships in the past and how they have changed. Like Sbu, he described his coercive behaviour as something that was ordinary – it was expected that young men could demand sex from their girlfriends. In talking about his past, he also reflected on the guilt and remorse that he felt. He admitted that his behaviour was tantamount to rape, and said he had apologised to his past girlfriends, even those he had not seen for some time:

> Even today, I still look at myself and say, hey, I'm so proud of myself with the fact that even if I go out with a girlfriend and with the intention that maybe we might go out and then come back and spend a night together, and suddenly she says no, I'm not in the mood to have sex with you, I would immediately accept that and say yes, that there is this thing that whenever a woman says so, you have to respect that. Because, you know, previously there were other relationships that I had where when she says no, I would go even further to say, no, she's actually lying. She wants to say yes. So, I had to influence her somehow and later on I even feel guilty. After some workshops I have been through I sometimes felt so guilty, how many girlfriends have I actually manipulated by persuading them to sleep with me. I realise somehow that I'm also part and parcel of those who are going to be part of the rape of women. (Interview, 13 February 2003)

Respect from family, friends and partners has often been exacted through the use of force. Many of the men's relationships have been structured through violence. Edwin spoke of the pain associated with becoming a man. Being a man has always, he said, been about being able to inflict pain on others and 'take pain yourself':

> Look at this culture of going to mountain school. You are going there to be circumcised and when you come back you will be a man. So what makes you a man? A pain makes you a man. You had a pain in order for you to be a man, so everything you do should be by force, by pain. But you can't be a man now by force. You need to make yourself understood and not by forcing things. This is the society of Madiba [Mandela]. (Interview, 24 March 2003)

These narratives offer testimony to the pervasiveness and normality of violence (particularly against women), which makes their desire to be non-violent, to halt their particular cycle of violence, more striking. Political transition in South Africa, or 'the society of Madiba', has confronted and contested violent masculinities, creating the space for different, non-violent versions of masculinity, which some of these young men are seeking to embrace.

Violent fathers – violent sons

The roots of men's violence were as much psychological as social. Explanations given by the interviewees were multiple and included the violence of the environments in which they grew up; the violence of apartheid, of poverty; the densely populated urban township; and, within this, the violence of their schools. A striking feature of their narratives, however, was the presence of violence in their families. Ten men interviewed spoke of their father's violence when they were growing up, of either witnessing their mothers being beaten or fearing the regular and violent beatings they received themselves. These beatings had left deep scars.

Tshepo graphically described his violent father and the cycle of violence into which he was drawn:

> My father was a very abusive man. I became lost and thought this is the way of life. Abusing is the way of life; then you leave that life. I began to realise the effect on me of that abuse at home. It is very difficult; because if you are not careful you are going to end up being violent because these people violate you. (Interview, 7 March 2003)

David described the extreme beatings he used to receive as a child, the effects of which he still feels today. He said he was determined never to repeat the actions of his father:

> We as children, when we were growing up we were beaten up; you do something wrong, even something stupid, we would all get beaten up. At one point I was beaten so badly that I had to lie at school that I fell from a bench, whereas I was beaten by my dad. It is a reminder that if I have kids I must never do that to them. (Interview, 7 February 2003)

Being abused as children influenced respondents' relationships with other men and women and, unsurprisingly, shaped their views of fatherhood. To be feared as a partner or as a father was one of the worst of the effects of violence that men were seeking to shed. Child abuse, particularly infant rape, has received extensive media coverage recently in South Africa, where 'the spotlight of shame [has focused] squarely on men' (Posel 2003b:16). Posel (2003b) argues that the reputations of the family and fatherhood have been sullied, and that the public and some within government have identified and marked them as the source of moral decay. This discourse had not escaped the young men interviewed. They spoke of being viewed with suspicion by family members and friends reluctant to 'leave their children under their supervision'. They spoke of the hurt they felt at being lumped together with 'those men that rape'.

Such a view was captured by Charles, who spoke poignantly of the importance of fatherhood in his future, of being a father that his wife and children could trust, admire, respect and not fear:

> My future has to be financially secure. And to have a relationship, where she'll understand I'm a different man. That she'll understand our kids are safe with me. And whenever I sit with my daughter, I can hug her. I want that, to be able to reach out to my kids, and not be judged. (Interview, 13 February 2003)

Sam expressed similar sentiments:

> Well, in my future, to be honest, I'm looking at a life where I'll be in a position to take care of my son or daughter, be able to share and express myself very well. I would like my son to look at me as somebody that he can call a friend. Because we as young people are not in good relations with our own parents. (Interview, 4 February 2003)

Present in all these narratives was the interviewees' desire to have an 'alternative' experience of being a man – an experience different from their fathers', uncles' or elder brothers'. For these men, the costs of hegemonic masculinity – certainly of male violence – outweighed the benefits. Indeed, all explicitly rejected the use of violence.

But none spoke of the 'process of change' glibly. Rather, achieving a different version of masculinity represented a tremendous challenge, an ongoing struggle between traditional masculinities of the past and the demands of being a 'modern man' who is in control, respectable, rational, and responsible – the very expectations embodied in liberal constitutional sexuality.

One marker of this struggle between old and new was found when the interviewees talked of trying to form new (modern) relationships with women. This particular negotiation has always been circumscribed by gendered and generational parameters – traditional notions of what it means to be a man involve a 'natural order of gender relations in the family' (Sideris 2003:3). Thami described the clash of cultures and generations very clearly:

> Because of where we come from and the culture that we have – it's not an easy thing. I'm a Zulu and I am strong and she a woman – it's traditional … traditions encroach into the modern life … It's the modern life, learning that men and women can help each other. Sometimes it clashes because it is a matter of pride and you use the cultural thing. But you can try and say, if tradition and modern life can come together, how are we going to mix it and make it work? (Interview, 7 February 2003)

Their desire to be modern men and modern fathers was evident when respondents spoke of their dreams and aspirations. Yet their hopes for the future also reflected the deprivations of the past. Most spoke of wanting respect and responsibility, of wanting education, a home and a car, to own a business, to become entrepreneurs, to have a wife and a family – to embark on a life of 'domestic respectability and conformity' (McDowell 2002). Their male role models were very often ordinary men in the community who had 'made good'.

These young men are seeking to reject the gender order they grew up with, an order enforced by their fathers and accepted by their mothers, and fundamentally based on patriarchy in a social and economic context that was repressive, violent and impoverished. They are striving to be modern fathers, modern men, modern subjects. For them, the transition to democracy in South Africa represents both opportunities and obstacles. Democracy created the space for 'men to change' and the Constitution established the legislative and public framework that demand that they do so. Older versions of masculinity are at odds with newer ones, with very unsettling results.

Jabulani said, 'Before 1994, a real man was one who beat, now a real man is one who understands' (interview, 11 June 2002).

The young men's vision of a new masculinity that is non-violent, monogamous, modern, responsible, and built on respect (for themselves and of others for them) contrasts sharply with other very visible expressions of township masculinity, perhaps more hegemonic ones. Drawing on their research amongst young men in the same township, Selikow et al. (2002) argue that men have multiple sexual partners in order to achieve masculine status, prestige and popularity. There is little doubt that this version of masculinity has strong currency. But the somewhat new and alternate views expressed by the young men's narratives in this discussion represent a very different sense of manhood. And as it is residual and embryonic, it is a version which is often silent. Recently though, more vocal expressions (from men) of opposition to domestic violence and rape have been heard. Thousands of men recently participated in a march in Johannesburg against women and child abuse. Their statement of intent read: 'We, men and fathers of Gauteng, stand together to speak out against oppression of children and women. We stand in solidarity against domestic violence' (*Gauteng News* 2003).

Challenges of change

Meeting the demands of constitutional sexuality is challenging. While a growing number of organisations condemn domestic violence and urge men, for example, to practice safer sex and 'be faithful', the dominant form of masculinity, particularly in urban townships, is often the reverse. Selikow et al. (2002:7) found that, among their interviewees:

> In Alex[andra], the highest compliment is to be called an *ingagara*. The hegemonic construct of the *ingagara* refers to a male who is well respected and who is considered macho. [He] is associated with having many girlfriends, an expensive car and fashionable clothes.

Attempting to be something other than the 'macho' norm is often met with surprise and disdain not only by men but by women as well. James commented:

> Sometimes I feel silly. I date, try to get to know the person, try to get to like them, try to go slowly with women but sometimes I find that they are not prepared for that change, so maybe they don't hang around. (Interview, 11 July 2002)

Recent research on masculinity in Soweto shows that men who do not drink, smoke and hang out with other men are referred to in insulting and belittling terms. 'Terms like *ibhari*, *cheese boy*, *umzalwana* are very derogative and they are often associated with how a man behaves in the presence of others and also his lifestyle in general' (Mfecane 2002:5). Similarly, Selikow et al. (2002:11) have shown that the opposite of an *ingagara* is an *isithipa* (sissy or dumb person):

> An *isithipa* does not have many girlfriends, does not wear fashionable clothes, does not do crime and wants to achieve educationally. These traits are not seen as desirable in popular township culture and an *isithipa* would not be particularly desirable to many women who often desire material benefits which an *isithipa* cannot offer ...

Negotiating relationships with women that are framed by new and different versions of masculinity can pose difficult challenges. As Charles said:

> I need to be in control of my emotions, when to say no and when to say yes. How do I talk with women now, how do I say, I don't have money and I can't buy you this? How do I get in control of this, because I am confused about it?' (Interview, 24 March 2003)

Resisting the pressures that women place on men to conform to more hegemonic notions of masculinity is clearly very difficult. The consequences of failing to provide, for example, can be extremely harsh, as Thabo describes:

> I had failures but right now I am striving towards my goal. I want a better life, to be employed and to stay in my own house with my wife and children. The reason is that at the present moment my girlfriend is pregnant so I don't want her to end up having an affair with someone just because that person is working and my child would be raised by a stepfather. (Interview, 4 February 2003)

The men interviewed expressed tremendous difficulty in coming to terms with their own violence and different practices of manhood in an environment which is unreceptive, defensive and intolerant.

> All I can say is that it doesn't come easily. Who I am, where I am going, what I am doing. I am not sure of this. But I don't see myself as abnormal. It is what you want for yourself, for your children. My father said, 'You became the copy of me. This is something terrible that you copied from me, so I am glad that you stick to your ground to say I can't continue, this is wrong'. (Interview, 11 June 2002)

Yet in spite of this environment, most rejected the use of force in favour of understanding and negotiation. Sizwe spoke of this:

> I am a Tswana-speaking person, and in Setswana we say, 'A coward's family never cries'. So when you are a coward, you always run away, you do not harm anyone. So there is no one you are hurting or anything. The minute you start being violent as well then you will have a very bad scar. And that will make you cry. As long as you are 'a coward', you will never hurt someone. (Interview, 20 March 2003)

But, if the fear of being 'cowardly' is an obstacle to change, so too are poverty and unemployment. Half of the men interviewed were unemployed. Others were studying or working in a voluntary capacity in non-governmental organisations. Poverty and unemployment were seen as serious impediments to change, particularly for men, and an unanticipated dimension of post-apartheid South Africa. Political liberation was expected to bring material reward and entitlement, not increased deprivation. The young men interviewed stated that it remains their role to earn and provide for their families and communities – a responsibility they find increasingly intense and daunting in the context of rapidly rising unemployment.

If counselling and support through MFC provided a space for confession and healing for these men, so too did the church. Many of them described themselves as religious, and were actively involved in the work of the church (primarily the Roman Catholic Church), running youth groups, for example. Indeed, many came to know of MFC through their church. Some described their religion as very 'powerful' and as 'providing a sense of purpose', and others spoke of 'being in the hands of God'. It is perhaps unsurprising that religion provides parameters of social and emotional stability in a context of extreme insecurity. For many, the healing power of reflexivity (mediated in part through counselling) acts in tandem with what they see as the healing power of God.

The reflective dimension of informants' narratives of healing and change resonates strongly with Barker's research in Brazil and the USA on alternative masculinity (1998, 2000). His work amongst low-income male youth suggests that certain key experiences have the potential to make young men 'more gender equitable'. These include, for example, their reflecting on the costs of traditional manhood; their constructing a coherent life narrative of themselves as different from most men around them; their having been victims of violence, having witnessed people being victimised or having engaged in violence themselves; and their being able to reflect on the costs of their roles and responsibilities in positive ways (Barker 2000). Conversations with young men in Alexandra reveal some of the features Barker describes. They also echo the findings of ongoing research in the Nkomazi district of Mpumalanga. Writing of men who are older and located in a rural setting, Sideris (2003:17) details male behaviour which is 'different'. She describes a small group of men who have rejected violence, engaged with human and gender rights, performed 'women's work' and relinquished control over family income. These men, she suggests (using Morrell's typology) represent 'progressive responses to social forces that pull in the opposite direction' (2003:17). Hunter's (2003) work on *isoka* masculinity (an *isoka* is a man who is successful with women) provides another contemporary example of new masculinities in South Africa. He argues that *isoka* masculinity, prevalent in the past, is increasingly being questioned by men and women today. His research in KwaZulu-Natal suggests that men are more inclined to see having multiple sexual partners as associated with irresponsibility than success. This, he argues, is partly the result of the AIDS epidemic, where death, which is now so common, has had an inhibiting impact on sexual practices.

Conclusion: new masculinities?

Do the versions of masculinity described in this paper reflect alternative, 'gender-equitable' or more progressive and just expressions of masculinity? Drawing on Messner's work on men's movements in the USA, Morrell (2002) has examined men's collective responses to gender transitions in South Africa. He identifies three categories of responses, those protecting privilege, those responding to a 'crisis of masculinity', and those fighting for gender justice (Morrell 2002:12). The men I interviewed fall into all three categories, although this typology locates them only in the last group. Their sense of male selfhood has been destabilised, and their ideas of what is 'right' for men to do (to be a 'real man') have arguably been changed. And they are making sense of this in a context of competing masculinities both old and new. Situating men as either for or against (or even in between) is too rigid and clear-cut. This research with young men in Alexandra reflects only the views and insights of a small group of men who want and need to be different – different from what they were in the past, different from their fathers, different from many of their peers – young men attempting to reclaim and remake their lives. Embedded in this process is a realisation that past versions of masculinity which may be violent, authoritarian and 'traditional' may represent a 'masculinity which has gone too far' (Hunter 2003:25). Arguably, these masculinities are not gender-equitable, alternative or progressive but rather new embryonic forms of male selfhood vying for space and expression.

There is little doubt that the transition to democracy and the very liberal version of sexuality embodied in the Constitution have had a series of highly contradictory effects. MFC largely owes its very existence to those processes. It is legitimate now for men to embark on a 'reflective' and introspective journey. Old masculinities have been exposed, and the lid on sexual violence has been lifted. Confusion and uncertainty around the nature of masculinity and male sexuality, and the expectations men have of themselves, each other and women are contested and in crisis, giving rise to new notions of manhood.

Acknowledgements

I should like to thank my colleagues at WISER for useful discussions and comments, which have informed this chapter.

Notes

1. The concept of masculinity is used loosely here, starting from the idea of masculinity as achieved – a set of practices (Wetherall and Edley 1999), performative acts (Butler 1990) or ways of 'doing gender' which are related to the social environments in which they occur. Or, as Connell (1995) suggests, masculinity is accomplished through the exploitation of available cultural resources such as the ideologies prevalent in particular societies (Frosh et al. 2002).
2. Alexandra is an old and very impoverished township (established in 1912), densely populated and characterised by high levels of violence.
3. For an excellent discussion on masculinities and their history in South Africa, see Morrell (2001).
4. 'Sub-Saharan Africa is now home to 29.4 million people living with HIV/AIDS. Approximately 3.5 million new infections occurred [in the region] in 2002, while the epidemic claimed the lives of an estimated 2.4 million Africans in the past year' (UNAIDS 2002).
5. The names of all interviewees have been changed to protect their identity.
6. I am not in a position to assess whether this violence has ceased. I have not conducted interviews with their partners or family members. All these interviewees were receiving counselling through MFC.

References

Barker, G. (1998) Non-violent males in violent settings: low income adolescent males in two Chicago neighborhoods. *Childhood: A Global Journal of Child Research*, 5, 4, 437–461.

Barker, G. (2000) Gender equitable boys in a gender inequitable world: reflections from qualitative research and programme development with young men in Rio de Janeiro, Brazil. *Sexual and Relationship Therapy*, 15, 3, 263–282.

Butler, J. (1990) *Gender Trouble.* (Cambridge: Polity).

Connell, R.W. (1995) *Masculinities.* (Cambridge: Polity).

Dowsett, G. (2002) Uncovering the men in men's health: working with desire, diversions and demons. Paper presented at the Wits Institute for Social and Economic Research.

Dworkin, A. (1997) *Life and Death: Unapologetic Writings on the Continuing War against Women.* (London: Virago).

Faludi, S. (1991) *Backlash: The Undeclared War against Women.* (London: Vintage).

Frosh, S., Phoenix, A. and Pattman, R. (2002) *Young Masculinities.* (Hampshire: Palgrave).

Gauteng News. (2003) Newsletter of the Gauteng Provincial Government, April.

Hassim, S. (1999) From presence to power: women's citizenship in a new democracy. *Agenda*, 40, 35–46.

Hunter, M. (2003) Masculinities and multiple-sexual partners in KwaZulu-Natal: the making and unmaking of *isoka*. Paper presented at the *Sex and Secrecy* Conference, University of the Witwatersrand, Johannesburg.

Johnson, L. and Budlender, D. (2002) *HIV Risk Factors: A Review of the Demographic, Socio-economic, Biomedical and Behavioral Determinants of HIV Prevalence in South Africa.* Monograph No 8. (Cape Town: Centre for Actuarial Research, University of Cape Town).

Marks, S. (2002) An epidemic waiting to happen? The spread of HIV/AIDS in South Africa in social and historical perspective. *African Studies*, 61, 1, 13–26.

McDowell, L. (2002) Masculine discourses and dissonances: strutting 'lads', protest masculinity, and domestic respectability. *Environment and Planning D: Society and Space*, 20, 97–119.

Mfecane, S. (2002) Report on an Ongoing Study on Masculinity and HIV/AIDS. (Johannesburg: Perinatal HIV Research Unit, Chris Hani Baragwanath Hospital).

Morrell, R. (ed.) (2001) *Changing Men in Southern Africa.* (London: Zed Books).

Morrell, R. (2002) Men, movement and gender transformation in South Africa. *Journal of Men's Studies*, 10, 3, 309–321.

Posel, D. (2003a) 'Getting the nation talking about sex': reflections on the politics of sexuality and 'nation-building' in post-apartheid South Africa. Seminar paper presented at the Wits Institute for Social and Economic Research.

Posel, D. (2003b) The scandal of manhood: unmaking secrets of sexual violence in post-apartheid South Africa. Paper presented at the *Sex and Secrecy* Conference, University of the Witwatersrand, Johannesburg.

Reid, G. and Dirsuweit, T. (2002) Understanding systemic violence: homophobic attacks in Johannesburg and its surrounds. *Urban Forum*, 13, 3, 99–126.

Selikow, T., Zulu, B. and Cedras, E. (2002) The ingagara, the regte and the cherry: HIV/AIDS and youth culture in contemporary urban townships. *Agenda*, 53, 22–32.

Sideris, T. (2003) Non-violent men in violent communities: negotiating the head and the neck. Paper presented at the Wits Institute for Social and Economic Research.

Smith, C. (2001) *Proud of Me. Speaking out against Sexual Violence and HIV.* (London: Penguin).

UNAIDS (2002) The global HIV/AIDS epidemic 2002–2003. UNAIDS 2002.05CD. (Geneva: United Nations).

Wetherell, M. and Edley, N. (1999) Negotiating hegemonic masculinity: imaginary and psycho-discursive practices. *Feminism and Psychology*, 9, 335–356.

Whitehead, S.M. (2002) *Men and Masculinities*. (Cambridge: Polity).

Xaba, T. (2001) Masculinity and its malcontents: the confrontation between 'struggle masculinity' and 'post-struggle masculinity' (1990–1997). (Morrell 2001:105–124).

8
Male-male sexuality in Lesotho: Two conversations

Marc Epprecht

Context

Basotho men have historically possessed a 'macho' reputation in relation to other African peoples of southern Africa.[1] They have long been reported to be among the toughest, most pain-insensitive workers; the fiercest gangsters; the proudest, most independent-minded nationalists; and the most devoted to idealised patriarchal 'traditions' in the region. They are also known to be among the most incorrigible womanisers, with a cultivated refusal to act upon sexual alternatives to de facto polygyny. Heterosexual promiscuity for men continues to be celebrated by Mosotho men – and bemoaned by Basotho women – in media as diverse as popular travel songs and pseudo-academic studies.[2]

As one might expect from such an assertively masculinist culture, male–male sexual relationships are virtually non-existent in the ethnography. The very first enquiry by the colonial government into traditional Sesotho mores and law (1873) found that 'unnatural crime' was so rare that it had no punishment. Another enquiry in 1907 found that Basotho men were among the least likely of all African groups working at the South African gold mines to practise the male–male sexual relationship known as 'mine marriage' or *inkotshane*. Also, in sharp distinction to the predominantly Xhosa and Zulu criminal gangs in the Johannesburg areas in the 1910s to 1940s who practised a system of male-male sexual relations, Basotho gang members made the sexual exploitation of women central to their gang ethic and organisation. As a protectorate of Britain, Lesotho was meanwhile largely spared from the kind of economic and infrastructural development that is typically associated with 'situational' homosexuality in southern Africa (cosmopolitan cities, same-sex hostels, boarding schools, prisons, Portuguese or Arab traders, a European military or tourist presence, and so on). Even as late as the 1990s, a gay journalist who was specifically looking for evidence of gay life off the beaten tracks of urban southern Africa came up virtually empty-handed in his search when he dropped in on Lesotho (Luirink 2000).

The public performance of masculine sexuality in Lesotho would thus appear at first glance to confirm claims coming from a variety of sources that homosexuality is 'un-African' or a 'white man's disease' that can be resisted with an appropriately patriarchal culture of masculinity.[3] Yet evidence has begun to emerge that not only challenges the implicit stability of heterosexuality among the Basotho, but also causes us to query the assumed relationship between gender identity and sexual practice. Not long after the Basotho were exonerated of *inkotshane* in 1907, for instance, a Sotho-ised version of the word (given as *boukoutchana*) and a sexually ambiguous Mosotho character appeared in a missionary novel about mine life (Junod 1911:254). South African officials as early as 1914 felt that the Basotho were put at serious risk of infection by the practice and recommended swift action to protect the men. Those efforts apparently proved to no avail. By 1941 Basotho at the mines had reportedly not only adopted *inkotshane* as a mass practice but also public cross-dressing and same-sex marriage ceremonies (Epprecht 2004). When asked politely in the mid-1980s, David Coplan's informants freely admitted as much, and also admitted to the attractions of having sex with 'boys' when away from home (Coplan 1994:141). Arthur Blair and John Gay's unpublished study of Basotho childhood and adolescence further noted that practices from the mines were being imported into Lesotho and that as a result, in rural Lesotho in the late 1970s, 'sodomy is very common' (Blair & Gay 1980:109).

That these snippets of information did not enter the realm of public debate in Lesotho can partly be explained by Basotho men's discretion. Colonial officials also seem to have suppressed discussion of the topic, concerned as they were to avoid any scandals that might compromise the smooth flow of Basotho labour to the South African mines. Yet discretion and denial continued after independence from the British, even in professional academic circles. The historian Tshidiso Maloka, for example, conceded that mine marriage may have taken place among other Africans but thought that it 'was an impossibility for most if not all Basotho migrants' (Maloka 1995:306). Most other scholars simply avoided enquiry altogether or, like J.M. Mohapeloa, characterised male-male sexuality in highly pejorative terms (Mohapeloa 2000:273). This continues even to the present, notwithstanding the by now ample evidence that the practice exists. Oppong & Kalipeni (2004), notably, do not specifically refer to the Basotho. However, in a sweeping critique of ethnocentrism or racism in Western scholarship on HIV and AIDS, they too attempt to shoot down calm discussion about even the possibility of bisexuality among any African men.

The Mosotho male's enduring reputation for heterosexual virility, in other words, owes its existence at least in part to the blindness, myth-making and self-censorship of heterosexist or homophobic Western and Western-trained scholars. Tellingly, as something of an exotic construction, this reputation commands only lukewarm loyalty among the Basotho themselves. Indeed, secrets that contradict the relentlessly virile profile are actually not all that difficult to uncover for those who care to look. Even I – straight, white, and non-Mosotho – was able to find a small but vibrant and uninhibited community of self-identified gay Basotho men less than 24 hours after beginning to ask around.

This article focuses on that brief, non-systematic research experience. Most basically, I want to draw attention to the existence of gay and bisexual Basotho men and to allow them to share their own insights into same-sex sexuality and masculinity in contemporary Lesotho.[4] Perhaps this will satisfy those scholars and activists who strangely persist in claiming that there is 'not a shred of evidence' (Oppong & Kalipeni 2004:53) of homosexuality or bisexuality in Africa.

I would like also to promote reflection upon the importance of sexuality studies to our understanding of other gendered social relations, including race, class, and ethnicity, both as these relations play out in African societies today and as they have been structured into professional academic enquiry in southern Africa. Kalipeni et al. (2004) and Lyons & Lyons (2004) are among many to have made the point that we need to understand better how ostensibly scientific or neutral discourses have historically been imbued with misleading assumptions about African sexuality. Correcting these, or at least reflecting upon them, acquires some urgency when we hope that our scholarship can be applied to address contemporary development frustrations (in general) and HIV/AIDS (in particular). Lesotho needs help on both scores. According to UNAIDS, Lesotho has slipped in recent years to become one of the poorest countries in the world, has very high levels of gender violence, and has an HIV prevalence rate of an estimated 31 percent of the adult population, making it among the very worst hit countries in the world. The last fact alone underscores the point that the time has surely passed for Africanist scholars to shield African men from truths about their sexual behaviour and attitudes. Those who care about the well-being of the Basotho, or indeed any group of people, do a clear disservice when they shy away from the honest discussion of sexuality in all its forms, whether out of misplaced respect for masculinist African 'traditions' and Western academic conventions, or from their own queasiness around the topic.

Inspiration and setting

In 1988 T. Dunbar Moodie published his ground-breaking article on male sexuality in the mine compounds in South Africa. His thesis was that male African migrant workers had engaged in sexual relationships with younger male migrants in large numbers while they were at the mines. They did so in part to protect themselves from expensive and risky sexual encounters with scarce and often diseased and demanding town women. Sex with males allowed the men to save their money and preserve their health so that they could eventually return home as respected, heterosexually married and virile members of a patriarchal community. Patrick Harries corroborated much of this argument with his publication of a similar study of Tsonga or Shangaan men at the mines (Harries 1994). Moodie's subsequent book and another article upon the vicissitudes of male sexuality then linked the rise and decline of mine marriages to changes in the political economy. He posited that African migrant workers today no longer have sex with males, in part because their sense of masculinity is no longer rooted in the rural areas (Moodie 1994:2001).

The first scholarly response to Moodie's and Harries's work as it pertained to the Basotho came from the anthropologist David Coplan (1994). As with the play *The Hill* (Mda 1990) and the novel *Teba*

(Mokhoane 1995), Coplan's informants confirmed that Moodie's claims about widespread and relatively non-controversial male–male sexual relationships applied to Basotho men as they did to the Mpondo or other African migrant mine-workers. Mda, Mokhoane and Coplan imply, moreover, that Moodie was wrong to portray these relationships as strictly a thing of the past. Two documentary videos and recent gay journalism also suggest that male–male sex remains a contemporary phenomenon at the mines (Edkins 1992, Alberton & Reid 2000, Mkhize 2001). It may no longer be a 'system', but it has not entirely withered away as structural conditions changed. They suggest, moreover, that the miners' sex life may not be as hermetically sealed off from more modern forms of gay sexuality as has tended to be assumed by academic researchers.

All of the above reflects the invigoration of gender studies in the West by queer critiques of Marxist and feminist research.[5] Above all, queer theorists have noted how homophobia, or more commonly, heterosexist assumptions and blind spots, weakened or betrayed the analytic power of the older radical approaches to social science research. Coplan tacitly conceded to this by admitting to his initial reluctance to delve into the topic of male–male sexuality. Others have been less willing or able to reflect upon their personal discomfort or ignorance around homosexuality. Indeed, in one of the first and most ambitious attempts to apply queer theory to African material, Rudi Bleys (1995) showed how the early ethnography about Africa was imbued with the European authors' unexamined anxieties around gender and class conflict in Europe. The creation of the stereotype of a sodomy-free black Africa, he argued, served bourgeois white male interests at least as much as it reflected the diverse and often contradictory empirical evidence from Africa. This early stereotype then coincided with the rise of 'respectable' African opinion, to be further reified through the politics of African nationalism in the mid- to late 20th century (see, for example, Dunton 1989, Holmes 1994). To use Lyons & Lyons's apt metaphor, the African evidence was initially conscripted to serve European and American debates but has since been drafted to elite African agendas. That the stereotype still persists today even in sexuality studies and in critical AIDS discourse is a remarkable testimony to its power (Achmat 1993, Phillips 2004).[6]

The subjectivity of Africanist scholars who pride themselves on their scientific or objective approach and tools cannot, in other words, be understood without reference to the sometimes subtle contests around masculinity in Europe and America, contests in which homophobia emerged as a fundamental characteristic of the hegemonic gender roles (Fone 2000). This is manifest in academic conventions around professionalism that for a long time tended to define sexuality as non-historical, non-political, unknowable and basically uninteresting (see, for example, Lyons & Lyons 2004 with respect to anthropology). Same-sex sexuality tended to be regarded as even more marginal, freakish, and professionally demeaning to talk about. Yet such conventions served to buttress or naturalise a particular construction of masculinity that was as alien to Africa as tea and crumpets. As queer scholars are now beginning to uncover, African societies in fact historically allowed for and at times celebrated a wide range of same-sex behaviours with sometimes important ramifications to the political economy, for example ritual gender inversions and spirit possession as means to buttress political authority (see Murray & Roscoe 1998, Epprecht 2004).

The existence of a hidden, indeed mostly unconscious agenda in the early Africanist scholarship holds enormous implications for African studies today, for our understanding both of the durability of old stereotypes around African masculinity, and of why some intellectuals and politicians protest so violently against challenges to those stereotypes. Undoubtedly, much of the emerging queer scholarship and journalism in Africa has been flawed and overeager in its revisionism, my own contributions included. The reaction against it, however, has at times exceeded the bounds of what could be considered reasonable critique.[7] Bleys's work suggests that the occasional visceral hostility to queer research by scholars working in older academic traditions and (more commonly) their apathy toward pursuing queer lines of enquiry is reflective of a specific culture of masculinity that is entrenched or implicit in the dominant expressions of Africanist research. That culture remains an active and corrosive influence.[8]

My own belated engagement with these ideas came about by happenstance. In May 1995 I took up a position in the History Department at the University of Zimbabwe. Right around that time, the chancellor of the university and president of the country, Robert Mugabe, began to make a series of speeches in which he vilified gays and lesbians as 'un-African'. I began checking the historical evidence from Zimbabwe to test what intuitively seemed to be a deeply implausible claim. I also determined to revisit the sources that I had used in an earlier project to check for hitherto unsuspected heterosexist assumptions in my research. This took me to Lesotho in March 1996. There, in addition to discovering Chris Dunton's brilliant analysis (1990) of the portrayal of homosexual lust among Basotho migrants in *Blanket Boy's Moon* (Lanham & Mopeli-Paulus 1953), I came upon Maloka's flat denial of that very lust. Once again, I was inspired to test a seemingly implausible assertion against such empirical evidence as could be found.

As noted above, that test proved remarkably easy to do. An anonymous article had appeared a few years earlier in the Maseru newsletter, *Work for Justice,* arguing the case for social acceptance of homosexuals in the name of human rights. I simply called up the editor, explained my problem, and asked if he could give my name and telephone number to the author. That evening, I received a call from Gerard Mathot, a Dutch educationalist who had been living in Lesotho for many years. He offered to take me to a gay-friendly bar to see for myself how 'impossible' it was for Basotho men to have sex with each other. The next day we met, struck up an immediate rapport, and then travelled to an informal settlement on the outskirts of the capital city. Down a bumpy dirt road we went, thence to turn into the courtyard of a bottle store attached to a set of one-room 'apartments'. Gerard introduced me to the owner, 'M,' a Mosotho in his mid-40s, who also happened to be a flamboyantly 'out' queen. I explained my research in Zimbabwe and how I had just read that people like 'M' could hardly exist. He laughed and invited me to return the next day to meet some of his friends so that we could set the record straight (so to speak).

I did so, on foot and armed with a pen and paper. By light of day, the area looked indistinguishable from the rest of the periurban sprawl that creeps up the jumble of rocks and over the erosion gulleys that surround Maseru. The bottle store itself, with its corrugated roof, concrete floor, rudimentary furniture, and little black ghetto blaster, could probably be replicated in ten thousand townships around southern Africa. On the way in, I saw goats, cattle, and a flock of egrets. In the courtyard, chickens scratched. Women with their infants were carrying out various womanly tasks. The language was Sesotho, although patrons kindly accommodated my lack of fluency in the language by switching to English after I had introduced myself. This place was clearly not, in other words, a slick gay bar in a cosmopolitan centre. I was the only *lekhooa* (white) there.

'M' greeted me fulsomely, then took me to a table in the courtyard to meet 'P'. I bought us a round of Lion, the clear beer preferred by Basotho men because of its reputed strength and manliness. I described the situation in Zimbabwe and how I hoped my research could help counter the homophobic statements of certain Zimbabwean politicians. They agreed that the situation sounded bad in that country and offered to answer any questions if indeed I thought it might help. I said that stranger things had happened, so you never know, it might. They agreed that I could jot down notes as we chatted and that I was welcome, as a teacher, to use the insights I gained. We then chatted for a couple of hours until the light began to fade and I had to make my way home.

In the following section I reproduce the interview-like part of these conversations – the eloquence and self-confidence of my informants invite that respect. I make no claims about methodological rigour in this, and indeed, I suspect real anthropologists will be embarrassed by my efforts.[9] On the other hand, conventional standards of enquiry on masculine sexuality in Lesotho have not been notably impressive. My convivial, Lion-fuelled conversation may actually be an improvement, at least as a starting point in deconstructing some of the more dangerous masks of Basotho masculinity.

'M'

'M,' it turns out, had been to university and had travelled internationally. His lisp and effeminate demeanour were 'sissy' in a stereotypically Western manner. They could in no way be seen as an exaggerated or mirror image of Basotho femininity. On the contrary, in all my time in Lesotho, I have never seen an actual Mosotho female behave in any way even remotely like such florid, yet demure, coquettishness. Yet if he were not a typical Mosotho by class or gender identity, 'M' nonetheless grew up in an underprivileged rural household. Moreover, he had opted out of a Western-style gay life that his level of education and travel experience potentially afforded in South Africa or beyond. He struck me as happy and self-confident in his life, managing a small saloon that catered overwhelmingly to working class and unemployed Basotho. He was just a bit on the chubby side.

> ME: I guess my first question comes from the rumour that homosexuality among Basotho men started at the mines in South Africa long back. Nowadays, so they say, it has more or less gone away because of different factors like there are more women in town than before and so there is no need for men to have sex with men. Have you ever heard anything about that?
> M: I don't know much about the mines, I never was there. I do know that there are some men who travel to the mines to earn money. To this very day, say, on the weekend, they just go there and charge a certain amount. Then they return to here, perhaps with some fancy things from town. And when the money runs out, they go back. The men there are willing to pay.
> ME: What do they pay for, exactly?
> M: They sometimes demand anal sex but this is a new thing, maybe only since about two years ago. (Shudders). I don't like it myself, it's dirty, it can hurt and tear. Ugh.
> ME: You say anal sex is a new thing? Then what would they do before?
> M: Between the thighs, of course, as our grandfathers did. Buttocks up, or buttocks down. You should try it (patting me on the thigh flirtatiously).
> ME: Mmm, no thanks. In fact, I have a wife.
> M: But she is not here!
> ME: Well no, but you know, I am really square.
> M: Shame. You can always change your mind.
> ME: You are right about that. But please do tell me more. What you are telling me is really making me wonder about other things I've been reading. Like, when you say your grandfathers did that, do you mean that men desiring to have sex with other men is not something really new? You don't blame the whites, yourself?
> M: Maybe it came from the mines, maybe it came from the whites, but really I doubt it. It just comes to us, one generation after the next. Of course I like white men ...

ME: But you don't blame them for your gayness?

M: No, that comes from inside. I think you know that.

ME: Yes, but it's good to hear you say that as a Mosotho. Other people may be surprised that such things could happen in Sesotho culture.

M: Although I am not saying that it [male–male sex] doesn't change. In fact it can change as the culture is changing. The culture changes, as you know. We are becoming more modern. So in the past it used to be just feeling [lust, the desire to have an orgasm regardless of who the partner was]. But there is love now, there is love.

ME: And yourself, how did it come to you, I mean, the knowledge that you were a gay person?

M: Me? It was just there ever since I was a young child. I looked girlish and I felt different from what I was supposed to be. Even when I was two or three years old I always played with the girls. Then I became a herd boy, which is what boys must do in our Sesotho culture. Other boys took me as a girl. They jumped me and poked me. I started to like it – there was nothing to do but learn to like it. Even now I still like it.

ME: What did your family say?

M: (shrugs) My uncle observed me with my boyfriend one time when I was a teenager. He had known it at the mines and he asked my cousin, 'What's this? I thought that thing was only for the mines.' So he was surprised that it was happening here in Lesotho. I do not think he was condemning it, but then we never talked directly.

ME: So when you say there is love now, do you mean men really prefer to have sex with men and have emotional ties as well as simply coming on, or in, somebody?

M: That is true. Look at all these handsome boys, they like it here.

ME: Is everybody here gay then?

M: (laughs) No, no.

ME: But some of you are. Like yourself, so out! Don't you worry that there might be a reaction against such things as I was telling you is happening in Zimbabwe? Do you feel society is now approving or disapproving of people who come out as gays?

> M: No, people don't mind us. See that one there? He's big, oh my! Once he and another of the boys were necking, mmm, mmm, mmm, right here. The women and children just laughed. In the old days you would never see that.
> ME: But outside of here? In town? Do you ever get mockery or experience threats or even gay-bashing?
> M: I have never experienced violence myself. Even when I ask a straight man in a bar if he would like to have sex with me, there is no reaction against it.
> ME: Really? You are lucky then. In my country, to try to pick up a straight man might result in a serious beating.
> M: I'm sorry. (At this point, 'M' tried to convince me once again that I might enjoy a little cuddle with him more than I thought. When I hesitated, he shrugged, then politely took his leave to return to tending the bar. I moved over to join 'P'.)

'P'

'P' was a quiet, self-effacing man of about 50 years. His English was not as polished as that of 'M', and his life experiences had been more parochial. Still, he was clearly not a 'typical' Mosotho in that his father had been a policeman with a good regular salary and no need to leave the country to earn money to pay for his son's high school education and marriage. 'P' conformed, in his demeanour and attire, to the picture of a healthy, handsome, heterosexual Mosotho man. In no way did he appear to be 'degraded' or having lost 'self-respect and sense of responsibility,' as Mohapeloa (2000:273) would have us believe is the outcome of homosexual relationships.

> ME: So, 'P', what of your own family? Do they know that you are a homosexual?
> P: My parents and my children, they know it. But it is not because I told them. This is my father, right here. (He introduces me to a youthful-looking, cheerful man, whose level of inebriation unfortunately precludes much more than an exchange of greetings and banalities.)
> ME: And when did you know yourself that you were gay?

P: Long back. I began to realise myself when I was about ten years old. It looks like the manner that homosexuality comes into a man is the same with most men: playing with girls and imitated mannerisms. I used to play with girls and they liked me very much. I did not know that I was also handsome, so much that some older boys in my village used to kiss me romantically like if I was a girl.

ME: Your parents knew this? How did they explain such a thing? What did they do?

P: My parents thought it was caused by not looking after cattle, sheep and other animals, which most boys do, but since my father was a policeman, I did not. They then decided to let me grow up with a relative's family in the mountains. I tried the boys there, but they are stiff [that is, dogmatically heterosexual]. It was boring and I fought to go back to Roma, my real home. I then went to St Thomas boarding school in Mafeteng where I fell in love with one older boy, who was about ten years older. We used to eat together, hide in darkness, fondling each other and he used to have sex with me between the thighs. It continued for three years, after which we went to different schools.

ME: Would you describe that as a love affair?

P: Yes. It is nice when this is done in love. It brings such passion to the couple.

ME: So you yourself don't blame not herding cattle or the mines as the cause of homosexual feelings?

P: Of course not. It is done at the mines, that is true, but I still believe this is done because of loneliness, just like in the prisons. Some men happen to adopt it permanently, why? Because it is fascinating.

ME: Yet I understand that you married a woman.

P: That is true. I tried very hard to do the proper thing by my family although my feelings were different.

ME: Can you explain?

P: I had girlfriends but not because of my own desire but mostly for show to my friends. But finally I was nagged and nagged into marriage. That irritated me but I had to accept it. What else can you do? Here in Lesotho, without children, who will support you when you get old?

ME: And so you married …
P: Yes, and I now have two children. 'M', maybe he told you, is very worried not to have children. He tried to have a husband but the man ran away, so now he is alone.
ME: Then what did your wife say when she learned?
P: We had a good marriage. She understood me. As I was fulfilling my obligations to her then she accepted that I had this need. In fact, she noticed that I was not able to be excited sexually with her, although we had children.
ME: Is this then a common thing? Is it a secret thing?
P: I know that many men who come here [to this bar for sex] are married. Their wives know. In fact their wives don't like me. Sometimes they shout at me, but I just shout back. Then we get to understand each other.
ME: Do you mean that there are straight men who come here not knowing it is a gay bar?
P: But as I said, this is my father. Do you think this is a gay bar? And these young children?
ME: No, no, what I mean is that there are definitely more gay people here than one usually sees in Lesotho. So my question is: do some straight men come here not knowing about that? Or do they know and prefer to have sex with men even though they are married?
P: Some men don't know at first, that is very true. They think I am a woman until … then they know. They do it, even though they may be surprised. Then they come the second time, the third time, and they like it.
ME: So do you find that these men are also really gay or bisexual, though they do not admit it?
P: In fact there are lots of gay men in Lesotho, but most of them suppress themselves. They do not want to come out, even if they feel themselves attracted to other men. We also have high government officials who are gay and some of my best friends too.
ME: So they come here?
P: Sometimes, as I said. But at M's joint you meet mostly his sissy friends. Personally I do not like those. Real men fascinate me, especially when I can play the part of a female.

ME: Do you know if some of these are the same men who travel to the mines and that that is where they learned the practice?

P: Maybe. I have heard that at TEBA [The Employment Bureau of Africa, the recruitment centre for migrant workers for South Africa], agents could recruit a certain number of underage boys, illegally, the prettiest-looking ones, who can go there to the mines to become wives. But really, we have a word in Sesotho for this, which makes me think it is not from the mines but has always been here. Our grandfathers did it.

ME: May you tell me the word? The missionaries who wrote your dictionaries somehow failed to include it.

P: (whispering) The word is *maotoane*, although this means between the thighs, not through the anus.

ME: And does that mean the Basotho do not go for anus-style?

P: (shrugs) There is no Sesotho word for it. Of course this is not something we talk about. Even when men do sex with women, they won't be giving such details. Those are really private for the lovers. Personally, though, I am fully accepting myself and I am enjoying it. I am not ashamed to tell you that since 1981, when I temporarily separated from my wife, until now I have never had the taste of a woman and I vow I will never as long as boys are there. I mostly like to fuck, anal or between the thighs (this is called 'in the passage' here). Interestingly, sometimes I like to be fucked by these manly men I have talked about before.

ME: And so these manly men don't object to fucking another man?

P: Not really, no. It's just feeling [lust], it's animalistic. I myself sometimes have such feeling. What I mean is that sometimes it is done through lust, or when one is lonely. You sometimes imagine/think of someone who thrills you and immediately you feel an erection, which can drive you to pick-ups.

ME: Do you feel safe here, as a gay man?

P: It is a good place. You might find me here almost every day. It makes me sad to hear what you have said about Zimbabwe. By the way, do you have any lesbians in Zimbabwe?

ME: Not many, I don't think. And you, do you have any here in Lesotho?

P: Plenty!

Conclusion

Gay Basotho men offer hitherto uninterrogated perspectives upon the dominant culture of masculinity in Lesotho. Their testimony, indeed their very existence, calls into question some of the most deeply-held assumptions about gender and sexuality in the region. Clearly, more thorough research needs to be done here. I would suggest that there is some urgency to this, not only because the toll from AIDS is growing so relentlessly, but also due to the risk that Robert Mugabe-esque forms of homophobic nationalism could emerge in Lesotho to close down research opportunities.[10] In the meantime, I would like to draw the following tentative conclusions.

First, gay Basotho men make it clear that they did not require lessons from foreigners to realise their preference for sex with males, although they do tacitly concede that modern innovations like the mines, like boarding schools, and like good highways have made the actualisation of their preference in mutually agreeable (non-violent) ways more possible than was likely the case under precolonial conditions.

Second, gay Basotho men provide the shred of evidence of bisexuality (or LGBT or MSM, however one chooses to describe it) that true believers in the imperative of heterosexual virility for African men have denied. This raises the possibility that HIV/AIDS in the region may not be transmitted by unprotected heterosexual sex as overwhelmingly as is generally assumed. If bisexuality or casual male–male sexuality exists even in Lesotho, where gender difference is so pronounced, then positing it elsewhere in Africa (see, for example, Aina 1991) is probably also warranted. This is not to suggest that MSM should suddenly unseat the priority given to addressing young women's vulnerability to infection by heterosexual intercourse. It is to say, however, that anything that helps to pry open 'secrets' about African masculinities is likely, ultimately, to be of value in reducing those women's vulnerability to infection by men.

Third, gay Basotho men give remarkable testimony to the ability of men to say one thing but to do another, that is, to perform a public masculine persona while engaging in a private sexuality that seemingly contradicts that persona. Basotho men are certainly not unique in this respect. However, the apparent frequency with which self-identified 'normal' Basotho men 'mistakenly' or opportunistically have sex with gays suggests that there is less internalised stigma to the act than is typically encountered in the West. Indeed, the possibility of straight men's unspoken (and plausibly deniable) preference for such 'mistakes' suggests that Basotho men's sense of masculine identity may owe less to their actual sexual behaviour than is the case for men in the West. In the West, heterosexuality is not only expected as the dominant public performance but is enforced through internalised homophobia. In Lesotho, by contrast, despite some mention of 'stiffness' about same-sex sexuality in the most isolated mountain areas, my informants attest to straight men and youths who are apparently untroubled by having sex with males. The relative lack of homophobia as a comprehensive underpinning of the dominant discourse of Basotho masculinity is particularly striking to anyone who came of age as a boy in, for example, a North American school.

A study of informal marriages among the diamond-diggers in the far uplands of Lesotho provides insight into an analogous flexibility around gender roles and sexuality that might help us understand the point above. Motlatsi Thabane (1995) describes how male and female diggers formed temporary marriages that would have been utterly scandalous in more traditional settings. In the freezing and isolated circumstances at the diggings, however, they were accepted as a necessary adaptation of culture. 'Given that the diggers were part of a society which took unkindly to extra-marital relationships, the extent of sympathy and rational view towards these liaisons is remarkable,' Thabane observes, concluding that 'there is nothing shameful about living together as man and wife for practical purposes' (1995:107). Indeed, social condemnation where it occurred was not directed against those who so cohabited, but against those who seemed openly to prefer it. Appearances, rather than actual practices, carried the greater weight.

This is not to deny that Sesotho culture can be oppressive to people who do not conform to heteronormative expectations. It should, however, make us question the assumption that 'modern' or 'Western' is necessarily more liberal or tolerant of sexual difference than 'primitive' or 'traditional', as Kendall (1999) has so eloquently shown with respect to female–female sexuality in Lesotho. 'M' and 'P' were clearly not traditional Basotho. But they did live openly gay lives in a community that was relatively less Westernised and more underdeveloped than the norm for the region. They sympathised with their less fortunate brothers and sisters in more developed Zimbabwe. This suggests that there may be good potential to develop effective sexual rights campaigns that take an alternative cultural route to those pioneered (with mixed success) in the West.

Finally, gay Basotho men's presence and approachability in Lesotho give insight into how the dominant culture of masculinity there has been cultivated by academic researchers. With rare exceptions, the latter have not shown much interest in questioning the stereotypes, ideals, and boasts about the heterosexual virility of Basotho men, notwithstanding that that masculinity so clearly and directly produces injustice and oppression against Basotho women. Academic research has also clearly served to buttress racist, capitalist, and patriarchal structures more widely in the region. Scholars' failure to critically assess easily accessible and long-standing contradictory evidence about Basotho masculinity and sexuality is thus striking. It would appear to confirm the queer critique of how heterosexism and homophobia have been structured into conventional academic discourse. To put it another way, Africanist 'macho' is implicated in the construction of African 'macho.'

This particular construction of masculinity today evidently fuels the devastating spread of heterosexually transmitted diseases, including HIV. Perhaps as the voices of African gays are heard, this reluctance will be made more visible, and closer attention will be paid to the ways that oppressive and unhealthy masculinities are reproduced over the generations. At the risk of overstating my case, the evidence here supports the argument that I have made elsewhere. The so-called invisibility of non-normative sexuality in Africa is a cultural artefact that was partially created and conscripted to serve in struggles around hegemonic, modern masculinity. To stretch the metaphor, the time has come for that conscript to go AWOL. We could then begin to design sex education and other gender, health, and human rights interventions that better resonate with lived experience in communities in Africa that are heavily affected by HIV and gender violence.

Notes

1 Research for this chapter was supported by the University of Zimbabwe and the Social Sciences and Humanities Research Council of Canada. Special thanks to John Gay, Judy Gay and Gerhard Mathot for facilitating it in Lesotho, as well as to my informants. An earlier version was published under the same title in *Journal of Men's Studies*, 10, 3 (2002), the editors of which kindly gave their permission to republish.

2 The literature on Basotho masculinity and sexuality in historical context is discussed in greater detail in various sources. On travel songs, see Coplan (1994); on Basotho gangs, see Kynoch (2001); on 'mine marriage', including mine marriage among Basotho workers, see Moodie (1994, 2001); and for a polemical defence of Basotho gender relations, see Bereng (1982). Basotho masculinity can be contextualised by the comparative studies offered in Morrell (2001), Murray & Roscoe (1998), Epprecht (2004) and GALZ (forthcoming), which also offer an entry into the theorisation of masculinities and homosexualities that guides the present study. The relationship between Basotho masculinity on the one hand and Basotho women's struggles and changing notions of femininity/female sexuality on the other is discussed in a rich literature that includes Gay (1985), Kendall (1999), and Epprecht (2000). Caveats on the choice of terminology are discussed in footnote 4, below.

3 The 'homosexuality is un-African' claim is helpfully analysed in, among other places, Murray & Roscoe (1998), Aarmo (1998), and Hoad (1999).

4 Big problems with terminology around 'heterosexuality', 'homosexuality' and 'bisexuality' have been identified and debated by queer scholars and activists. Some have proposed 'LGBT persons' or 'MSM' (men who have sex with men but do not identify as homosexual) as a way around some of these problems. Complicating matters in both this study and a related exercise in oral history in Zimbabwe is that the informants tend to use the old terms to refer to themselves, or some even older and more 'politically incorrect' ones. For the sake of simplicity I will stick with their preference, although acknowledging the importance of the critique.

5 In addition to the works cited in footnote 2, see Murray (2000) for a provocative engagement with the burgeoning field of queer theory, also developed with respect to Africa in Bleys (1995) and with respect to HIV/AIDS discourse in Africa by Phillips (2004).

6 This same argument could, of course, be turned against Achmat, Phillips, and indeed the present chapter, that is, we conscript select African evidence to the cause of counter-hegemonic masculinity in our own privileged communities. Mea culpa, with the proviso that I have

been explicitly aware of this critique from the start of the research process and have tried to limit the effects of my personal agendas on the evidence to the best of my professional ability. For the record, I do acknowledge growing up in a racist, sexist and deeply homophobic milieu; I had and still have many gay friends; I married a feminist woman, with whom I have three children; and I lived in rural Zimbabwe and Lesotho for extended periods while still at a young, formative age. I currently embrace the concept of sexual rights as enunciated by the All Africa Rights Initiative's Johannesburg Statement (2004). For further reflections on queer and feminist methods in post-colonial contexts, see Wolf (1996), Blackwood & Wierenga (1999a) and Epprecht (1999).

7 Here I would simply like to mention Amadiume (1987), who denounced Western lesbians who speculated about the sexuality within woman–woman marriages in Africa, Oppong and Kaliperi (2004), who deride an article that posited bisexuality among African men as a possible factor in the transmission of HIV, and Phimister (1997), who heaped scorn upon my own earlier work. Caldwell et al. (1989) are also interesting in that they manage entirely to ignore the issue in their purportedly authoritative survey of African attitudes toward sexuality.

8 Here I would like to draw attention to Kendall (1999). Although she does not specifically discuss masculinity, she makes the point that the appearance of homophobia in Lesotho can be linked to modern, Western discourses around sexuality, a thesis also implicit in Jeater's analysis of the creation of (heterosexual) perversion in colonial Zimbabwe (Jeater 1993).

9 The conversations took place on 16 March 1996, at Motimposo. From previous experiences of interviewing in Lesotho I did not even bother to ask permission to tape-record the event. Instead, I took shorthand notes that I then reconstructed as soon as I got home. Because I did not anticipate ever actually using the interviews beyond making a general point or two, I did not at first bother to send the transcript to my informants for their approval. Only much later did I realise that I would like to use them for placing my Zimbabwe research in context and for developing a more regional understanding of the historical construction of African masculinities. By that time, sadly, 'M' had died and I was about as far away from Motimposo as one can get in the world. I sent the transcript electronically to Gerhard and thence to 'P', who approved of my rendition. He also added some autobiographical detail which, for the sake of coherence, I have retroactively worked into the original 'interview'. Caveat anthropologus.

10 On a follow-up visit to Lesotho in 2000, for example, I found that 'M' had joined the burgeoning statistics of young people dying and that his bar

had passed into gay-unfriendly hands. I also found that the national archives, which provide probably the only documentary source for male–male sexual behaviour in Lesotho (criminal court cases), had been physically removed from their housing at the university and closed to public access. Many of the circumstances that have contributed to the emergence of state-sanctioned homophobia elsewhere in Africa (such as high unemployment, foreign domination, women's assertion of new autonomies, AIDS, and political malaise or corruption – see Epprecht 2004), are all very much present in Lesotho.

References

Aarmo, M. (1999) How homosexuality became 'un-African': the case of Zimbabwe. (Blackwood, E. & Wieringa 1999:255–80).

Achmat, Z. (1993) 'Apostles of civilised vice': 'immoral practices' and 'unnatural vice' in South African prisons and compounds, 1890–1920. *Social Dynamics*, 19, 2, 92–110.

Aina, T.A. (1991) Patterns of bisexuality in sub-Saharan Africa. In Tielman, R., Carball, M., and Hendriks, A. (eds.). *Bisexuality and HIV/AIDS: A Global Perspective*. (Buffalo, New York: Prometheus), pp. 81–90.

Alberton, P. and Reid, G. (directors/producers) (2000) *Dark and Lovely, Soft and Free*. (São Paulo: Franmi Produções and Gay and Lesbian Archives of South Africa).

All Africa Rights Initiative. (2004) Johannesburg Statement. http://www.mark.org.za, accessed 24 November 2004.

Amadiume, I (1987) *Male Daughters and Female Husbands: Gender and Sex in an African Society*. (London: Zed Press).

Bereng, P.M. (1982) *I am a Mosotho*. (Roma: National University of Lesotho).

Blackwood, E. and Wierenga, S. (1999a) Sapphic shadows: challenging the silence in the study of sexuality. In (Blackwood, E. & S. Wieringa 1999b:39–63).

Blackwood, E. and Wieringa, S. (eds.), (1999b) *Same-sex Relations and Female Desires: Transgender Practices across Culture*. (New York: Columbia University Press).

Blair, A., and Gay, J. (1980) Growing up in Lesotho (A Basotho Interpretation). Unpublished paper. (Roma: Dept of Education, National University of Lesotho).

Bleys, R.C. (1995) *The Geography of Perversion: Male–Male Sexual Behaviour Outside the West and the Ethnographic Imagination*. (New York: New York University Press).

Caldwell, J.C., Caldwell, P. and Quiggin, P. (1989) The social context of AIDS in sub-Saharan Africa. *Population and Development Review*, 15, 2, 185–233.

Coplan, D. (1994) *In the Time of Cannibals: The Word Music of South Africa's Basotho Migrants.* (Chicago: University of Chicago Press).

Dunton, C. (1990) Mopeli-Paulus and Blanket Boy's Moon. *Research in African Literature*, 21, 4, 105–120.

Edkins, D. (director) (1992). *The Color of Gold.* (New York: Icarus Films).

Epprecht, M. (1999) The Gay Oral History Project: black empowerment, human rights, and the research process. *History in Africa: A Journal of Method*, 26, 25–41.

Epprecht., M. (2000) *'This Matter of Women is Getting Very Bad': Gender, Development and Politics in Colonial Lesotho, 1870–1965.* (Pietermaritzburg: University of Natal Press).

Epprecht, M. (2004) *Hungochani: A History of a Dissident Sexuality in Southern Africa.* (Kingston: McGill-Queen's University Press).

Fone, B. (2000) *Homophobia: A History.* (New York: Metropolitan Books).

GALZ. (forthcoming) *African Homosexualities: A History.* (Harare: Weaver Books).

Gay, J. (1985) 'Mummies and babies' and friends and lovers in Lesotho. *Journal of Homosexuality*, 3, 4, 93–116.

Harries, P. (1994) *Work, Culture and Identity: Migrant Laborers in Mozambique and South Africa, c. 1860–1910.* (Portsmouth, New Hampshire: Heinemann).

Hoad, N. (1999) Between the White Man's Burden and the White Man's Disease. *Journal of Lesbian and Gay Studies*, 5, 4, 559–584.

Holmes, R. (1994) White rapists make coloureds (and homosexuals). In Gevisser, M. and Cameron, E. (eds.). *Defiant Desire: Gay and Lesbian Lives in South Africa.* (Johannesburg: Ravan Press), 284–94.

Jeater, D. (1993) *Marriage, Perversion and Power: The Construction of Moral Discourse in Southern Rhodesia, 1890–1920.* (Oxford: Clarendon).

Junod, Hi. (1911). *Zidji: étude de mœurs sud-africaine.* (St Blaise: Foyer Solidariste).

Kalipeni, E., Craddock, S., Oppong, J.R. and Ghosh, J. (eds.).(2004) *HIV and AIDS in Africa: Beyond Epidemiology.* (Oxford: Blackwell).

Kendall (1999) Women in Lesotho and the (Western) construction of homophobia. (Blackwood & Wieringa: 157–178).

Kynoch, G. (2001) A man among men: gender, identity and power in South Africa's Marashea gangs. *Gender and History*, 13, 2, 249–72.

Lanham, P. and Mopeli-Paulus, A. S. (1953) *Blanket Boy's Moon*. (London: Collins).

Luirink, B. (2000) *Moffies: Gay Life in Southern Africa*. (Cape Town: Ink Inc).

Lyons, A.P. and Lyons, H. (2004) *Irregular Connections: A History of Anthropology and Sexuality*. (Lincoln and London: University of Nebraska Press).

Maloka, E.T. (1995) Basotho and the Mines: Towards a History of Labour Migrancy. PhD dissertation, University of Cape Town.

Mda, Z. (1990) *The Plays of Zakes Mda*. (Introduction by A. Horn). (Johannesburg: Ravan).

Mkhize, V. (2001) A Gay Zulu Language. Behind the Mask. www.mask.org.

Mohapeloa, J.M. (2000) Tentative British Imperialism in Lesotho, 1884–1910. Unpublished manuscript. (Morija: Morija Museum and Archives).

Mokhoane, M. (1995) *Teba*. (Manzini: Macmillan Boleswa).

Moodie, T D. (2001) Black migrant mine labourers and the vicissitudes of male desire. In Morrell, R. (ed.) *Changing Men in Southern Africa*. (Pietermaritzburg: University of Natal Press, and London: Zed Press).

Moodie, T.D. with Ndatshe, V. (1994) *Going for Gold: Men's Lives on the Mines*. (Berkeley: University of California Press).

Moodie, T.D. with Ndatshe, V. and Sibuyi, B. (1988) Migrancy and male sexuality on the South African gold mines. *Journal of Southern African Studies*, 14, 2, 229–245.

Morrell, R. (ed.) (2001) *Changing Men in Southern Africa*. (Pietermaritzburg: University of Natal Press, and London: Zed Press).

Murray, S.O. (2000) *Homosexualities*. (Chicago and London: University of Chicago Press).

Murray, S.O. and Roscoe, W. (eds.). (1998) *Boy Wives and Female Husbands: Studies in African Homosexualities*. (New York: St Martin's Press).

Oppong, J.R. and Kalipeni, E. (2004) Perceptions and Misperceptions of AIDS in Africa, (Kalipeni et al. 2004:47–57).

Phillips, O. (2004) The Invisible Presence of Homosexuality: Implications for HIV/AIDS and Rights in Southern Africa. (Kalipeni et al. 2004:155–66).

Phimister, I. (1997) From Ian Phimister. *The Zimbabwean Review*, 3, 4, 31.

Thabane, M. (1995) Individual Diamond Digging in Lesotho, 1955–970. PhD dissertation, University of Trondheim.

Wolf, Diane L. (ed.) (1996) *Feminist Dilemmas in Fieldwork*. (Boulder: Westview).

9

'A man is a man completely and a wife is a wife completely': Gender classification and performance amongst 'ladies' and 'gents' in Ermelo, Mpumalanga

Graeme Reid

This chapter is based on fieldwork undertaken in 2003 and 2004 which forms part of a larger research project that seeks to explore the making of gay identities and the creation of public spaces in the wake of political transformation in South Africa. I am interested in emergent forms of gay identities outside of metropolitan centres, in rural and small-town South Africa. I started my research by focusing on a network of gay hairstylists, and was surprised at the level of acceptance and integration which coexisted with the more anticipated experiences of harassment and violence. My research base is Wesselton township, Ermelo, in the Mpumalanga province of South Africa, although 'the field' also extends to surrounding towns such as Bethal, Standerton and Piet Retief. Even so, given the nature of networking and the constant movement of people, goods and ideas, 'the field' extends way beyond any neatly defined geographical parameters.

Ermelo is situated about 250 kilometers east of Johannesburg and constitutes a regional centre for agricultural and mining activities. On the route to Swaziland and one possible route to the Kruger National Park, the town has also benefited from the post-apartheid tourist boom. Several guest houses, some of which promote an eclectic African theme, have opened and thrive on the patronage of salesmen and tourists passing through. In fact for anyone with the means and the luxury of leisure travel, 'passing through' is what one does in Ermelo. 'Oh, Ermelo? I think I passed through there once' is a common response to mention of my primary fieldwork site. The township of

Wesselton, established as a black residential area under apartheid's Group Areas Act, does not receive many tourists, although recently the local newspaper, *The Highvelder*, reported that a busload of French visitors had enjoyed an evening of dancing and conviviality at the Back of the Moon nightclub in Wesselton.

Despite Ermelo's comparatively large population and its role as an economic node for mining and agriculture in the region, it is a marginal and peripheral setting, far removed from the gay centres of Johannesburg, Cape Town and Durban. It is also a place where identities are being self-consciously produced, through experimentation and innovation. The quest for identity characterises many of the social activities and daily practices amongst the gays of Ermelo. A patchwork of identities provides insight into the ways in which this quest continues to play an important role in developing a more or less coherent concept of self, especially in an environment of rapid political and social change. The appeal to certain concepts of African tradition and custom, the effects of the Constitution and the impact of global gay identities all circulate as powerful ideas that shape individual identities. However, identity is also remarkably malleable. In this chapter I will show that there is a complex interplay between identity as both malleable and a compelling force that can shape even the most intimate spheres of individual desire. Nowhere is this interplay between creativity and constraint more evident than in the performances that characterise gender relations between 'ladies' and 'gents'. This chapter will attempt to map the role of this basic identity in everyday life. In spite of the malleability and creativity invested in making new identities, there is a remarkable adherence to rigid and inflexible gender norms, roles and practices. I will pay particular attention to prevailing ideas about masculinity and femininity, and to marriage and engagement ceremonies where masculine and feminine ideals are valorised through ritual performance, but simultaneously undermined by rumour and gossip.

This perspective suggests several questions: What does this material say about local understandings of gender, sex and sexual difference? If gender is to be understood primarily as performance, what are the possibilities of the performance of gender, and what are the constraints on it? If gender is relational and exists in the context of social interactions, to what extent are 'ladies' and 'gents' able to mould and transform gender and sexual identities, and to what extent are they constrained by social norms and expectations? What are the erotic dynamics that produce and sustain these gender dichotomies? Can sex and gender be neatly separated, as a body of feminist scholarship would argue, or do 'ladies' and 'gents' confirm cross-cultural accounts which suggest that this separation is an ethnocentrism (Yanagisako & Collier 1987)? Are 'ladies' men and are 'gents' gay? Or do 'ladies' constitute some sort of third gender, existing outside of the neat categories 'male' and 'female'? These questions of sex, gender and sexual difference are of immediate and compelling interest to the 'ladies' and 'gents' of Ermelo. They come up frequently in conversation, discussion and argument. They are the focus of workshops and are raised in religious meetings. They are performed in day-to-day interactions, enacted in ritual ceremonies and displayed in beauty pageants. They are also a site of speculation and contestation and hence defy clear definitions and consistent norms or practices. An ethnographic study of the gays of Ermelo, for whom these questions hold a profound fascination, also provides fertile ground for exploring the nature of 'masculinities' and 'femininities' in a South African context.

Gender in feminist anthropology

The publication in 1935 of Margaret Mead's *Sex and Temperament in Three Primitive Societies* was something of a milestone in gender studies in the field of anthropology. Mead's study questioned essentialist assumptions about the nature of gender by showing that social ideals of masculinity and femininity were culturally specific, shaped by history and subject to change. In addition, she attempted to apply the insights derived from fieldwork in Oceania to the social situation prevalent in American society at the time, thereby suggesting the possibility of making useful cross-cultural comparisons. In so doing she inaugurated an enduring tendency within feminist anthropology that has sought both to understand the specificities of particular cultural organisations of gender and to use these for the purpose of generalisation. Anthropology, by insisting on cultural specificity, has had a strong influence on the development of an understanding of gender as socially constructed rather than biologically determined, while feminist scholarship in anthropology has also attempted to explain the apparently universal phenomenon of the subordinate social position of women. In this paradigm, various theories have been developed, the most resilient of which is the idea that women are associated with nature and the private, domestic sphere, while men are associated with culture and the public, civic sphere. These theories were offered as explanations for the seemingly universal discrepancy in social status between men and women (Ortner 1972, Rosaldo 1974a). However, the usefulness of the category 'woman' was brought into question by subsequent work which challenged the universalising assumptions that underpinned this social category, stressing instead the plurality and specificity of women's experiences. Yet both approaches, whether the emphasis was placed on universal commonality or cultural specificity, retained a neat division between sex and gender. Sex featured as an obvious biological fact, and gender as the socially constructed dimension of sex.

Masculinities

A similar development can be seen in relation to understandings of 'masculinity'. In the quest to explain, from a feminist standpoint, the social position of women in a range of cultural settings, 'masculinity' initially tended to feature as part of a shadowy terrain of power and privilege. In other words, 'masculinity' was seen as part of a wider political problem, and analytically as somewhat homogeneous and evasive of scrutiny, rather than as an area of study in and of itself. The past two decades have seen the emergence of 'masculinities' as an arena for more focused social enquiry. Recently, gay studies in anthropology and history have also contributed to an understanding of masculinity by exploring the ways in which ideas about masculinity and femininity interact in a same-sex context (Besnier 1997, Kulick 1997, Epprecht 1998). A more nuanced understanding of gender dynamics has thus been developed by unpacking the concept of 'masculinity'.

However, masculinity continues to shadow-box with neat definitions, prompting the theorist R.W. Connell to observe:

> 'Masculinity', to the extent the term can be briefly defined at all, is simultaneously a place in gender relations, the practices through which men and women engage that place in gender, and the effects

of these practices in bodily experience, personality and culture. (2001:34)

As a 'place in gender relations', masculinity became the subject of renewed theoretical interest, spearheaded by the work of Connell (1995). He emphasised the role of race, class and sexual locations in determining men's ability to access and wield power, reflected in the concepts of hegemonic and non-hegemonic masculinities (Connell 1995, Whitehead 2001). In this model, gay men are seen to be one of the main objects in the subordinating impulse of hegemonic masculinity: 'Oppression positions homosexual masculinities at the bottom of a gender hierarchy among men' (2001:40). Connell argues that masculinity, as a structure of social practice, can be seen to be beset by a series of 'crisis tendencies' that are evident, for example, in the dramatic shift in power relations between men and women, changes in production relations towards a more equitable distribution of economic power and changes in the nature of the social structure which shapes sexual norms and emotional mores (Connell 2001).

Thus in feminist anthropology and masculinity studies a common understanding of gender as a relational set of social practices emerged. The terms 'feminine' and 'masculine', far from being homogeneous and universally applicable, revealed themselves as remarkably heterogeneous, fractured and contested. The work of Butler (1990) took this a step further by emphasising the central role of performance in the construction and deployment of gender as a form of social and cultural interaction. Anthropology has played an important role in destabilising the neat distinctions between sex and gender by showing that the idea of sex as a self-evident biological fact and gender as a social construct are culturally specific notions that cannot be plausibly sustained in the light of cross-cultural scrutiny.

Getting engaged

Henrietta Moore (1994) suggests that the analytical focus on gender as performance (Butler 1990) resonates strongly in anthropology, as ethnographic material demonstrates that gender classifications are based on roles – what men and women actually do, rather than on anatomy:

Ethnographic accounts often give a very vivid sense of people's perceptions of their 'lived anatomies', and of how understandings of bodies, gender identities and sexual differences are given substance through involvement in repetitive daily tasks and through the concrete nature of social relationships. (Moore 1994:24)

Certainly my fieldwork demonstrates that 'gender identities and sexual differences' are central to the ways in which gay identities are produced and performed. It is a complex terrain and I will introduce the topic through a description of an engagement party which took place in Ermelo in December 2003. It is during events such as these that gender differences are highlighted through an elaborate, and, in this particular instance, highly improvised yet culturally constrained performance.

The engagement party

In the early evening of 12 December 2003 a group of 'ladies' find themselves outside the local supermarket in Ermelo surrounded by shopping bags, looking tired, a trifle stressed, primarily exuberant. These ladies are in fact young men.[1] I arrive and my car is soon loaded with as many ladies and groceries as can fit in. I drive to Wesselton township, situated on the outskirts of Ermelo, and park the car outside Bhuti's place. Bhuti stays in a room next to a busy, noisy shebeen – 'full of thieves' remarks Paul, a visitor from Standerton, and he is perhaps right. Later tonight Bhuti will throw three unwelcome male guests from his room, accusing them of theft and attempted rape of one of the ladies. But that is later. For now, arrangements are still in full swing for the engagement that is to take place in Ermelo tomorrow afternoon. Once the groceries are offloaded I again drive back towards town. A symphony of cellphone ring tones accompanies the 'jolly talk' (camp banter and gossip) in the car.

Word has reached Andrew, the bride-to-be, that Bruce from Durban has arrived and is waiting at the taxi rank in town. Andrew has invited Bruce to the engagement as a blind date for Tsepo. As we travel towards the taxi rank all attention is focused on Tsepo, who is animated with anticipation. He touches up his hair playfully in the mirror, and briefly brushes a piece of imaginary fluff from his shirt pocket. Andrew alights to find Bruce and, once he is out of earshot, someone exclaims, in the spirit of 'jolly talk', 'You can see that the bride is a bitch, he knows all these men'. There are a few tense, speculative moments as we wait to see the elusive Bruce, who travels light, a bag slung over his shoulder. He is handsome and aware of his good looks. A beret sits askance on his head in a gesture of masculine bravado. This blind date is to end in heartbreak and a discussion on the nature of betrayal, with Tsepo resolving to find a white boyfriend. But we don't know that yet, and in the meantime we share with Tsepo his sense of initial excitement, and his dreams of romance kindled at this moment by a frisson of lust.

Meanwhile the groom, Sifiso, is hungry. He calls Andrew several times on his cellphone, demanding to know when supper will be ready. In the car there is talk of divorce before marriage – because the groom is already hungry and wondering where his bride-to-be is. Andrew pacifies him over the phone until we get back to Bhuti's place. At Bhuti's place the groom and his friends are sitting separately from the ladies, smoking, drinking Hunter's Gold and waiting for supper. It is a very masculine space. In the next room, the kitchen is a hive of activity as groceries are unpacked and supper prepared by the ladies amidst laughter and chatter. Bhuti leaves his guests to get on with it while he steals some time to have his hair plaited by a neighbour in preparation for the big day. 'Is the groom still angry?' he asks, grimacing as his hair is tugged and deftly woven by a young woman who keeps an eye on the *The Bold and the Beautiful*, a popular television soap opera, while working with his hair.

Mxolisi, who has traveled from Standerton, is relieved to have made it to Ermelo at all. His boyfriend did not want him to come and had argued with him before he left. Mxolisi told him that the bride-to-be was 'not just anybody, he is my friend'. The boyfriend eventually relented on condition that Mxolisi ironed his clothes and made him supper before he left. The boyfriend reminded Mxolisi, 'When we are married, then you will have to obey me.' However, Mxolisi is not so keen on marriage as he does not trust his boyfriend completely. He explains that his boyfriend is straight and he suspects that he also has a girlfriend because he sometimes comes home very late at night or even early in the morning without a plausible explanation.

That night I am accommodated in a nearby house, sharing a small room with Paul, who has recently moved from Soweto to Standerton. Paul is struck by differences and similarities between gay life in his Soweto home and in Mpumalanga and is keen to share these insights with me, so we talk late into the night. 'Most Zulus are gay,' Paul observes, having lived in Standerton for little over a month and having received many propositions from men. However, he explains that:

> Here it is unlike in Johannesburg or Cape Town where you find a gay partner who does not have a girlfriend. Here maybe he is gay but he has a girlfriend. You start to ask 'Is this person gay, or what?'

The next day, several hours later than planned, the engagement ceremony takes place on the outskirts of Ermelo. Thulani starts the formal proceedings by welcoming the guests and asserting that the engagement gives expression to 'something that is within us. We are not faking it.' He introduces Pastor Nokuthula from a gay Pentecostal church community in Johannesburg, who officiates at the ceremony. She grew up in the town of Volksrust, not far from here, so the ceremony has special resonance for her, even though she has conducted several similar services in her Johannesburg congregation. She expresses regret that the bride and groom's family members are not present. 'Part of me feels so disappointed when I don't see the family. It kills me somehow.' She bewails the fact that gay marriage is not yet legal but says that she hopes and prays that one day God will make it possible.[2] She gives advice to the assembled guests on the nature of true love – and the obstacles and pitfalls in its path. A speaker explains that he was there when the couple met while shopping at Shoprite. 'From now on I'm going to shop until I drop until I find the one,' he declares. Engagement rings are exchanged and to end the day's formal proceedings a bouquet of flowers is thrown to the single ladies present and much pleasure and enjoyment is derived from the fact that Emmanuel, who catches the bouquet, is ignorant of its meaning and significance. Unwittingly he (or she) has placed herself next in line for engagement and, possibly, marriage.

The gender hierarchy

A striking feature of the engagement is the extent to which there is a sharp distinction between 'masculine' and 'feminine' which has the strong imprint of a heterosexual model. In local terminology there are 'ladies' and 'gents'.[3] Ladies are gay. To be a lady does not mean that you want to be a woman, although some pass quite successfully as women. In fact Nathi, a hairstylist, is so successful that he has been able to compete professionally against other women in beauty pageants and was recently placed in the top five in the 'Miss Ermelo' competition. To be a lady is to be a gay and to be gay is to be socially effeminate and sexually passive.

Ladies occupy traditional feminine spheres both at work and at home. Many ladies are drawn to hairstyling, where they are often highly regarded, sought after, and very successful. Ladies are seen as relatively affluent and are often the victims of muggings, bag snatchings and cellphone theft. They organise social functions, they take care of the detailed planning of events (such as the engagement ceremony), and they do the housework – they cook and clean and iron. Amongst themselves they gossip about each other and about their men in the form of 'jolly talk'. They often provide materially for the gents. It was Andrew who paid for the engagement party, incurring significant debt, which he is paying off to this day. Ladies are understandably wary of 'gold-diggers', a frequent topic in 'jolly talk'. There is a social convention that a lady should be faithful to one gent. But in practice this seldom happens. Unlike gents, ladies must be discrete about their infidelities or risk being beaten. Gents, on the other hand, are not gay. As a relational concept, 'masculinity' is usually defined as 'not feminine' or 'not female' in this context: it must also be seen as 'not gay'.

During the preparations for the engagement the gents keep themselves separate from the ladies, opening bottles of Hunter's Gold with their teeth, smoking cigarettes held between thumb and forefinger, talking in low subdued tones, listening to music and generally doing what gents do. Gents are boyfriends to gays and their lives are not atypical compared to those of other men in Wesselton. They usually have irregular, poorly paid manual work. Drinking is an important part of entertainment. They exercise control over and occasionally discipline, punish and beat their ladies. As mentioned, Mxolisi was nearly prevented from attending the engagement ceremony by an irate boyfriend who insisted that domestic duties came before independent travel.

In another example a gent discovered the photograph of a rival boyfriend and a few personal effects belonging to him discreetly concealed in a shoe box for the duration of his conjugal visit from an East Rand township. Furious, he shouted and interrogated his lady, demanding to know the truth, and beating her occasionally. She begged him to stop, but in her traumatised state used the name of her other lover, which led to a more severe beating. Afterwards she said she loved him 100 percent and they made up by making passionate love during the night and the next morning too. The lady displayed a large 'love bite' that her gent had given her, apparently to stop any other man looking at her, at least for the duration of the weekend. A day later her gent disappeared, taking a substantial portion of her wardrobe, as well as her cellphone, with him. Cellphones often feature in domestic disputes. Another lady had her cellphone confiscated by her gent, who then monitored all her calls. This was a prelude to another form of punishment in the form of restricting her movements. He insisted that she no longer visit friends after work but rather report to him, as it were, on her way home.

Gents frequently have multiple sexual partners, both ladies and women. Multi-partner sexual arrangements are justified as an expression of male sexual needs (including the 'bisexual' needs of a straight man) and may even be formally arranged on the model of a polygamous marriage. In one case the male partner, Brian, has a lady 'wife', and a number of younger, junior lady partners who need the senior lady wife's permission for sexual congress with the husband. Brian also has a girlfriend, who is pregnant with his second child. To him fatherhood has been a great affirmation of his masculinity. 'When the baby was born it made me feel like a real man,' he said.

A crisis of masculinity?

In masculinity studies 'crisis tendencies' are symptomatic of the vulnerable nature of masculinity, of achieving and sustaining a masculine identity. 'Most studies show masculinity as rather fragile, provisional, something to be won and then defended, something under a constant threat of loss' (Wood & Jewkes 1997:42).

The 'crisis of masculinity' has become an accepted trope for looking at, inter alia, the gender-based conflicts and disturbances that arise in times of social and political transformation. In this respect South Africa presents a remarkable case study. As scholars have shown (Posel forthcoming, Walker 2005, Gear 2005, Niehaus 2003), the fault lines of social and political change, of thwarted ambition and threatened patriarchal privilege, are evident in an exponential increase in gender-based violence, the nature of sexual assault, risk-taking behaviour and a dramatic increase in male suicide rates. Endemic unemployment, coupled with the failure to establish viable alternative role models that would enable young men to achieve successful masculinity, is cited as part of the evidence which points to 'a crisis in masculinity'. Morrell (2001a) argues that two key historical factors have had a disproportionate influence on the construction of South African masculinities, namely rural life and migrant labour. He shows how rural patriarchal and gerontocratic arrangements left an indelible imprint on the forms of masculinity that developed in an urban context in the wake of proletarianisation. These were reflected in the survival strategies that men adopted in order to cope with the extremely harsh conditions experienced by migrant labourers, especially on the mines.

Drawing on Connell's model, Morrell suggests that South African men have responded to crisis in three broadly defined ways – by reacting against change in an attempt to protect privilege; by accommodating some changes while resisting others; or, in a responsive and progressive way, by actively fighting for gender justice. He states:

> The absence of any widespread opposition to the improvement in women's positions and to the tolerance of gay men is possibly the most impressive testimony to the accommodationist position, although misogyny and homophobia have far from disappeared. (2001a:31)

Like Connell, he also sees gay emancipation and its associated public visibility as evidence of an intrinsically progressive response, embracing change in the gender hierarchy and in so doing challenging accepted norms of hegemonic masculinity. This assumption is not supported by my research findings, where forms of hegemonic masculinities are reproduced in a same-sex context and where marginal masculinities are not as subordinate as they may at first appear.

If one of the preconditions of 'crisis' is the fragile nature of masculinity then 'the ladies and gents' of Ermelo do show that masculinity is extraordinarily provisional, contextual and tentative. They raise the question, 'What is masculinity?' Do we accept the ladies' self-definition as non-masculine, or is being a lady in this context just one of many ways of being a man? Sometimes ladies do indeed become gents. This was a topic of intense speculation when a well-known lady met and struck up a relationship with a woman. 'Jolly talk' suggested that he had even begun to walk and talk differently. Indeed one gent revealed to me in an interview that he thinks he might be a lady. Sometimes he goes with the ladies and sometimes with the gents. In 'jolly talk' he would be known as a 'Greek Salad', someone who does not know who he is. He has valorised the ideal of a monogamous relationship, which he articulates in terms of his religious convictions and family background. His dilemma is that he must be one thing or the other – a husband or a wife. In his words, 'A man is a man completely and a wife is a wife completely.'

To what extent do the ladies and gents of Ermelo support or contest the notion of a crisis in masculinity? It could be argued that the improved social status and economic power of the ladies impacts on the gents' sense of masculinity: in other words, there is a strong parallel with the arguments put forward in a heterosexual context where traditional male roles have been undermined by the changing economic realities and shifts in social and political power towards a more gender-equitable arrangement. It is true that the ladies are generally better off and enjoy a certain social status in the community often associated with fashion, beauty and style. If we follow this line of argument it would suggest that the Constitution and the rhetoric of gay rights have empowered the ladies. It is the ladies, after all, who are gay. It is not my intention here to demonstrate the veracity or otherwise of the 'crisis' argument in relation to men and masculinity in South Africa. What is pertinent is that the same arguments that are applied to the social position of women in relation to men can equally be applied to ladies in relation to gents.

Liberated 'modern' ladies in Ermelo are beginning to run workshops on 'how to be a real gay', empowering workshops which question whether a gent should be shared with a heterosexual woman, for example. They may also offer advice on domestic violence. The workshops articulate something of a liberal feminist position. The gender hierarchy remains intact, boyfriends are still gents, and gents are still straight – but they need to behave better. Ladies are said to be 'doing it for themselves'. The financially independent modern lady can set the agenda. The workshops also fulfil another important need – gays acquire a better self-knowledge and are thus in a position to answer difficult questions from an inquisitive public:

> The next person in the taxi will ask how can a man be a woman? They need to know, is it your sexual orientation, or your whole body that is a woman?

This example, one of many drawn from day-to-day conversation, reveals the complexity of individual understandings of gender, sex and sexual orientation. It is perhaps not surprising that the workshops organised by the ladies pay such close attention to terminology. 'Butch', 'femme', 'gay', 'dragging queen', 'transvestite' are discussed and infused with local meanings that bear little resemblance to their etymology but do reflect local gender norms and practices. Gendered performances do change remarkably quickly. When three young gay men 'came out' in Wesselton township in 1994, they flamboyantly signalled this by wearing skirts and make-up to school. Evidently all the younger gays also started 'dragging', as this was seen to be the way of expressing 'being gay'. In recent years this practice has changed and it is now even frowned upon in some gay circles to wear drag all the time. 'She is too much' is a remark that I have heard directed at Emmanuel, who is never seen without a skirt. Yet the same person who made the remark competed in, and in fact won, the 'Miss Gay Ermelo 10 Years of Democracy' competition in evening wear, formal wear and casual wear. Some ladies wear masculine attire, albeit infused with a certain style, while others go for a more androgynous look in their dress code. The contestations and disagreements about gender norms and practices point to instability and hybridity in the making of gendered identities. Some of this confusion is evident in public responses to ladies, as the following incident illustrates.

Nathi, (I heard during the launch of the Mpumalanga fellowship of a gay church community, which took place in the town of Bethal), had been stabbed several times in the neck and arm in a gay-bashing incident in Wesselton township. When the formalities of the church launch were concluded we rushed to the Ermelo Provincial Hospital to visit him. It was soon clear that his life was not, in fact, in danger. He was in the women's section, in a private ward, with his hand bandaged. He had indeed received a deep cut to his left hand as he had resisted, in vain, the theft of his cellphone. He said that he had asked to be moved to a private ward because the general ward had, according to him, been 'too much', with several young women in what appeared to be terminal stages of illness. For the duration of his hospital visit Nathi felt that it was prudent to give up the artificial breasts that he normally wore in the form of slightly inflated condoms tucked under his blouse. On discharge, one of the nurses who had cared for Nathi gave him his follow-up appointment card in which he was addressed as 'Ms'. His close friend, Dumiso, a lady, was surprised and questioned Nathi about this. Nathi felt that it was appropriate. Dumiso turned to me for clarity. 'Shouldn't they write "Mr"? If you are a gay, aren't you still a Mr?' Still dissatisfied, he turned to the nurse. 'Why does it say Ms?', he asked her. 'Oh, is she married?' was the reply.

Masculine and feminine performances

For the ladies and gents of Ermelo, sexual difference is not determined by who you are but by what you do. A lady is a lady, not because of biological signifiers, but because of everyday social practices and performances. Similarly, a gent becomes a gent based on a set of social relationships and practices, and not because of a fixed biological essence. Sis' Fiki, an older figure regarded as a kindred spirit by the ladies of Ermelo, claimed not to know the meaning of the word 'gay', and described herself instead as *isitabane*, which roughly translates as 'two organs' or hermaphrodite. When I asked her, through a lady interpreter, whether she played an invariably passive role in her sexual relationships, the interpreter was unable to ask the question because he found it so funny and so ludicrous that I could even imagine it to be any other way. Again, Sis' Fiki is feminine, not because of physical traits, but as a result of social practices and gendered performances. Whether

Sis' Fiki is intersexed or not is incidental and immaterial in this particular configuration of gender and the performance of gender relations.

Both ladies and gents are constrained by rigid ideas about gender norms and practices, but paradoxically ladies also experience elaborate possibilities for improvisation facilitated by the conflation between sex and gender. 'You are what you do' allows their 'doing' to have a more profound influence on their 'being' than is the case with the gents, who by and large experience an overlap between sexual and gender identities, shaped primarily by the weighty influence of hegemonic ideas about masculinity. Social pressure on men as gents is perhaps greater than that on men as ladies, because the ladies have a more flexible script based on public recognition of performance as constitutive of their gendered selves. If masculinity is a fragile thing it is perhaps the more so when negotiating same-sex relations with ladies. For gents, the masculine model remains intact and is only potentially troubled if the gender of the ladies, as sexual partners, is brought into question or if a gent becomes a lady. This is why an informant experienced such intense anxiety about his indecision as to whether he was a lady or a gent. While he did not mind being either, he could not live in the in-between zone, a no-man's-land without an appropriate script or a clear set of daily practices.

Who then are the gents having sex with? Public health discourse has popularised the phrase 'men who have sex with men' to target those, like the gents, who do not regard themselves as gay but who have sex with other men. This understanding assumes a neat division between sex and gender. In Ermelo, while the gents are certainly men, are the ladies also men? The feminine performances of the ladies are both facilitated and curtailed by the gender hierarchy. For example, Dumiso took a calculated risk in relocating to a one-horse town (appropriately named Perdekop, 'Horse Hill'), where he felt his skills as a hairstylist would be sought after and appreciated. However, his business failed to thrive, due to a lack of customers. 'I was thinking that they don't know about our style. I wanted to improve them. People came for new styles, but not enough.' So he turned to trade (sex work) to supplement his income. But first he had some explaining to do. When he was propositioned by a man, he explained that he was a gay. He was asked 'What is a gay?' and he explained that 'We feel like them but we are homos.' The clarifications did not end there. 'When I explained "homosexual" they wanted to know what that meant. I explained they are girls, but with no breasts. They took it easy as they were very understanding.' He claims that his side business thrived as his male clients discovered the joys of anal sex:

> I took them to bed to demonstrate. I throw them to my Durban (anus). Because you know that Durban is too small. They scream and scream and say 'Oh, if I can stay with you, baby, you are hot!' You are hotter than women.

The men started coming as clients to his saloon, mainly for popular styles such as s-curl and waves. They also retained their girlfriends but continued to enjoy Dumiso's 'special cake'. Dumiso demonstrated how his deft use of a towel concealed his penis from view and sustained the jointly maintained myth that he was 'a queen in town and they rushed to their queen'. Thus Dumiso, who felt that his friend Nathi should be referred to as 'Mr' on his hospital appointment card, went to great lengths to be a 'Ms' in Perdekop. He felt sorry for the one gay in Perdekop, who he says was forced to go out drinking and socialising with other men against his wishes, whereas Dumiso was accepted, not as a gay, but as a girl. 'I was comfortable in Perdekop because they know me as a girl, not a gay.' A fieldwork assistant, Bongani, who grew up in the rural enclave of Driefontien (about 100 kilometers from Ermelo) but who has lived in Johannesburg for several years, liked to cause consternation amongst some of the ladies by saying that he was gay. Bongani is well-known in the district as a gent, both in appearance and through reputation, so this revelation sparked confusion and disbelief. Nathi abandoned a client in the Professional Hair Salon to discuss this matter privately with Bongani and myself in the street outside. He said that people were saying that Bongani was gay. 'Yes, I am gay,' answered Bongani, which left Nathi exclaiming in disbelief, hands cupped over his mouth. Similarly Bongani's expressed desire to 'do Mandla', a prominent gent in Wesselton, astounded and amused the ladies present: 'No, he is a boy.' To which Bongani responded, 'That does not mean anything to me. When you get into bed you can talk. We do the same things. He can be surprised, he can do these things.'

It seems to be that erotic dynamics are critical to the creation and maintenance of gender classifications. Amidst all the innovation and creativity in the realm of gender, one thing appears to remain constant and that is the erotic necessity that there should be gents and ladies. Sex cannot happen between two ladies or two gents. This was clearly articulated in a discussion about a marriage. Lucky was talking about the impending marriage of his boyfriend to a woman. He still hoped that, even at the eleventh hour, his gent might choose him over her. When asked why he and his close and intimate friend, Paul, did not form a relationship rather than hoping for the enduring affections of a straight man, he replied, 'Oh, I love him very much, but I am not a lesbian!' To be desirable to the ladies, a gent needs to be a real gent. This includes being straight, and a girlfriend or wife is reassuring proof of that. A gent may drink too much from time to time; sometimes he may even beat his lady. He may have several other wives or partners. But the lady is likely to continue to love him completely, because all this is part of what a lady expects from a real gent.

Marriage and respectability

Same-sex engagement and marriage ceremonies which take place in the region are events where traditions are both evoked and reinvented. They constitute significant social occasions where the performance of gender is enacted in a particular, ritualised way. These events are also topics for seemingly endless speculation, rumour, gossip and fantasy. For example, during the course of my fieldwork there was a rumour doing the rounds that the British Broadcasting Corporation (BBC) was looking to make a documentary on 'an African gay wedding'. The story was that the BBC had approached the Hope and Unity Metropolitan Community Church (the gay Pentecostal Church in Johannesburg) and the news had spread from there. Most importantly, the BBC would 'sponsor everything'. When Andrew (who was already engaged at this point) first heard about it he suggested to his friend Bhuti (who is also a lady) that he should get married that year. Bhuti was skeptical: 'Can you meet someone and get married in the same year?' Meanwhile Bhuti elaborated on his own extravagant wedding fantasy, located, somewhat modestly, on the banks of the Vaal River in Standerton and peopled with a chaotic throng of well-wishers from his home base in Sakhile township. In the glare of the television cameras he would marry his one and only love, who had recently shifted in status from secret admirer to lover. If that was not possible he would throw his 'love heart' in the water and never love again. The image of the television cameras created an imaginary setting in which Bhuti could invent a playful and extravagant soap opera script of romantic love, community acceptance and social recognition.

Marriage is indeed an avenue to respectability, but it is one that is also being constantly undermined by gossip. In Bhuti's fantasy, the chaotic throngs of well-wishers are a powerful reminder of the strength and importance of social institutions such as marriage, and why, of all rights secured by Constitutional equality, this is the one most frequently spoken about and discussed. It is significant that while the South African Law Commission continues to prevaricate in a mire of legislation concerning the regulation of traditional marriage, religious marriage and same-sex marriage, some gays in Ermelo and elsewhere are simply going ahead and getting married, in form if not in legal substance. Oliver and Muntu are one such couple; however, if gossip is to be believed, it is extraordinary that their relationship has survived the troubles and turbulence that have beset their recent marriage. The gossip revolves around familiar themes. Muntu, the husband, is a gold-digger and used Oliver to finance liaisons with women, and most outrageously, to throw a party for his girlfriend. Then Oliver, the wife, was accused of brazen infidelity. It was an indiscretion that was said to have taken place at Andrew's pre-engagement party with the fiancé's best man. As Andrew remarked: 'Shameless, and with the ring on!' However, similar stories plague Andrew's engagement.

Another significant feature of both the marriage and engagement ceremonies is the absence of important family members. When Oliver's mother discovered that he had got married in secret and without her knowledge or involvement she insisted on a subsequent ceremony to bless the marriage. Oliver and his husband then moved into her home, where they remain to this day, sharing the house with several other relatives. Andrew, who continued to live with his mother, hid his engagement photographs and concealed his ring. But his mother heard the increasingly persistent rumours circulating in Driefontein and she eventually confronted him about them. Pastor Nokuthula made this point strongly at the engagement ceremony when she said, 'It kills me somehow.'

While Bhuti may have fantasised about a white wedding and honeymoon, Zakhi of Bethal aspired towards a more 'traditionally African' engagement and wedding ceremony, which includes *lobola* negotiations between the respective families. He described the engagement or *umhlambiso*, suggesting that the groom's family would come with a cloak, a shawl and a 'don't touch scarf' which would be tied around the bride's neck 'like a ring in an African way', which signals that 'this is a wife not to be proposed by anyone else'. Seen from this perspective, Andrew's engagement was 'too much Westernised', and I was told, 'Usually we have an *umhlambiso* followed by a white wedding – a traditional engagement with a white touch.' Zakhi explained that while protocol does not allow for a discussion of the actual bride price, which is a private matter, he is confident that because he has his own home (albeit a makeshift corrugated iron house with a mud floor, subject to periodic flooding) and has 'adopted' a niece (there is a strong value placed on child-bearing capacity), he should fetch in the region of about R5000.[4] Another advantage for a prospective husband is that Zakhi is also independently employed. While he has largely given up hairstyling, except for occasional braiding work, because, he claims, he was bewitched by jealous rivals, he now runs a relatively busy shebeen from his home, which is situated on a main thoroughfare in the township. While the details of his imminent engagement were presented to me almost as a fait accompli, it is difficult to separate the facts from the fantasy – what the engagement ceremony may or may not look like when it actually takes place, which members of the respective families will participate and how much *lobola* will actually be paid. For instance, Andrew assured everyone that his mother would be present and actively involved in his engagement ceremony and yet, as we have seen, she only found out about it in retrospect through the reliable grapevine.

Marriage signals a pinnacle of social acceptance and equality before the law. The fact that individuals are getting married in spite of the law suggests that social acceptance and the quest for respectability is a primary motivating factor. Yet a constant stream of rumour and gossip undermines these aspirations, not only of those who are already married or on the path towards marriage, but of those who apparently aspire towards marriage. Clearly these rumours are derived from actual circumstances or are based on symbolic truths. The gossip that has plagued the engagement and wedding ceremonies is perhaps symptomatic of the impossibility of keeping a 'straight man' indefinitely. It is accepted as a truism, as in the case of Lucky's boyfriend, that straight men inevitably end up with women. It is also the case that in both the engagement and the marriage, it is the ladies who bring money and a degree of affluence to the relationships. But it seems that the rumours of gold-diggers (and the constant warnings to be alert to this in any relationship) are also about the discrepancy in emotional investment. In a relationship between a lady and a gent, a gay and a straight, the emotional costs are perhaps inevitably somewhat one-sided. The negative, undermining gossip that runs parallel to the aspiration to be married also seems to represent a disbelief in the possibility of marriage, beyond the realm of fantasy and soap operas. It is a context in which 'love hearts' must inevitably end in the Vaal River, or as Paul explained to me:

> Another thing that I have noticed is that gays here are struggling to get the right partners. The community understands, but gay people are so lonely, they don't have dates and all those things.

Thus, while engagements and marriages are performed and these do have tangible results in the form of enhanced social status, acceptance within the family or as a form of integration into a wider social network, the gossip highlights the innovative and tentative nature of the events themselves and emphasises the precarious social position of the ladies within these relationships. It seems that underlying the rumour and gossip, the simultaneous idealising and undermining of marriage, is also a question of authenticity. Can institutions such as marriage really be adapted to meet the needs of ladies and gents in Ermelo? Will they be taken seriously by the broader community and hence ensure acceptance and respectability? Do they involve substance as well as form? These concerns were expressed during the preparations for the engagement ceremony, where organisers were anxious that the event should start on time and that there should be a pastor officiating, otherwise the community would not take them seriously. The master of ceremonies at the engagement ceremony made the point that 'we are not faking it'. One organiser told me that people wanted to be the first to get engaged or married to enhance their social status. He complained that in gay weddings there was far too much emphasis placed on superficial things such as rings, food and especially clothing, at the expense of more substantial issues such as the quality of relationships.

On the edge: Jezebel

Of course marriage, while it may be presented as an ideal, remains the exception to the rule. Only a handful of engagement and marriage ceremonies have taken place in Ermelo and surrounding areas in the past few years. If marriage represents the desire for respectability, what would be its counterpoint? An extreme position, located in direct opposition to marriage, is that represented by Thulani, or Jezebel, as he is often called. Thulani has a string of lovers, and is always accused of stealing other ladies' boyfriends in Ermelo. His sexual conquests are legendary and are by no means limited to Ermelo but extend to Durban and Johannesburg as well. Once during the 45-minute drive from Driefontein to Ermelo he produced a list of the men that he seduced in the preceding six months. An impressive list, even though one name was erased and presumably deleted from memory. One significant snippet of gossip to emerge from the gay gossip column, or 'ggc' as it is referred to in 'jolly talk', is that Thulani, a lady and a Jezebel, played the role of a gent in his brief and sporadic sexual encounters with a white man from Durban. The white man was spoken about both as a victim and a fool. He was seen as a victim because he bought Thulani a lot of things and Thulani apparently evaded most of his sexual advances, and as a fool because it seemed so obvious to everyone, except himself, that he was being taken for a ride. It was also rumoured that Thulani had had a 'lesbian experience', by having sex with another lady in Ermelo. These rumours illustrate the fact that Thulani falls outside of the parameters of generally acceptable behaviour. Operating on the edge of traditional norms and codes that govern gender, he is able to be a gent with a white man[5] and a lesbian with another lady. Like Jezebel before him he is seen to be an extremely bad influence. He is seen as dangerous, threatening and disruptive. If misfortunes, such as robbery, befall him these are seen as his just deserts. Jezebel, as we know from 1 and 2 Kings in the Bible, came to a particularly sticky end. Yet Thulani is also an ambiguous figure who is seen as powerful and independent. Thulani is better educated than his peers and he enjoys the economic advantages of a relatively lucrative job. He owns a car and lives outside Wesselton township in a rented room in one of Ermelo's historically white, lower-middle-class suburbs. He is prone to flaunt his wealth and status, and to use these attributes to his advantage in the fine art of seducing men. He is the source of intense gossip amongst the ladies and the object of resentment as well as envy.

Jezebel is the counterpoint to the respectable (married) lady. Marriage and engagement ceremonies are particularly powerful occasions in which ideas about gender are imagined and performed. But figures who operate on the margins of decorum also serve as signposts marking the edges of acceptable behaviour. Their actions serve as a warning to others to stay within the bounds of what is deemed appropriate. Jezebel's conduct transgresses gender norms and values. But he, and others like him, also play an important role in monitoring the rules of gender. Evoking 'traditions' in the form of a marriage that is 'too much Westernised', a traditional *umhlambiso* or a combination of both, as in a 'traditional engagement with a white touch' offers the promise of social integration, affirmation and a sense of belonging to the ladies; and financial security and domestic comfort to the gents. However, as a cultural innovation based on a traditional form it also carries associated risks and constraints. One risk is that of the perception of 'authenticity' and the social acceptance, or respectability, which goes with it. And the constraints are evident in the enactment of conventional and highly regulated gender norms and practices. Paradoxically in a context where the making of identities is extraordinarily malleable and adaptable, gender remains an area in which roles and norms are quite fixed and inflexible. This is particularly evident in these stylised performances of gender and the intense speculation, rumour and gossip that follow in their wake.

For the ladies, engagement is a prelude to the social status of 'married woman'. This is a particularly significant ritual event in the performance of 'gender', which emerges from and reflects a myriad of daily practices as well as other periodic public performances, such as beauty pageants. Social relationships and gendered performances clearly take precedence over categories of 'male' and 'female'. Gender is not synonymous with biological sex, it is a consequence of social practice. And sexual relationships are highly constrained by gendered rules and the viability of erotic desire. Ladies and gents are a prerequisite for sexual relationships. Marriage is one of the ways in which these gender ideals are expressed, while rumour and gossip play an important part in policing the parameters of acceptable behaviour. But these identities are in many ways up for grabs, hence the constant discussion about what terms mean, how to behave, and the arguments and discussions about what it means to be a lady. The contestations that take place within the scope of what it means to be a lady allow for considerable room to manoeuvre. The terrain is a flexible one and, within certain parameters, there are indeed many ways to be a lady. For gents, the possibilities are perhaps more limited, as the conflation between sex and gender offers more constrained possibilities than for their lady partners who manage to dodge sex in favour of gender and thereby win some space to manoeuvre. I never did answer Dumiso's question, 'If you are a gay aren't you still a "Mr"?' In this context it seems that you are and you are not. To the extent that gender is primarily social and enacted through performance you are both a Mr and a Ms. And to the extent that the engagement ceremony was a ritual performance of a set of rigid gender norms, I must agree with the nurse from the Ermelo Provincial Hospital who recognised that when you are married to a gent you do indeed become a Mrs.

Acknowledgements

Research was funded by the Netherlands Foundation for the Advancement of Tropical Research (WOTRO) of the Netherlands Organization for Scientific Research (NOW).

Notes

1. From here on, the terms 'ladies' and 'gents' will be used without inverted commas. Pseudonyms have been used throughout.
2. In November 2004, the South African Supreme Court of Appeal declared that the current legal definition of marriage was discriminatory and proposed a revised, gender-non-specific, wording.
3. To avoid confusion I will adopt this term when referring to same-sex partnering.
4. Approximately €600.00
5. Tsepo's note of despair when his blind date dumps him for Jezebel and he resolves to get a white boyfriend also evokes the possibility of escaping and transcending the options available in this particular arrangement of gender norms and values.

References

Besnier, N. (1997) Sluts and superwomen: the politics of gender liminality in urban Tonga. *Ethnos*, 62, 5–31.

Butler, J. (1990) *Gender Trouble: Feminism and the Subversion of Identity*. (London: Routledge).

Collier, J. and Yanagisako, S. (eds.) (1987) *Gender and Kinship: Essays toward a Unified Analysis*. (Stanford: Stanford University Press).

Connell, R.W. (1995) *Masculinities*. (Cambridge: Polity).

Connell, R.W. (2001) *The social organization of masculinity*. (Whitehead & Barrett 2001:30–50).

Epprecht, M. (1998) The 'unsaying' of homosexuality among indigenous black Zimbabweans: mapping a blindspot in an African masculinity. *Journal of Southern African Studies*, 24, 4, 631–51.

Gardiner, J.K. (ed.) (2002). *Masculinity Studies and Feminist Theory*. (New York: Columbia University Press).

Gear, S. (2005) Rules of engagement: structuring sex and damage in men's prisons and beyond. *Culture, Health and Sexuality*, 7, 3, 195–208.

Hekma, G. (2000) Queering anthropology. (Sandfort et al. 2000:81–97).

Kulick, D. (1997) The gender of Brazilian transgendered prostitutes. *American Anthropologist*, 99, 3, 574–585.

Mead, M. (1935) (1963). *Sex and Temperament in Three Primitive Societies.* (New York: Morrow).

Moore, H.L. (1994) *A Passion for Difference.* (Cambridge: Polity Press).

Morrell, R. (2001a) *The times of change. Men and masculinity in South Africa.* (Morrell 2001b:3–37).

Morrell R. (ed.) (2001b) *Changing Men.* (Pietermaritzburg: University of Natal Press).

Niehaus, I. (2003) 'Now everyone is doing it': towards a social history of rape in the Southern African Lowveld. Paper presented at *Sex and Secrecy*, the Fourth International Conference of the International Association for the Study of Sexuality, Culture and Society (IASSCS), University of the Witwatersrand, Johannesburg, 22–25 June, 2003.

Ortner, S.B. (1972) (1996a). *Is Female to Male as Nature is to Culture?* (Ortner 1996b).

Ortner, S.B. (1996) *Making Gender: The Politics and Erotics of Culture.* (Boston: Beacon Press).

Posel, D. (forthcoming) Sex, death and the fate of the nation: reflections on the politicisation of sexuality in post-apartheid South Africa. *Africa.*

Rosaldo, M. (1974a) Woman, culture and society: a theoretical overview. (Rosaldo & Lamphere 1974b:17–42).

Rosaldo, M. and Lamphere, L. (eds.) (1974b) *Woman, Culture and Society.* (Stanford: Stanford University Press).

Sandfort, T., Schuyf, J., Duyvendak, J.W. and Weeks, J. (eds.) *Lesbian and Gay Studies.* (London: Sage).

Walker, L. (2005) Men behaving differently. *Culture, Health and Sexuality,* 7, 3, 225–238.

Whitehead, S.M. and Barrett, F.J. (eds.) (2001) *The Masculinities Reader.* (Cambridge: Polity Press).

Yanagisako, S. and Collier, J. (1987) Toward a unified analysis of gender and kinship. (Collier & Yanagisako 1987:14–50).

Index

Achmat, Z. 91–2, 102, 105
African sexuality 3–6, 139–40, 185
Alexandra 161, 166–7, 179; case studies 168–77
alternative masculinity 149, 178–9
Arendt, Hannah 52
Arnfred, Signe 4

baby rape 9, 37, 55, 118, 165; media coverage 34–7, 173; *see also* moral panic
Baby Tsephang 34–6, 40
Barker, G. 178
Bill of Rights 31, 161, 163; *see also* South African Constitution
bisexuality 185, 197, 212, 214, 219
Bleys, Rudi 187–8
Bushbuckridge region 66–9, 72, 81
Butler, J. 92, 100, 103, 209

Caldwell, J.C. and P. 3–4, 139–40
carceral identities 90–4; *see also* mine compounds; prison
child abuse 22, 32, 172–3, 175; sexual 8–9, 27, 32, 34, 36, 46, 83
child rape 22, 33, 38, 43, 50, 71, 165; as punishment 78–81; media coverage 33–5; silence about it 27–8; statistics 34–5, 38, 65, 166
Chiloane, Jackson 73–5
Christianity 146–7

Cohen, Stanley 41
confession 23, 46–55; as an act of healing 45, 54–5, 178; public 22, 39–40
Connell, R.W. 2, 7, 10–11, 120, 140, 208–9, 215
Coplan, David 184, 186–7
crisis of masculinity 10–11, 119–20, 161–3, 166, 179, 209, 214–18; impact of Constitution on 119, 133–4, 161, 163, 166
culture and cultural politics 4, 112, 140, 152, 155–6, 174; and masculinity 113, 129; and the power of sexual difference 121, 130–1, 133; attitude towards secrecy about sexual violence 27–8; change of 140, 156; of multiple sexual partners 148, 151, 155–6; *see also* tradition

death penalty 22, 35
Dirsuweit, T. 9, 91–3, 164, 166
domestic violence 9, 31, 111, 124, 163, 165, 175; and masculine domination 70–1; in Nkomazi region 114–16, 124–6; sexual 42, 45–6
Domestic Violence Act of 1999 126
Dunton, Chris 189

Ermelo region 205–6, 218; and emergent forms of gay identities 205–7, 216–17; engagement party 210–13, 222–6; same-sex marriage ceremonies 221–7

family relations 26–7, 112–13, 133, 135, 174; *see also* household relations
fatherhood 10, 39, 214; abuse of own children 31, 125; and violence 172–5; as head of family 129–35; control over resources 127–9; control over spouses and children 126, 133; shared decision making 127–9; *see also* masculine domination
female: initiation 4; sexuality 123, 145–7
feminist anthropology 207–9
femininity 96, 207–8, 213

gang rape 73–5, 82
gangs 183; *see also* prison gangs
gay identity 6–7, 187, 209–10; in Ermelo region 205–6, 217–18; in Lesotho 185, 191–4, 197; in period of democratic transformation 9, 16, 164, 166
gender: as performance 209, 217–19, 221, 227; classifications (based on roles) 209–10, 221; differences 197, 210; dynamics 208–9; hierarchy 213–14, 219; in feminist anthropology 207–9; inequalities 65, 111, 115; justice 162, 179, 215; shifts in order 10–11, 164, 168, 198, 209
gender-based violence 8, 135, 150, 165–6, 215

gender equality 1, 31, 46, 48, 83, 113, 163–4; as challenge to men's privileged status 117, 168; attempts at in Nkomazi region 111, 116, 124, 126–9; in decision making 127–8
gender identities 70, 121, 130–3; as socially constructed 207–9; in Ermelo region 206–7, 217; redefinition of 118, 134–5, 165; relationship with sexual practice 184, 209–10, 218–21, 227
gender relations 11, 117, 120–1, 123–4, 174, 219; between 'ladies' and 'gents' in Ermelo region 206–7; masculinity's place in 208–9; reorganisation of 10–11, 134–5, 174, 179; *see also* Nkomazi region
general violence 117, 172, 186
gerontocratic social systems 4, 91, 215

HIV/AIDS 33, 50–1, 55, 123, 139–40, 151–2; and sexual violence 33, 49; effect on *isoka* masculinity 151, 156; in Lesotho 186; men's role in epidemic 9, 33; pandemic 48, 117–18, 165 179; prevention and education programmes 5, 8–9, 48–51, 153–5; spread of 197, 199; statistics 68, 139–40; women's position 5, 151; *see also* multiple sexual partners
Harries, P. 90–2, 186
hegemonic masculinity 209, 215–16, 219
homelands 121–2
homophobia 166, 187–8, 190, 198–9

homosexuality 215; in Africa 5–6, 185; in Lesotho 183–5, 189–99; in southern Africa 183–4, 219–20; increased visibility of 166, 215; reluctance to admit to and research into 6, 187–8
household relations 120, 126–9; *see also* family relations
human rights 10, 45–6, 48, 112, 119, 163, 189; abuses 54; acknowledgement of in Nkomazi region 124, 126; international 52–3; *see also* Bill of Rights; South African Constitution
Hunter, M. 118–19, 178–9

Impalahoek 66, 68–73, 80–1
incest 26, 43, 80
indecent assault 25, 29
Interdenominational Prayer Women's League 30
isoka masculinity 118–19, 141, 143–6, 148, 151–2, 156, 178; *see also* multiple sexual partners

Khosa, Solanka 75–8
KwaZulu-Natal (KZN) 140–1, 144, 154, 179

Lesotho 186; homosexuality in 183–5, 189–90; 'macho' reputation of men 183–5, 190, 199; male–male sexual relationships 187
lobola 27; as earned through mine wifehood 91; dependence on wage labour for 148; for same-sex marriage 223; in KwaZulu-Natal 141, 147, 149; in Nkomazi region 115, 135; in the Bushbuckridge region 66–8
loveLife 51, 154–5

Mabaso, Mary 27–8, 30–1, 43
Makandeni 73–5
male–male sexuality 183; in Lesotho 183–5, 197–8; on mine compounds 186–7
male: prisons 90, 93–4, 101, 106; sexuality 34, 161, 179–80, 186
Maloka, Tshidiso 184–5, 189
Mandela, Nelson 50
Mandeni 142, 152–4
marital rape 30, 71, 163
marriage: in the Bushbuckridge region 66–8, 70–1; in KwaZulu-Natal 143, 146; rates of 148–9
masculine domination 7, 46, 50–1, 83, 111–13, 117–18, 120, 135, 140, 152; and rape 65–6, 69–73, 80–1; and violence 118, 139, 168–72; changing of 123, 128, 134, 162, 164–5; power v. authority 120, 122, 124, 128–34, 156; *see also* fatherhood
masculinity 2–3, 70–1, 113, 134, 140, 208–9, 214, 216; African 156, 188, 197; amongst 'gents' 213–14, 219; and violence 70, 168–73, 179; Basotho 190, 197–9; history 142–8, 155; homosexual 208–9; in Europe 188; in prison 95–7, 101, 106; in South Africa 7–8, 117, 135, 140, 207–8, 215; post-apartheid 156, 161; reworking of 155, 166–73, 176–7; sexual entitlement as feature of 65, 70–1, 95–7; studies

6–9; urban 149–50, 175; *see also* alternative masculinity; crisis of masculinity; hegemonic masculinity; *isoka* masculinity; sexuality

masculinity, changing concepts of 1–3, 8, 11, 46, 113, 118, 120–1, 161, 178–80; as in Alexandra case studies 168–77; as in Nkomazi region 111–12, 126–31, 135

Mashile, Aaron 71

Mathebula, Khazamula 81

Mbeki, Thabo 35–6, 40, 50

Mead, Margaret 207

medical discourse, influence on study of sexuality in Africa 4–6

Men for Change (MFC) 152, 166–7, 169–70, 178–9

migrant labour 5, 7, 67–8, 71, 115, 121–2, 144, 147–8, 196, 215; from Lesotho 7, 183–5, 187, 189; influence on women's extra-marital affairs 145–6; *see also* male–male sexuality; mine compounds; mine marriages

mine compounds 8, 90–2, 94, 186–7

mine marriages 90–1, 183–6, 196

mines and mining 7, 68, 187; influence on masculinity 7–8, 215

Mohapaloa, J.M. 185, 193

Moodie, T.D. 90–2, 186–7

Moore, H. 69–70, 80, 209

moral panic 10–11, 34–40, 65, 82–3, 118

Morrell, R. 1–2, 7–8, 117, 121, 179, 215

Mpengesi, Mandisi 32–3

Mugabe, Robert 188–9

multiple sexual partners 118–19, 139, 152, 175, 179, 214; because of social structure 139–40; by women 152–3; history of 141–56; in East Africa 150; *see also isoka* masculinity

National Association of People Living with HIV/Aids (NAPWA) 38

Ngwenya, Shelly 73–5

Nkomazi region 111–17, 133, 135, 178; case studies 125–33; control over family income 127–9; gender violence 114–17, 123, 125–6; status of manhood in 122–4, 133–4; violence against children 115, 125–6

Nyathi, Doris 76–7

patriarchy 1, 4, 91, 113, 124, 161, 174, 183–4, 215; and sexual violence 24–6, 42–5, 69, 80, 82; as 'used' in prisons 106; power v. authority of 120–2; *see also* crisis of masculinity; masculine domination

People Against Women Abuse 30

Posel, Deborah 11, 82–3, 118, 120–1, 149–50, 173

poverty 8, 50, 96, 123, 150, 155, 164–5, 177, 186; and multiple sexual partners 141, 150; in Nkomazi region 115–17, 127

Prevention of Domestic Violence Draft Bill 31

Prevention of Family Violence Act of 1993, 30

prison 90; culture 89–90, 94, 102–3; gangs 8, 89–90, 94–5, 98–100,

103, 105; identities in 90, 105; marriages 94–8, 103, 105; sexual transgressions in 103–5; sexual violence in 36, 95–9; sexuality in 89–90; 'womanhood' in 94–6, 98–103; *see also* male prisons; women's prisons

proletarianisation 7, 121–2, 215

Promotion of National Unity and Reconciliation Act of 1995 54

protest against: sexual violence 22, 30–1, 33–5, 38; violence against women and children 38, 118, 175

rape 8, 29–30, 36, 40, 45, 55, 82, 166, 168; as assertion of power of men 71–2, 80; during apartheid era 24–6; history 21–2, 24–5, 30; increase in 69, 82, 165; inquiry into laying charges 29–30; media coverage 33, 35–6; policing of 25–7, 29–30; public concern and interest 21–2, 29, 37, 50; statistics 65, 71–3, 80, 165; *see also* baby rape; child rape; gang rape; marital rape; serial rapists; secrecy and silence

Reid, G. 9, 164, 166

rural life 8, 178, 205; influence on masculinity 7, 215; multiple sexual partners in 144–8; relations of power and authority in 121–2; *see also* Nkomazi region

safer-sex practices 8–9, 49, 51, 118, 153–4, 175

same-sex: context 208, 215–16; identities 5, 92, 219; marriage ceremonies 221–7; sexuality 188

secrecy and silence 27, 39–46, 49, 83; about AIDS 33, 51; about rape in prison 95, 102; about sexual violence 21–4, 28–9, 33, 40, 43–6, 55, 82–3; as a site of power 42–6; cultural incentives to 27–8; politicisation of 23, 25–6; *see also* confession; moral panic

Segal, L. 120

serial rapists 75–8

sexual: crimes 22, 25, 28, 166; difference *see* gender identity; networking 139–40

sexual violence 21–3, 29–30, 37–8, 44, 117–18, 166; and AIDS 33, 49; during apartheid era 21, 24, 27, 42; exposé of 23, 32, 35–6, 46, 48–50, 165, 179; history of 21–2, 24–6, 30; in zones of domestic or familial intimacy 26–7, 31–2, 38, 42–4; media coverage 22, 34–5, 118; post-apartheid 32, 37, 42, 65; protection against 24–5, 31, 47–8, 66; public debate on 23, 32, 35–6, 38, 83; *see also* protest

sexuality 2–3, 9, 23, 51, 118, 147–8, 152, 155, 165–6,188, 198; study of in Africa 3–6; visibility of 9, 47, 49, 164, 166; *see also* femininity; masculinity

Sideris, Tina 10–11, 178

Silberschmidt, Margrethe 10, 150

Simelela, Nono 33

situational homosexuality 183–4, 197

Smith, Charlene 33

South African Constitution 163–4, 166; constitutional change 9, 47, 175–9; constitutional sexuality

48, 163–5; and crisis of masculinity 119, 133–4, 161, 174–5, 179; and gays 9, 16, 166, 206, 216; consequences of 165–6; gender equality 1, 46, 48, 111, 163–4, 222; perceptions of 168–9
South African Council of Churches 30
South African Law Commission 29–30, 222
South African Men's Forum 38
South African National Council for Child Welfare 33–4
South African Police 25–7, 29, 44
'struggle masculinity' 8, 165

Thabane, Motlatsi 198
township culture 175–6
tradition 121–3, 127, 134–5, 148, 206; *see also isoka* masculinity; lobola; multiple sexual partners
transition to democracy 1–2, 9, 116, 124, 129; and crisis in the order of gender relations 134, 163–5, 179; and gay people 9, 164, 205–6; and masculinity 8, 10–11, 117–19, 163, 174–5
Treatment Action Campaign (TAC) 155
Truth and Reconciliation Commission (TRC) 48, 52–5
truth commissions 53

Tshabalala, Patience 33
Tutu, Desmond 54

unemployment 128, 141, 164, 177, 215; and rape 72–3, 82–3; effect on men's capacity to provide 123, 151; in Bushbuckridge region 68, 72–3; in East Africa 150; in the Nkomazi region 116–17; since 1994 148–9, 154–5, 177–8
urbanisation 7, 149–50, 153–5, 175

Van Onselen, C. 90–2
Vaughan, Megan 4
Vilakazi, A. 144–5
virginity testing 4, 123, 144, 147, 154

Walker, L. 118–19, 152
Whitehead, S.M. 162
Wilson, Monica (née Hunter) 143
women 25–6, 31, 148, 164, 168; and sexual crimes 25–6, 65, 83, 166; empowerment of 4, 113, 168–9, 215
women's: movement 11, 29–31, 163; prisons 92–4; subordinate social position 4, 163, 207–8

Zandela, George 78–80
Zuma, Jacob 36–7